W9-BOP-732

Henry & Delia Meyers Library

ANTI-SEMITISM
& JEWISH
NATIONALISM

662
PiL
1427

To My Parents

Copyright © 1981 by Jay M. Pilzer

All rights reserved, including the right to reproduce this book in any form whatsoever without permission in writing from the publisher, except for brief passages in connection with a review. For information, write: The Donning Company/Publishers, 5041 Admiral Wright Road, Virginia Beach, Virginia 23462.

Library of Congress Cataloging in Publication Data

Main entry under title:
Anti-Semitism and Jewish nationalism.

Bibliography: p.
1. Antisemitism—Addresses, essays, lectures.
2. Jewish question—Addresses, essays, lectures.
I. Pilzer, Jay, 1946-
DS145.A63 301.45'19'24 79-11650
ISBN 0-915442-89-2

Printed in the United States of America

Contents

Foreword

The essays in this book deal with the "Jewish problem" over three generations of European culture. That the very presence of Jews in Europe constituted a "problem" is in itself an indictment of the European self-image of progress and civilization. As two world wars were to demonstrate, Europe's political and social health was an illusion which masked a seriously ill society unable to cope with the rise of modern nationalism and the search for social justice within the framework of participatory democracy. The disease of anti-Semitism was symptomatic of a much more grave social condition, yet for years Jewish protests were commonly dismissed as exaggerations.

Europe has never been very hospitable to Jews, who were usually regarded as intruders whose presence could be tolerated at some times but not at others. The historical reasons for this are complex; they began during the Middle Ages, when the presence of Jews was a constant reminder of the rejection of the Christian message. For some, religious justice required the persecution of the "Christ-killers"; therefore in the Crusades of the eleventh and twelfth centuries, the massacre of Jews was pursued as a legitimate Christian endeavor. The scenario was to be repeated all too many times in European history, with and without official government or church sanction. Spontaneous pogroms even took place after World War I in celebration of Polish independence. In all of these events, there was the attitude that the Jew is an outsider, and must be regarded as evil, malignant, and dangerous, a threat to society and therefore legitimately the object of official control at least.

In West Europe this view had substantially decreased in popularity by the late nineteenth century. In fact, by 1880, when the essays

1

in this volume first appeared, there had for all purposes developed two very separate Jewish populations, those of West Europe and those of East Europe. In the East, where the majority of Europe's Jews lived, Jewish life was universally harsh, usually impoverished, and the outlook for improvement dim. The passage of overtly anti-Semitic laws in the Russian Empire of the 1880s and government tolerance, if not encouragement, of pogroms augured poorly for the future of East European Jews.

The world of the West European Jew, in contrast, seemed open, if not wholly accepting. West Europe prided itself on its continued dynamic of growth. In varying degrees, democratic procedures were the rule in most countries, and democratic ideals were presumed to be the norms of society. In virtually all fields of endeavor—science, technology, the arts, government, etc.—West Europe was a self-proclaimed model of progress. In this setting the Jew was presumably free to participate, to contribute, and even to benefit; in fact, it appears that many did, although in the long run their integration into western society proved to be the greatest illusion of all.

Even before the virulent anti-Semitism that surfaced with the Dreyfus Case of the 1890s [see Part I, Chapter 6], resistance to accepting Jews as part of the larger society had become stronger. It continued to grow even after Dreyfus' vindication. Even Jews who had "made it" still remained outsiders. Degas, one of the best known French artists of the times, could never overlook or accept the Jewishness of his contemporary Pissaro; Bleichroder may have been Bismarck's banker and as such responsible for the creation of the German Empire, but he was not socially welcome at the Imperial German court; Freud, neither flaunting nor denying his Jewishness, was mired for years in the lower ranks of acadame while Mahler's genius was rewarded only when he ceased being Jewish and converted to Catholicism. These people were not being confronted directly by anti-Semitism but by the persistence of the European feeling that Jews were different and had to be kept at arm's length. When the youthful Hitler first saw strangely garbed Jews in the streets of Vienna and wondered out loud whether these people were Germans, too, he was not putting forth any new theory, but merely echoing his generation's rejection of Jews as Europeans.

Obsessive fear of Jews pervades these essays; people who had never been in situations where they had direct contact with Jews, or who lived in countries where Jews were at best a politically weak minority, still regarded Jews as a latent threat. These essays were widely read in the European press; for this reason these writers reinforced each others' fears and contributed to the persistent mythology of a Jewish menace. The celebrated *Protocols of the Learned Elders of Zion*, which purported to be a Jewish plot to take over the world, was easily proven to be a clumsy forgery, and yet it was readily believed in the first quarter of this century [see Part II, Chapter 3], and in fact is enjoying a revival in the 1970s. Many centuries ago, Machiavelli spoke of the desirability of being feared, but his observation was addressed to those in power. For those who are powerless, being feared can be dangerous.

The essays treat the rise of modern Zionism only sparingly, but they contribute to an understanding of its origins among European Jews as eternal outsiders. Of course, the dream of returning to the ancestral land has been part of the Jewish liturgy for centuries. Yet only in the twentieth century has there been any *major* movement of Jews towards re-establishing a national state. Though the modern state of Israel, officially born in 1948, may well claim a several-thousand-year heritage, its development in this century has been the direct result of the failure of Europe to solve its Jewish "problem." Europe had proven unable and unwilling to understand and accept the fact of a Jewish identity within the larger society; yet, in the final analysis, it was the Jews and not Europe that paid the price of this failure. This is the sad moral that Dr. Pilzer traces in his "essays without hindsight."

WARREN LERNER
Duke University

Preface

This is a book of opinions. The authors of these essays, Jews, non-Jews, anti-Semites, and philo-Semites, all wrote either to explain or propose a solution to the "Jewish Question." This term, common between 1880 and 1939, covered a wide range of ideas and beliefs all of which dealt with the issue of defining what Jews were and what their place was in European life and society. Many of the most dynamic aspects of recent Jewish history were discussed as parts of the Jewish Question.

The nucleus of the Jewish Question after 1880 and before the outbreak of the Second World War lay in two movements which would have decisive impacts on Jewish life. On one hand, the ancient hatred of Judaism and Jews took on new forms with the emergence of political anti-Semitism, and, on the other hand, Jewish nationalism was born as a modern political movement. While Jews came to be despised as a race by many Europeans, Jews themselves rediscovered their national unity and forged a new movement—Zionism—to give the nation substance. The former led to the destruction of one-third of the Jewish people; the latter led to the creation of Israel as a Jewish state.

These two events caused me to compile this series of essays. The Holocaust and the formation of Israel are apocalyptic events in Jewish history, and it is difficult, if not impossible, to see some aspects of Jewish life and politics before 1939 clearly with these events so prominent in our thoughts. Yet, if we are to understand how these events came about, we must be able to see developments in the Jewish past without the blinders of hindsight. Hannah Arendt has called anti-Semitism "an outrage to common sense," and it is difficult for the contemporary world to comprehend how that movement grew and how it came to have such a devastating impact on European Jewry. The articles in this book all have one thing in common—for their authors, the Jewish Question was an issue of impelling gravity that demanded a solution. Neither the Holocaust nor Israel came quickly; both were the result of years of ideological and political preparation. This book is an attempt to recapitulate that process.

All of the articles are from British or American periodicals and were written for the informed layperson. Articles from Central and Eastern Europe could have made this work more comprehensive, but they also would have served to add obscurity in a book designed for a Western audience. Thus, I decided to sacrifice some breadth for the clarity which I believe is an essential part of this work. Few of the essays were written by direct participants in the many controversies which surrounded Jewish life in the period. The authors were attempting either to explain or convince. As such, they offer us an opportunity to see the issues as they did—without the veil of time. Anti-Semitism, the value of a Jewish identity in a secular society, the relationship of Jews in the Diaspora to a Jewish state, and other aspects of the Jewish Question are still major issues today. It is hoped that this book will offer a different context in which to examine these concerns.

This book will add to the understanding of any person interested in the recent Jewish past. But beyond that, I have tried to assemble articles which reflect a wide spectrum of opinion so that thought and discussion will naturally arise from the reading. The initial idea for this work came in 1972 while I was teaching a course on Zionism for members of the Norfolk, Virginia, Jewish community. In that course, and in several that have followed over the years, I found that readings of the type presented here provided an effective springboard for discussion of both the past and the present. I hope that others who teach or lead discussions concerned with the Jewish past will find similar value in this work; no other provides the same intimacy with the debate on the Jewish Question before the Second World War.

I have edited many of the articles to make them more readable for a modern audience, but have not changed the authors' views in any way. In my brief introductions, I have set out only to give the broadest outline of some aspects of recent Jewish history. These are designed to put each section and each article into its historical context.

There are many people who have helped me in this work. Dr. Warren Lerner of Duke University not only contributed his fine foreword, but he and his family provided me with a magnificent long distance research service. Fran and Suzy I thank you. Dr. William E. Scott, also of Duke University, will always deserve my thanks for the training he gave me as an historian. I also wish to thank the administration and the Research Committee of Norfolk State University for their support of this project. Last, I happily admit my dependence on my family. My wife, Betty, lent her insight; my sons, Joshua and Ethan, observed the sanctity of the study, and their futures make this exploration of the Jewish past even more worthwhile.

PART
I

THE
NEW HATRED,
THE NEW NATION:
1880-1913

The period from 1880 to the beginning of the First World War was a time of great change in European Jewish life. The relationship of Jews to other Europeans was in 1914 fundamentally different from its nature in 1870. The root of this change was the spread of conservative nationalism, particularly in Central and Eastern Europe. Nationalism did not speak of the glory of Germany, Rumania, or Russia as states; rather, it glorified the Germans, Russians, Poles, and other groups as peoples all believing in their own mission. The state was not merely a political entity, but the repository of the national destiny. The state became the embodiment of the nation. As such, many believed that it had to be free of "foreign" influences.

The increasing tide of nationalism had an enormous impact on Jewish life. Heretofore, Jewishness was seen by most as a religious distinction. The Jew, in those earlier times, had suffered greatly, but as religious toleration had grown in the late eighteenth and nineteenth centuries, particularly in Western and Central Europe, the Jews had gained increasing civil rights. These rights were based on the belief that Jews were a people who followed a particular religious creed. After 1880, however, many Europeans began to redefine what it was to be a Jew. As Germans, Englishmen, Poles, and Frenchmen were nations, or races in their terms, so too were Jews. And this race of Jews, they went on, was spread throughout the world, forming a racial impurity within the nation-states of Europe. Here was a new definition of Jewishness, and with it came a different and more deadly rationale for agitation against Jews. No longer would Europeans base their hatred of Jews solely on religious differences; now a new word was coined to describe a new movement directed not against Judaism, but against the Jewish people. That word—that movement—was anti-Semitism. It was a movement that would come to draw support from all classes of European society—from the lower and working classes to the intellectual and political elite.

In Russia, which of course included Poland, agitation against Jews climbed to a fever pitch after the assassination of Czar Alexander II in 1881. The archaic Russian government needed a way to shift attention from its own failures, and the Jews, long despised throughout Russian society, provided a focus for the growing frustration of the peasantry. The Russian press repeatedly wrote of secret Jewish conspiracies, and the government supported "spontaneous" pogroms. Physical attacks against Jews increased in frequency and intensity, and the May Laws of 1882 proclaimed a new legal attack on Russia's Jewish communities. These laws placed even greater disabilities on the Jews than had already been in force. The Jews were portrayed as a foreign and corrupting influence within the Slavic empire.

Anti-Semitism was not confined to Eastern Europe. In Germany and Austria anti-Semitism had, by 1880-90, become a political movement with parties founded on the dual principles of the great destiny of the German race and the belief that Jews were racial foreigners in these lands. Even in France, the first country to emancipate the Jews, anti-Semitic agitation threatened the Jewish community. The Dreyfus Case was many things, but chief among them it was a signal for virulent anti-Semitism in France. Hatred of Jews, it seemed, had become an international movement.

There were many results of this wave of anti-Jewish feeling. In Russia, with its massive Jewish population, the new agitation was, for many, positive proof that Jews could not hold even the slightest hope of acceptance in Russian life. Several movements were part of the reaction to this conclusion. The first was a growing belief among many Eastern European Jews that they, too, were a nation, and as such should be allowed a national destiny. An important aspect of this Jewish nationalism was the issue of Jewish economic life. Jews were primarily distributors in Europe, and many believed that Jewish economic life had to become more diverse if Jewish life, either in Europe or elsewhere, was to change. Some believed that Jews could develop a national life in Europe, but many of the nationalists believed that the recent agitation against Jews was evidence that Jews could no longer live in Europe. The religious dream of a return to Zion began to emerge as an activist political philosophy, and with the advent of a dynamic leader—Theodor Herzl—Zionism became a movement dedicated to securing a national home for the Jewish people. Herzl, himself an assimilated Austrian Jew, was not wedded to the idea that the Jewish homeland must be in Palestine, but he came to see that the Jews of Eastern Europe, who were his mass of support, would accept no home other than Zion. He then bent all of his efforts towards gaining international recognition for a Jewish home in Palestine.

Two non-national movements also resulted from the horrors of

Jewish life in Eastern Europe. The first was the emergence of Jews as leaders in European socialism. These Jews believed that anti-Semitism was a phenomenon of capitalism and would disappear in a socialist world.

The second non-national approach was the great emigration of Eastern Europe's Jews to the West. The United States received the vast majority of these refugees, but many settled in England and other European states. With this influx of poor, ill-educated Jews, the fears of both Jewish and non-Jewish Americans, Englishmen, and others were raised. The non-Jews, aside from a general animosity towards Jews, feared economic competition, and the Jews believed that these immigrants could threaten their status. This flood of immigrants to America and England, and the fear of Socialism, played an important role in focusing attention on the Jewish Question.

The essays in the first part of this book all reflect a growing concern over who and what were Europe's Jews and what should be done with them. The basic question was one of definition. Were these people a race, a religion, or perhaps a "tribe"? Were they racially only suited to business; could they become producers, which would be essential for the creation of a Jewish homeland; or were they forever destined to be distributors, or economic middlemen, as they had become in Europe? The following essays portray the debate on these issues as it actually took place. The authors knew nothing of the Holocaust or the creation of the Jewish state. Nevertheless, these writers, and others like them, provided much of the basic groundwork for both of those events.

THE
JEWISH
QUESTION

by Goldwin Smith

[A major facet of the new anti-Semitism was that many of its spokesmen were well-respected intellectuals. In Germany Heinrich von Treitschke was the intellectual leader of anti-Semitism; Goldwin Smith was one who played that role in Britain and Canada. Smith (1823-1910) was a respected historian and educational reformer.

In this article, published in 1881, Smith examined the Jewish Question in a way that became standard in anti-Semitic literature. His basic assumption was that Jews were a racial, not a religious, entity and that they were economic parasites wherever they lived. The article is a reply to one written by Lucien Wolf, a British Jew who was a champion of Jewish rights. Wolf's piece had decried the recent outburst of anti-Jewish activity in Europe.]

"The Jewish Question" by Goldwin Smith, first published in *Nineteenth Century*, 10 (Oct. 1881), 494-515.

It had happened that when I was last in England we were on the brink of a war with Russia, which would have involved the whole Empire. The Jewish interest throughout Europe, with the Jewish press of Vienna as its chief organ, was doing its utmost to push us in. At such a crisis it was necessary and right to remind the English people that Israel was a separate race, with tribal objects, and that its enmities could not be safely allowed to sway the councils of England.

I heartily supported, and, were it needful, would heartily support again, the political enfranchisement of the Jews, though I do not pretend to believe that people who intrench themselves in tribal exclusiveness, refuse intermarriage, and treat the rest of the community as Gentiles, are the very best of candidates for citizenship. But the franchise is a trust, in the exercise of which every one must expect to be watched, especially those who are liable to any peculiar bias, above all when their allegiance is divided between the nation and some other power or interest. Especially is vigilance needful when the equivocal influence is exercised through the secretly enslaved organs of an ostensibly independent Press.

If patriotism means merely a willingness to perform all social duties and to do good to the community, nobody can deny that it may be possessed in the largest measure by the kinsmen of Sir Moses Montefiore. But if it means undivided devotion to the national interest, there is difficulty in seeing how it can be possessed without abatement by the members of a cosmopolitan and wandering race, with a tribal bond, tribal aspirations, and tribal feelings of its own. Far be it from Liberals to set up a narrow patriotism as the highest of virtues, or to make an idol of the nation. There is something higher than nationality, something which nationality at present ought to serve, and in which it will ultimately be merged. Mazzini taught us how to think upon that subject. But tribalism is not higher or more liberal than nationality; it is lower and less liberal; it is the primeval germ of which nationality is the more civilised development. Nor does the narrowest patriot make such a religious idol of his nation as the Jew makes of his tribe. All the other races profess at least allegiance to humanity: they all look forward, however vaguely, to a day of universal brotherhood; they cannot help doing this if they are Christian, and have accepted the ideal of the Christian Church. The Jew alone regards his race as superior to humanity, and looks forward not to its ultimate union with other races, but to its triumph over them all, and to its final ascendency under the leadership of a tribal Messiah. I mean of course the genuine, or, as the Americans would say with rough picturesqueness, the "hard-shell" Jews. About the position of these alone can there be any question. As to the men of Jewish descent who have put off tribalism altogether, we have only to welcome them as citizens in the fullest sense of the term and to rejoice in any good gifts, peculiar to their stock, which they may bring to the common store.

Of the existence of Israel as a power and an interest apart from the nations, though domiciled among them, there can scarcely be a doubt. One who has deeply studied the question, Mr. Oliphant, in his recent and very interesting work *The Land of Gilead*, dwells more than once on the great advantages which any European Government might gain over its rivals by an alliance with the Jews. "It is evident," he says, "that the policy which I have proposed to the Turkish Government (*i.e.* the restoration of Palestine) might be adopted with equal advantage by England or any other European Power. The nation that espoused the cause of the Jews and their restoration to Palestine would be able to rely on their support in financial operations on the largest scale, upon the powerful influence which they wield in the Press of many countries, and on their political co-operation in those countries, which would of necessity tend to paralyse the diplomatic and even hostile action of Powers antagonistic to the one with which they were allied. Owing to the financial, political, and commercial importance to which the Jews have now attained, there is probably no one power in

11

Europe that would prove so valuable an ally to a nation likely to be engaged in a European war as this wealthy, powerful, and cosmopolitan race." Perhaps the writer of these words hardly realises the state of things which they present to our minds. We see the Governments of Europe bidding against each other for the favour and support of an anti-national money power, which would itself be morally unfettered by any allegiance, would be ever ready to betray and secretly paralyse for its own objects the Governments under the protection of which its members were living, and of course would be always gaining strength and predominance at the expense of a divided and subservient world. The least part of the evil would be the wound inflicted on our pride. It is the highest treason against civilisation that Mr. Oliphant unwittingly suggests.

The allusion to the influence wielded by the Jews in the European Press has a particularly sinister sound. This, as has already been said, is a danger the growth of which specially justifies our vigilance. In the social as in the physical sphere new diseases are continually making their appearance. One of the new social diseases of the present day, and certainly not the least deadly, is the perversion of public opinion in the interest of private or sectional objects, by the clandestine manipulation of the Press.

Mr. Wolf assumes that the main question between the Jews and their adversaries is one of religion, and that opposition to Jewish ascendency is a revival of religious persecution. To the full extent to which his belief is well founded, I share his "all-consuming indignation." Indeed the fear of seeming to abet anything like an attack on liberty of conscience makes me almost shrink from dealing with the subject. In this respect, however, I feel that I am tolerably free from reproach. I believe I have on all occasions to the utmost of my power supported the cause of perfect freedom of opinion. I have advocated unsectarian education in all its grades, and no one can desire more heartily than I do to see the last relic of intolerance swept away from the constitution of the House of Commons. But among the opponents of Liberal principles on both these points, as I am told, are rich Jews, who have apparently come to the conclusion that sectarian education and exclusive tests are useful guardians of certain special interest. It seems that in France corresponding phenomena present themselves. The French correspondent of a thoroughly pro-Jewish journal in this country remarks, with reference to the part played by the Jews in French politics, that "the Jew, when struggling, or merely rich, is Anti-Clerical and Liberal, but when he becomes a magnate and wants to marry his children to the sons and daughters of 'crusading' families of undoubted nobility, he becomes a supporter of moral order and all that is comprised in the term." It is possible, then, to be opposed to Jews and yet to be on the side of religious liberty. If I mistake not, the possibility will become more evident every day in proportion as Israel accumulates more wealth, and becomes more identified with the class to which the good things and the honours of the world belong.

For my part I have been all along persuaded that in these troubles religion is not the primary but a secondary cause; though, as it struck the eye of superficial observers most, it has been hitherto taken for the primary cause. The root of the mischief lies, I am convinced, not in the peculiar creed, but in the peculiar character, habits, and position of the Jewish people; in their tribal exclusiveness, their practice of the tribal rite of circumcision, the nature of the trades to which they are addicted, and the relation in which they stand to the native races of the countries wherein they take up their abode as a wandering and parasitic race, without a country, avoiding ordinary labour, and spreading over the world to live on the labour of others by means of usury and other pursuits of the same sort. They are not the only instance of the kind. The Armenians are another, the Parsees a third; the Greeks were fast becoming a fourth, when happily alike for them and other nations their country was restored to them. The Lombards and Cahorsins in the Middle Ages were examples of the same tendency on a smaller scale, as the Gipsies are in a different way. But the theological importance attached to the Jews and the belief in the divinely ordained and penal character of their wanderings has prevented their case from being referred to the historical class to which it belongs, and caused their dispersion to be regarded not only as far the most memorable, which assuredly it is, but as absolutely unique.

I had once been listening to a debate in the House of Commons on a motion brought forward by that most excellent scion of the Jewish race, the late Sir F. Goldsmith, respecting the maltreatment of the Jews in the Danubian Principalities, in which it was assumed both by the mover and by the Foreign Minister, who replied to him, that the case was one of religious persecution. At my side sat a friend who knew the Principalities well, who hated wrong and oppression of all kinds if ever man did, and who was not a Christian but an avowed Agnostic. He said that in his opinion the real point had been missed; that the case in its essential character was not one of religious persecution; that the people, a good-natured race, were not inflamed with fanatical hatred of the Jewish faith; that a Jewish synagogue in one of the cities received aid from the Government. The Jews, he said, came among a simple-minded peasantry, devoured its substance by usury, dispossessed it of its freeholds, and at the same time corrupted it by the practice of demoralising trades; hence attempts were made to exclude them from the country, and they were sometimes treated with cruel violence. In Russia the people regard religion very much as a question of nationality, deeming it perfectly natural that a man of a different race should also have a different creed, so that the inhabitants of Christian villages dwell peaceably side by side with the inhabitants of villages which are not Christian. Hence it would seem that in this case again religious fanaticism can hardly be the chief source of the popular excitement [against the Jews]. The Germans are being denounced as a herd of infuriated and brutal bigots; but they are in reality a kindly people, and their history is peculiarly free from the stains of religious persecution, especially if we take out the action of Austria, which is really not a German power. Mr. Wolf complains of the frequent Boycotting of Jews in the United States. He refers, I presume, to the refusal, some time ago, of New York insurance offices to insure the houses of the Jews, and to their recent exclusion from some hotels in the same State. At least I know of nothing else to which the term Boycotting could be applied. In both cases the reason may have been insufficient; but in both it was certainly commercial, not religious. No New York insurance office or hotel would ever refuse anybody's money on religious grounds. At the time of secession an order, the exact tenor of which I do not remember, was issued by a Federal commander against the Jews, who were plying their usual trades in the wake of war; but we may be quite sure that this was a military measure, with which bigotry had nothing to do. That the Jews should have exposed themselves to exceptional treatment in a country where the principle of religious liberty and equality is so firmly established, not only in the Constitution, but in the hearts of the people, as it is in the United States, seems clearly to indicate that there may be other than religious grounds for the popular feeling against them in other countries also. No man is responsible to his fellow-men for his beliefs, however strange they may be; but every man, whatever his beliefs, must take the natural consequences of his actions. He who plies an unpopular trade, or does what is offensive to his neighbours, at the same time treating them as Gentiles, will be sure to incur odium not only of the theological kind. That his ancestors, eighteen centuries and a half ago, instigated Pilate to crucify Christ is a very bad reason for maltreating any man at the present day; but it is an equally bad reason for allowing any man to behave offensively at the present day that his ancestors were maltreated in the Middle Ages.

The belief that these troubles are wholly or mainly religious flows naturally from the notion almost universally entertained, that Israel is merely a dissenting sect. Talleyrand, as a remarkable passage quoted by Mr. Wolf shows, fancied that a Jew was just like other citizens, saving his theological opinions, and that when toleration was extended to those opinions he would become like other citizens in every respect. The advocacy of Jewish emancipation in England proceeded on the same assumption, while the opposition was founded on that of a religious crime and a divine sentence. The result has proved that though emancipation was wise and right, the impression under which the debate was conducted was mistaken. We now see that Israel is not a sect, but a vast relic of primeval tribalism, with its tribal mark, its tribal separatism, and its tribal God. The affinity of Judaism is not to nonconformity but to caste. If Judaism were a religion as Christianity or Buddhism is, it would, like Christianity and Buddhism, proselytise: it did proselytise during that period of its history in which, under the influence of Greek philosophy and other liberalising agencies, it was tending from the condition of a tribal to that of a universal creed, though it subsequently fell back into tribalism.

It is partly under the influence of the same erroneous impression, as I venture to think, that Mr. Wolf ascribes whatever is not lofty in the commercial character and habits of the Jews to the "demoniac attitude" of Christianity, that he depicts the conduct of Christendom towards Judaism throughout history as "a persecution unexampled for its long duration and calculated malignity," that he speaks of the "brutality and infamous uncharitableness with which throughout the ages the Jews have been wantonly persecuted by the *soi-distant* votaries of a Gospel of Mercy." Such expressions, I submit, betray a misreading of history, and one which not only produces a misconception as to the main source of these calamitous conflicts in the past, but prevents the Jew from seeing what is the only real security against their recurrence in the future. The group of nations which makes up Christendom emerged from barbarism only by a very gradual process, as did also the nation which deemed that it pleased its God by the massacre of the Canaanites with their wives and children, and which penned the books of Judges, Chronicles, and Esther; but apart from any belief about revelation, and from theological questions altogether, it has as fair a claim at least as any other group to be painted with historical discrimination, and not carelessly daubed with black. Perhaps in regard to the Jewish question the self-accusation of Christendom, since its acceptance of the principle of toleration, has somewhat exceeded the fact, as the self-accusation of reformed sinners is apt to do. Mr. Wolf's sweeping language is enough in itself to suggest the need of historical revision, though by most of his Christian readers it will be accepted without criticism and echoed with a penitential sigh.

There are features common to the characters of Orientals generally, and visible in that of the Jew, for which Christendom plainly is not responsible. Nor is Christendom responsible for anything that originally marked, for good or for evil, either the Semitic stock generally or the Hebrew branch of it. It was not the attitude of Christianity that made the Phoenician a kidnapper or the Carthaginian faithless. It was not the attitude of Christianity that caused the Jews to adopt as a typical hero the man who takes advantage of his brother's hunger to buy him our of his birthright with a mess of pottage, or led them to record with exultation how they had spoiled the Egyptians by borrowing their jewels on a feigned pretext. It was not Christianity that penned passages in Hebrew books instinct with sanguinary tribalism and vindictive malediction. But a more unhappy element probably in the special character of the modern Jew than any Oriental or Semitic defect is the accumulated effect of the wandering life, with its homelessness, its combination of degrading vagrancy with unpopular exclusiveness, its almost inevitable tendency to mean and hateful trades. And to the wandering life the Jews were led partly by untoward circumstances, partly by their own choice, certainly not by the attitude or the conduct of Christendom. They seem to have been not less unpopular with the nations of the pagan world, including some even outside the pale of the Roman Empire, than they have been with

Christian nations; and their unpopularity seems to have arisen always from much the same causes. Either the whole human race except the Jew is demoniac, or there is something naturally unpopular in the habits and bearing of the Jew.

Into England the Jews streamed after the Conquest, as they follow in the train of modern war; and we may be sure that their presence was not the least part of the calamity which befell the hapless people. Through them the Norman and Angevin kings were enabled to organise vicarious extortion, and though the king squeezed the sponge when it had sucked up the money of the people, this process while it filled his coffers did not restore the popularity of the unfortunate Jews. Nor does it seem that the Jew, to make up for his exactions, when he had amassed wealth, bore himself meekly towards the natives. Our highest authority on medieval history, Mr. Freeman, says: "In the wake of the Conqueror the Jews of Rouen found their way to London, and before long we find settlements of the Hebrew race in the chief cities and boroughs of England: at York, Winchester, Lincoln, Bristol, Oxford, and even at the gate of the Abbot of St. Edmonds and St. Albans. They came as the king's special men, or more truly as his special chattels, strangers alike to the Church and the commonwealth, but strong in the protection of a master who commonly found it his interest to protect them against all others. Hated, feared, and loathed, but far too deeply feared to be scorned or oppressed, they stalked defiantly among the people of the land, on whose wants they throve, safe from harm or insult, save now and then, when popular wrath burst all bounds, when their proud mansions and fortified quarters could shelter them no longer from raging crowds, who were eager to wash out their debts in the blood of their creditors. The romantic picture of the despised, trembling Jew, cringing before every Christian whom he meets, is, in any age of English history, simply a romantic picture." The suppleness of the Oriental, which made him willing to be the chattel for the sake of the royal protection in his trade, might diminish the respect of the people for him, but would not diminish their hatred or their fear.

Like the expulsion of the Jews from St. Edmonsbury by Abbot Samson, the banishment of the whole race from England by Edward I was unquestionably intended by the king and welcomed by the nation as a measure of social reform and relief to the people. The execution of the measure was marked by savage outbursts of popular passion against the objects of general hatred; and Jewish writers may be easily forgiven for denouncing Edward as one of a set of "insolent, rapacious, and unprincipled tyrants whose virtues, if they happened to possess any, were overshadowed by their crimes." But this is not history. Edward was as great, as noble-minded, and as beneficent a king as ever sat upon the English throne; and he must have made no small fiscal sacrifice in sending away the luckless race whose craft had filled his coffers and those of his predecessors. The situation was throughout miserable; its consequences while it lasted were deplorable; its termination was hideous and heart-rending: but the English people had never invited the Jews to England.

In Spain the situation was still worse than in England, and the consequences were still more hideous. For centuries a struggle raged for the possession of the peninsula between Christendom and Islam, by which religious passion as well as antipathy of race was excited to the highest pitch. At last the Christian triumphed and the Mahomedan was ruthlessly driven out, as, we may be sure, the Christian would have been driven out from any realm of Islam in which he had planted himself for a time as an invader, unless he had preferred to banishment the most abject and wretched slavery. The Jew being connected with the Mahomedan, and bound to him by sympathy, shared his piteous doom. In the dreadful reign of persecution which followed, after the establishment of the Inquisition, the Jew or "New Christian" did not suffer more than the Christian who was suspected of heresy, or, to speak perhaps more correctly, of disloyalty to that religious union which the Spaniard had learned to regard as the palladium of national existence. Perhaps even in Spain the vast revenues of the State Church had as much to do with persecution as had the bigotry of the nation; and assuredly the religion of Jesus of Nazareth had nothing to do with the vast revenues of the State Church. All these horrors now belong to the past as completely as the massacre of the Canaanites.

During the Middle Ages intolerance was universal, perhaps inevitable, and the Christian heretic, though a native and a member of the commonwealth, was persecuted not less, but far more cruelly, than the Jew who was an intruder. In England the Jews were relieved of their political disabilities almost as soon as the Dissenters, and those who relieved them were of course Christians. It is tacitly assumed that all the time Judaism itself was tolerant and would have established religious liberty had power been in its hands. No assumption surely could be more precarious. Judaism persecuted Christianity while it could, calling in the Roman authority for the purpose. In a later age the heresy of Uriel D'Acosta was punished with forms apparently borrowed, as has been remarked, from the practice of the Inquisition. Spinoza was put in peril of his life. To burn or stone him, or any other apostate, was not possible where Jewish orthodoxy did not wield the civil sword. The works of Maimonides were publicly burned. Instances of anathema and ex-communication launched by the priesthood against freedom of thought abound in Jewish history; and Jewish writers acknowledge that bigotry capable of anything is to be found among the zealots of their race in Poland. Even so liberal an Israelite as Mr. Samuel, the author of *Jewish Life in the East*, speaks of "renegades," that is, converts from Judaism to Christianity, in a tone suggestive of social penalties if not of faggots. After all, whence did ecclesiastics in the Middle Ages chiefly derive their notions as to the duty of extirpating misbelief with the sword? Was it not from passages in the sacred books of the Hebrews? Was it not from the injunction to exterminate the idolatrous Canaanites, and the precepts of the law making death the penalty of apostasy, blasphemy, and religious perversion? Even the superstition of witch-burning, had it not its origin in an uncritical adherence to the Mosaic law which ordains that a witch shall not be allowed to live? Among rational Christians the Old Testament has given place to the New. But in the synagogue is not the Old Testament still read as the final expression of the Divine Will? Is not the Feast of Purim still kept by the Hebrew race? If so, Judaism ought to be cautious how it applies such epithets as demoniac to Christendom on account of any misdeeds of the ignorant and irrational past.

Mr. Wolf ascribes the abandonment of husbandry by the Jews to the cruel bigotry of Christian rulers, who forbade them to hold Christians as farm-slaves, it being regarded as out of the question that a Jew should put his own hand to the plough. Would the Jews in their own country, or in any other country where they were dominant, have allowed Christians to hold Jews as slaves? Mr. Samuel, the Jewish writer already mentioned, says, "A Jewish servant or labourer is almost unknown in Egypt, our people here as elsewhere being infected with that dislike for manual labour and that preference for earning their living with their heads which is at once the strength of our upper and the destruction of our lower classes." The destruction, then, of the lower classes among the Jews, their economical destruction at least, is not to be laid at the door of Christendom. Their propensities with regard to labour are the same in the East and in their own land as in the Christian countries of the West. It is true that in those happier days when, instead of Rabbinism and the Cabala, they were producing a great religion, and memorably contributing to the progress of humanity, the Jews were, as Mr. Wolf reminds us, a community of husbandmen; but they have now been so long a wandering race, "preferring to earn their living with their heads," that the tendency is ingrained, and cannot be altered by anything that Christendom can do. Not even in lands where they have been longest and most completely emancipated, such as Holland and the United States, have the Jews, it is believed, shown any disposition to return to the blameless industry any more than to the simple and devout character of the husbandmen who gathered in the Courts of Zion. The same thing would probably have befallen the Greeks had they, like the Jews, been permanently converted into a race without a home. For such habits, whether formed by an individual or a race, humanity is not responsible, nor can it prevent them from bearing their natural fruits. The one valid ground of complaint which the Jews have in this respect is the medieval prohibition of usury, which, so far as it was operative, tended no doubt at once to throw the trade into the hands of the Hebrews, and to degrade it. But this again had its origin mainly in the Hebrew law, though that law makes a tribal distinction between taking interest of a Hebrew and taking it of a stranger.

The idea that to exclude the Jew was to shut out commerce and prosperity is curiously at variance with the indications of the ethnographical map at the present day, from which it would appear that the number of Jews was nearly in inverse proportion to national well-being. In wretched Poland, including Posen and Galicia, the proportion of them is largest; they abound in Hungary, in Rumania, in the southern parts of Russia; in England and France there are comparatively few; in Scotland, the soundest and healthiest of communities, hardly any. Nothing can really increase the wealth of a country but productive industry, in which the Jews stand low. Mere money-dealing, though necessary and therefore legitimate, is not productive. That the presence in large numbers of a wandering race of money-dealers and petty traders does more harm to a nation than good is a fact which does not justify the maltreatment of any member of that race, but a fact it appears to be.

In cases where a military race has absolutely refused to engage in trade, and has prevented its serfs or rayahs from engaging, the Jew has found a natural opening; but while he has filled the gap, he has precluded native commerce from coming into existence, as otherwise in course of time it would almost certainly have done.

"The Jew," says Renan, "from that time [that of the final dispersion] to this has insinuated himself everywhere, claiming the benefit of common rights. But in reality he has not been within the pale of common rights; he has kept his status apart; he has wanted to have the same securities as the rest, with his exceptional privileges and special laws into the bargain. He has wished to enjoy the advantages of nationality without being a member of the nation, or bearing his share of national burdens. And this no people has ever been able to endure." There is no reason why any people should endure it, at all events if the number and influence of the intruders are such as to constitute a serious danger to the nation, and the parasite seems likely to injure the growth of the tree. In England the Jews are few; and though some of them have made colossal fortunes by stock-broking, the aggregate amount of their wealth is not great compared with that of the whole country. English writers are therefore able, much at their ease, to preach the lessons of a serene philosophy to the Germans, who have as many Jews in a single city as there are in the whole of England or France, and are moreover threatened with fresh eruptions from Poland, that grand reservoir, as even Jewish writers admit, of all that is least admirable in Israel. Seeing the growth of the Jewish power in Germany, the immense wealth which it has amassed by stock-broking, and which, refusing intermarriage, it holds with a grasp almost as tight as mortmain, its influence over the Press, the lines of sumptuous mansions which bespeak its riches and its pride, the rapid multiplication of its people and the reinforcements which it receives from abroad, its tribal exclusiveness and compactness, its disdain of manual labour and increasing appropriation of the higher and more influential places in the community, a German may be excused for feeling apprehensions which in an Englishman would be absurd. No wonder if he fancies, as he walks along the principal street of his chief city, that he is in some danger of being reduced to the condition of a hewer of wood and a drawer of water for an intrusive race in his own land. Not the German only, but any one who feels an interest in the fortunes of Germany, may well regard the growth of Jewish influence there with some anxiety, at least if he deems it best for the world that the great Teutonic nation, at last united and liberated by efforts so heroic and at so great a cost, should be allowed to develop its character, and work out its destiny in its own way. This revolt against Semite ascendency may be regarded in fact as a natural sequel of the revolts against Austrian domination and French intrigue. Crushed by a brood of petty despots, Germany, after the Thirty Years' War, had been lying depressed and torpid, the prey of all who chose to prey on her; she is now awakened to national life, feels the blood coursing through her veins again, and is successively casting off all her bonds. The economical yoke of the Jew becomes as irksome as the rest.

The situation is a most unhappy one. Such consequences as have flowed from the dispersion of the Jews are enough to prove to the optimist that there are real and lasting calamities in history. Repression, though duty imposes it on a government, does not seem hopeful; soldiers may be sent, and some of the anti-Semitic rioters may be shot down, but this will not make the rest of the people love the Jew. That the people should ever love the Jew while he adheres to his tribalism, his circumcision, and his favourite trades, seems to be morally impossible. It is not difficult to frame golden rules by which Jews and Gentiles as well as Magyar and Sclav, Anglo-American and Negro, shall live in philosophic amity; but it is too certain what the practical result will be. No real solution seems to present itself except the abandonment by the Hebrew of his tribalism, with its strange and savage rite, and of all that separates him socially from the people among whom he dwells. As to the hygienic practices, on the importance of which Mr. Wolf insists as a ground for separatism, there is not the smallest reason, if they are rational and good, why the Jew should not retain them himself, and impart them to other people. Thenceforth, if Jewish genius showed itself so superior as Jews assert that it is to that of people of other blood, and if any one sought to deny it a fair career, there would be justice in assuming him to be actuated by envy. We should all be bound to welcome it without prejudice as a purely beneficent power. In England and France such a solution seems possible—the Jewish element is here not so large as to defy assimilation and absorption; but in Germany and Poland it appears very remote.

What can, what ought, the Germans to do? It behooves them calmly to consider this question. Violence clearly in any form is neither right nor expedient. The Government is bound to put it down, and excesses which provoke a deserved reaction will only leave Semitism morally stronger and more formidable than ever. The withdrawal of political rights, once conceded, is also practically out of the question, more especially as the Jew has not only been permitted to vote but compelled to serve in the army. This last fact is decisive. On the other hand, no principle, political or moral, forbids a German to use his own vote for the purpose of keeping the government and guidance of the nation in German hands. Of course he is equally at liberty to encourage, or refuse to encourage, such journals as he thinks fit. Associations against anybody have a very ugly look, yet they may be justified by great compactness of tribal organisation and corporate activity on the side of the Hebrews. Restraints upon immigration are harsh and inhospitable, except in a case of absolute necessity. But a case of absolute necessity may be conceived, and the land of every nation is its own. The right of self-defence is not confined to those who are called upon to resist an armed invader. It might be exercised with equal propriety, though in a different way, by a nation the character and commercial life of which were threatened by a great eruption of Polish Jews. The Americans think themselves perfectly at liberty to lay restrictions on the immigration of the Chinese, though the Chinaman with his labourer's shovel is nothing like so formidable an invader as the Jew. In trade the sons of those who founded the Free Cities will surely be able, now that their energies have been restored and their shackles struck off, to hold their own, without legislative protection, against the Hebrew, preternatural as his skill in a special tone of business has become.

It has been said, and I believe truly, that religion is the least part of the matter. Yet there is between the modern Jew and the compatriot of Luther a certain divergence of general character and aim in life connected with religion which makes itself felt beside the antagonism of race, and the traces of which appear in the literature of this controversy. Judaism is material optimism with a preference to a chosen race, while Christianity, whether Catholic or Protestant, is neither material nor in a temporal sense optimist. Judaism is Legalism, of which the Talmud is the most signal embodiment, and here again it is contrasted with Christianity and the Christian Ideal; which is something widely different from the mere observance, however punctual, of the law. In the competition for this world's goods it is pretty clear that the legalist will be apt to have the advantage, and at the same time that his conduct will often appear not right to those whose highest monitor is not the law. The Agnostic, seeing what he deems the reveries of Christianity rejected by the Jew, and imagining this to be the cause of quarrel, is ready to take the Jew to his heart. But it may be questioned whether he will find the affinity so close as at first sight it appears. The Agnostic after all is the child of Christendom. He is still practically the liegeman of the Christian conscience, whatever account of its genesis he may have given to himself. He has a social ideal, not that of the Church, but that of humanity, which has come to him through the Church, and which is utterly at variance with the pretension of a chosen race.

Apart from these local collisions, there is a general curiosity, not unmingled with anxiety, to know what course in politics the enfranchised Jew will take. He is everywhere making his way into the political arena, which indeed, under the system of party government, suits his traditional habits almost as well as the stock exchange. A money power is sure in the main to be conservative, and the inclination of Jewish wealth to the side of reaction in England and other countries is already becoming apparent. Poor Jews will be found in the revolutionary, and even in the socialist, camp. But in whatever camp the Jew is found he will be apt for some time, unless the doctrine of heredity is utterly false, to retain the habits formed during eighteen centuries of itinerant existence, without a country, and under circumstances which rendered cunning, suppleness, and intrigue almost as necessary weapons of self-defence in his case as the sword and the lance were in the case of the feudal soldier. He will be often disposed to study "the spirit of the age" much as he studies the stock list and to turn the knowledge to his own profit in the same way. It is very likely that he may sometimes outrun and overact national sentiment or even national passion, which he does not himself share. This is one of the dangerous liabilities of his character as a statesman. It might have been supposed that the Jews, having been for so many centuries shut out from military life, would be free from militarism; indeed, a high rank in civilisation has been plausibly claimed for them on that ground. Yet a Jewish statesman got up Jingoism much as he would have got up a speculative mania for a commercial purpose, and his consuming patriotism threw quite into the shade that of men who, though opposed to Jingoism, would have given their lives for the country. Among the ablest and most active organisers of that rebellion in the United States which cost a thousand millions sterling and half a million of lives, was a Jewish senator from Louisiana, who when the crash came, unlike the other leaders, went off to push his fortune elsewhere. There was no particular reason why he should not do so, being, as he was, a member of a cosmopolitan race; but there was a particular reason why the people who had no other country should receive his counsels with caution in a question of national life or death. A political adventurer will not be sparing of that which in the pride of Jewish superiority he regards as "gutter blood." Joseph, being the Prime Minister of Pharaoh, displays his statecraft for the benefit of his employer by teaching him to take advantage of the necessities of the people in a time of famine for the purpose of getting them to surrender their freeholds into the royal hands. He would no doubt have played the game of an aristocracy or even of a democracy in the same spirit, though his natural taste, as an Oriental, would lead him if possible to be the vizier of an absolute monarch.

Mr. Oliphant, in the work to which reference has already been made, proposes that Palestine should be restored to the Jew, with some of the vacant country adjoining; and it appears that this plan is not unlikely to be carried into effect. The restoration of their own land may have the same good influence upon the Jews which it has had upon the Greeks. It is not likely that of those now settled in the West any considerable number would ever turn their steps eastward. We know the anecdote of the Parisian Jew who said that if the kingdom of

Jerusalem was restored he should ask for the ambassadorship at Paris; but the westward flow of migration might be checked, and from the eastern parts of Europe, where the relations of the Jews to the native population are very bad, some of them might return to their own land. Mr. Oliphant seems to have little hope of seeing the Jews, even in Palestine, take to husbandry, and proposes that they should be the landowners, and that the land should be tilled for them by "fellahs" [Arab peasants]. We must assume that fellahs convinced of the validity of the Jews' claim to exemption from the indignity of manual labour will be found. But necessity would in time compel the Jew once more to handle the plough. The situation at all events would be cleared, and the statesmen who are now inditing despatches about religious toleration would see that Israel is not a sect but a tribe, and that the difficulty with which they have to deal arises not merely from difference of opinion, or any animosities produced by it, but from consecrated exclusiveness of race.

I cannot conclude without repeating that if this was a case of opposition to religious liberty, I should thoroughly share the emotions and heartily echo the words of Mr. Lucien Wolf. But I have convinced myself—and I think Mr. Wolf's own paper when carefully examined affords proof—that it is a case of a different kind.

RECENT PHASES OF JUDEOPHOBIA

by **Hermann Adler**

*[Hermann Adler became the Chief Rabbi of Great Britain in 1891.
When he wrote this 1881 reply to Goldwin Smith he was the Chief Rabbi
delegate. Adler, like many Western European and American Jews, denied
that Jews were a race—Jewish identity was based on religion. He wrote
that Smith had totally misread both the Old Testament and the history of
the Jews in Europe. The economic life of Jews was dictated neither by
religious principles nor racial attributes. It was, instead, determined by the
hard facts of Jewish history. Jews had no choice, Adler wrote, than to
abandon agriculture and crafts when these occupations were closed to them
in the Diaspora.*

*Adler detailed the trials of Russian Jewry and noted German anti-
Semitism, but was hopeful that the Russian government did not support the
former and that the latter was a "phase" in German history and would
soon pass. Adler remained convinced the Jewish identity had no place for
either race or nation, and later in his career was an opponent of political
Zionism.]*

"Recent Phases of Judeophobia" by Hermann Adler, first published in *Nineteenth
Century*, 10 (May 1881), 817-29.

Professor Goldwin Smith renews his onslaughts upon Jews and
Judaism with an acerbity and virulence which I may be permitted to
term Hamanic. Each sentence is a barbed arrow; each barb is tipped
with venom. I do not propose to traverse the ground already covered
by my former replies to the Professor's attacks, but shall mainly
confine myself to the task of examining the new charges which he
brings forward, and of exposing his distortions of Judaism and his
perversions of Jewish history.

The main argument, stripped of its side issues, is contained in a
narrow compass. Mr. Goldwin Smith discusses the anti-Jewish agitation prevalent in Germany, and justifies it on various grounds. He

attributes the persecutions of the Hebrew, past and present, in the first instance to the tribal exclusiveness of the Jewish people. According to him the Jew makes a religious idol of his tribe. "All the other races profess at least allegiance to humanity; they all look forward, however vaguely, to a day of universal brotherhood. The Jew alone regards his race as superior to humanity, and looks forward, not to its ultimate union with other races, but to its triumph over them all, and to its final ascendency under the leadership of a tribal Messiah." I maintain that these statements are entirely opposed to fact. The great bond which unites Israel is not one of race, but the bond of a common religion. We regard all mankind as brethren. We consider ourselves citizens of the country in which we dwell, in the highest and fullest sense of the term, and esteem it our dearest privilege and duty to labour for its welfare. Is there aught incompatible with our devotion to humanity and with our patriotism, if, at the same time, we feel sympathy for those who profess the same religious faith and practise the same religious ordinances, whether they inhabit this country or other lands? If the bond which unites the Jew were, in truth, tribal, it would be a matter of perfect indifference to us what might be the religious belief or practice of our brethren in race. But the bare fact that we regard as apostates those of our fellow Jews who abandon their faith, is proof sufficient that religion is the main bond. So Mr. Goldwin Smith proposes, as his panacea, that the Israelite should abandon his tribalism, and "all that separates him socially from the people among whom he dwells." This means that he should give up his separate church, his religious rites and prayers, his seventh day Sabbath, and that in Turkey he should conform to Islam, in Russia to Greek orthodoxy—in other words, that he should cease to be a Jew; and in spite of this, the Professor claims that he upholds religious toleration and liberty of conscience. "I will tolerate you Jews," he would say, "when you cease to be Jews; I will tolerate your religion when you reject it."

Yet he himself demonstrates the worthlessness of his suggested remedy. In Berlin, the headquarters of anti-Semitism, are numbers of Jews who have discarded every trace of tribalism and intermarried freely with the general population. But against these, even more loudly than against the consistent, observant, "hard-shell" Jew, the modern "Hep! Hep!" is raised.

I emphatically contest the position that our objection to mixed marriages is the outcome of tribal exclusiveness. It is essentially a matter of religion. It is an indispensable condition of domestic peace and happiness, that two persons who have entered into a compact to pass their lives together should fairly agree in their views on religion, which, to those who possess any religion at all, is a paramount concern of life. Hence statistics show that in all religious denominations the parties who contract marriage usually belong to the same faith, and that, for example, alliances between Churchmen and Catholics are comparatively rare. Alliances between Christians and Hindus, between Christians and Mohammedans, between Greek Christians and

Protestants are still more rare, and probably in every case must practically (and especially for reasons connected with the religious education of the offspring) be attended with renunciation of faith by one of the parties to the marriage. Why, then, should the Jew specially be taunted and blamed for refusing intermarriage, seeing that it would practically necessitate the abandonment of a faith which he has ever felt dearer to him than life itself?

Next, our opponent taunts us with practising the rite of circumcision, as Apion in the days of Josephus did; for there is a strange coincidence of argument between the anti-Semites, old and new. He calls it a savage custom; though the pain of the operation is probably not equal to that produced by the barbarous custom of piercing children's ears, and certainly not more dangerous than the highly salutary operation of vaccination. Nay, most medical men agree that the practice of this rite is positively conducive to health. And what distortion of fact does it indicate to brand the accomplishment of this rite as a tribal mark! We initiate our sons into the covenant of Abraham not because we desire to indicate that we belong to the same tribe, but because we are thereby obeying what we believe to be a Divine behest. Does not Milton himself, first among sacred Christian poets, characterise this ordinance as "that great covenant which we still transgress?"

The allegation that we hope for a Messianic age not of universal brotherhood is altogether without foundation. All the predictions of our inspired seers point to precisely the opposite view. They prophesy, indeed, that Israel will be restored to his land, and that a wise and pious king of David's lineage will there rule over him. But this is not to be the crowning climax of that golden age. Not a tribal Messiah will govern the world, but the Lord will be King over all the earth! "And he shall judge among the nations, and shall rebuke many people; and they shall beat their swords into ploughshares, and their spears into pruning-hooks: nation shall not lift up sword against nation, neither shall they learn war any more." "Then will I turn to the people a pure language, that they may all call upon the name of the Lord, to serve him with one consent." This, it may perhaps be argued, was the spiritual teaching of prophets holding transcendental views, which, however, took no root among the mass of the people. Turn we then to the recognised liturgy of the Hebrews. At the period when the article on "the Jewish Question" appeared we were celebrating the most solemn festivals of the year. And the burden of our chief prayer was: "Inspire, O Lord our God, all thy creatures with the reverence of Thee, that they may unitedly perform thy will. Speed the time when the dominion of tyranny will be removed from the earth, when all iniquity shall be dumb, all wickedness vanish like smoke." At the conclusion of each one of our daily services throughout the year we supplicate the Lord "that He may cause us speedily to behold the time when all flesh shall invoke His name, when all the inhabitants of the world shall know and acknowledge Him, so that unto Him every knee shall bow, every tongue swear fealty." Does this look as if we believe in "a tribal God"? So, too, all the authorised expositors of our law agree in declaring that the supreme boon of the Messianic days will consist herein, that their blessings are not to be reserved unto us, but will be diffused throughout the earth, that those truths for which we have bled and suffered will be recognised by mankind, that racial antipathy will come to an end, that all religious hatred will cease, that all men will feel and consider themselves as brethren and will think and act as brethren, that one language will be spoken—the language of truth, mercy, and love. What aspirations can be nobler than these? Can there be an acknowledgment ampler than this, of hope and expectation of universal brotherhood in the days to come?

Mr. Goldwin Smith proceeds further to trace the persecutions of the Jews not to any religious fanaticism on the part of the oppressors, but to the peculiar character, habits, and position of the Jewish people. He stigmatises them as a wandering and parasitic race, without a country, avoiding ordinary labour, spreading over the world to live on the labour of others by means of usury and other equally discreditable pursuits. And he does not stay to investigate whether he may not be guilty of the crying injustice of making a whole community responsible for the wrong-doings of its black sheep. He does not stop to inquire whether any of these failings may not be due to a long-continued system of persecution unparalleled in the annals of humanity. No; he asserts that they are characteristics inherent in the Hebrew branch of the Semitic stock. "Otherwise the Jews would not have adopted as a typical hero the man who takes advantage of his brother's hunger to buy him out of his birthright with a mess of pottage, or they would not record with exultation how they had spoiled the Egyptians by borrowing their jewels on a feigned pretext." This is all that the Professor has to say in respect to the place occupied by the Jewish nation and the Jewish Scripture in the development of mankind.

Has the Jew indeed done nothing for the world but to live on the labour of others? I address myself to the great body of my English countrymen and countrywomen whose hearts will beat responsively to the noble reply once given by our Queen to an African prince. The prince sent an embassy with costly presents, and asked her to tell him, in return, the secret of England's greatness and glory. She sent him not the number of her fleet, not the details of the inexhaustible wealth of her country; but, handing the envoy a copy of the Bible, she said: "Tell the prince that this is the secret of England's greatness." Need I state, that three-fourths of this volume consists of the Old Testament, which by common consent of Christian theologians contains the germ and nucleus of the New? And it is the Hebrew who has written down, preserved, and treasured his Sacred Scriptures.

I am well aware that Mr. Goldwin Smith will not assent to this position. To him the records of the Hebrew Scriptures are not more hallowed than any other boulder of a primeval world. To us it is something far different. To us, Jews and Christians alike, it has been a guide, a solace, and a friend during long centuries of darkness; to our philosophers a never-failing well of profound thought; to our poets a rich mine of beauteous imagery; to our moralists a source of purity, love, mercy, and justice. When, then, our opponent attacks the Bible, he attacks Jews and Christians alike. With a well-assumed horror, he reviles the Bible because he finds in it the command to exterminate the Canaanites. Surely it is sufficiently clear from the narrative that they were doomed on account of those abominable crimes which "caused the land to spew them out." He makes the Bible responsible for the cruel murder of half-witted women reputed to be witches. Yet it is an undoubted fact that its command was directed not against the half-witted, but against those criminals who practised witchcraft in its most mischievous forms, and often with fatal results by playing upon the superstitious fears of the ignorant, and arrogating to themselves a divine power. But, amid all this criticism, we fail to see one word of generous acknowledgment of the sublime truth of monotheism which our Bible proclaims, the lofty morality which it preaches, the tenderness which it enjoins to the slave, the emphasis with which it insists on the rights of the poor, the intensity with which it admonishes us to love God and to love our neighbours, the fervour with which it commends the duty of purity and forgiveness, honesty and truth, not forgetful even of the right of the brute to our compassion and help. Again and again he holds up his gargoyle, the massacre of the Canaanites, as the justifying cause of every medieval act of bigotry and intolerance. But the Bible is certainly in no sense responsible for religious intolerance. It presents to us the beautiful picture of Abraham interceding for the sinners of Sodom. It teaches again and again, "And if a stranger sojourn with thee in your land, ye shall not vex him. The stranger that dwelleth with you shall be unto you as one born among you, and thou shalt love him as thyself."

To all these liberal features in our Bible the Professor is blind. He sees there nothing but the failings of the "base Judean." How can it be otherwise, he asks, than that the Jew should follow mean and hateful trades, when he adopts "as a typical hero the man who buys his brother out of his birthright with a mess of pottage"? It has been remarked that the Bible is more read, but that it is also more *misread*, than any other book, and this charge aptly illustrates the statement. There is no word in the Bible to justify the assertion that the dealings of Jacob with Esau are deemed praiseworthy, and that if the former is held up as the typical hero of the race—a position which may well be contested—it is on the score of an act of trickery and craft. The Bible conceals nothing, extenuates no fault, writes for us no history of saints and angels unapproachable by man; but tells of human beings like ourselves, with faults like our own.

The statement that the Hebrews spoiled the Egyptians by borrowing their jewels on a feigned pretext, will also, upon examination, be found incorrect. Biblical scholars are agreed that *Vayishalu* should not be rendered "they *borrowed*" but "they *asked*." The Israelites had served their task-masters for a long series of years, and therefore, when they were about to quit the land of bondage, they were told they had a right to demand some remuneration for long service, and a compensation for cruel wrongs. We are expressly informed that the Egyptians readily *gave* (not *lent*) what was asked for. It is then utterly absurd to speak of a "feigned pretext." There are no grounds whatever for assuming that the Egyptians were led to expect that the presents would be returned to them.

I have dealt with the Professor's misreadings of Scripture, but I find that he has not been less unfortunate in his treatment of Jewish history. He maintains that it is inherent in the character of the Hebrew to shirk honourable labour, to prefer to live by the work of his head rather than by that of his hand. I will not now stay to discuss the question whether it be not at least as honourable to eat one's bread earned by the sweat of the brain as to eat that earned by the sweat of the brow, but will at once show that it is entirely at variance with fact to make Rabbinism responsible for the transformation of the Jewish agriculturist and handicraftsman into a money-lender and hawker. For while Aristotle declared that mechanics should not be admitted to the rights of citizenship in his ideal Republic, and, indeed, maintained that only slaves should practise handicraft, the text-book of Rabbinism speaks enthusiastically of the dignity of manual labour. The Jewish sages declared it a duty incumbent upon every father to teach his son a mechanical trade; and, with something of Oriental hyperbole, they continue, "And if he fail to teach his son, it is as though he encouraged him to robbery." Such admonitions had the desired effect; for there is hardly one art or handicraft practised in those days, of which we do not find representatives among our people. It would seem, also, as though these different trades associated themselves in guilds; for there existed in Jerusalem a Synagogue of the Coppersmiths, a Street of the Bakers, the Gate of the Carpenters, a quarter of the city exclusively inhabited by Potters. In the grand basilica Synagogue of Alexandria, separate portions of the building were assigned to the Silversmiths, Weavers, and other trades. The Rabbins, the authorised expounders of the law, deemed it derogatory to receive any reward for the exercise of their spiritual, doctrinal, and judicial functions, and maintained themselves by the labour of their hands. And thus in the Talmud we meet in curious juxtaposition the Rabbi and his trade in such phrases as these: "It was taught by Rabbi Jochanan, the shoemaker." "This tradition was handed down by Jose ben Chalafta, the tanner."

Josephus was able to say truly of his contemporaries, that they applied themselves exclusively to mechanical occupations, and to tilling the soil of their fruitful country. Nor is there any trace in Roman literature and in the decrees of the Emperors to show that the Jews in those days followed commerce or devoted themselves to money-lending. History declares it as a positive fact "that the Jews did not embrace trade and commerce until they were actually compelled to do so, until they were excluded from following mechanical occupations by the establishment of guilds, and it was made absolutely impossible for them to practise agriculture, because they were not allowed to hold land."

A very trustworthy evidence of the fact that the Jews are not by nature averse to mechanical labour is afforded by our knowledge of the pursuits in which many thousands of the Jews in Russia are engaged. A few words must suffice with respect to those who inhabit the countries outside Europe. Sir A. H. Layard met with Jewish shepherds in Kurdistan, who pastured their flocks on the hills of Baschkala, as their fathers had done before them. In South Arabia the chief mechanical trades, such as those of armourers, masons, weavers, dyers, smiths, and metal workers, are entirely in their hands, since the Moslem inhabitants despise artisans, and look upon handicraft as a pursuit unworthy of the free Bedouins. The same holds good of the Jews in Persia, who are silk spinners, glass polishers, and manufacturers of chemicals, and who, it may be added, also practise in large numbers as physicians.

The question will naturally be asked, How is it that, in those countries where all restrictions have been removed, the Jew does not devote himself with greater eagerness to mechanical occupations? One reason is to be found in the circumstance that children preferentially follow the calling of their parents. But the main cause is probably that, being obliged by the dictates of his religion to rest on the seventh day, the Jew is practically debarred from entering upon those occupations in which journeymen are employed. He is compelled to resort to trades in which piece-work is possible, and in which he can take his work home with him, so that on the Sunday he may make up for the lost Saturday. This accounts for the preponderating number of Jewish tailors, cap and shoe makers, such trades permitting piece-work and not being necessarily associative.

But the list of indictments against us is not yet exhausted. Our opponent taunts us with being a vagrant race, with leading a wandering life, a homeless existence. Was ever more heartless gibe flung at a defenseless race? What is our medieval history other than a mournful record of our banishment and expatriation—measures which the Professor seeks to justify? And yet he reproaches us—driven to wander—with being wanderers. Should, then, all our ancestors have thrust the dagger into their breast, or plunged themselves into the foaming waves? Or should they have betrayed their holiest trust and hypocritically avowed their acquiescence in a faith to which their heart and intellect refused credence? The fact remains that the Jew, where he is degraded, owes his degradation to the acts of his oppressors. The usurer who became one by being excluded from every honourable occupation, might well reflect upon his revilers: "The villany you teach me I will execute."

Can we be surprised that the Jew addicted himself to commercial pursuits when this was the only mode of maintaining wife and children; that he became over-fond of amassing wealth, when gold became the only means by which he could buy safety and toleration? Can it be a matter of wonder to us, that in many instances he did become abject and cringing, when the iron hand of bigotry tried to crush all his attempts at mental and social elevation, when the soul-chilling venom of contempt, the "oppression that maketh the wise man mad," gnawed at his heart and cowed his nobler nature? And even then he was not altogether crushed. He strove manfully, and strove not in vain, to preserve those lofty aspirations that were inseparable from the memory of his former greatness. Even then he remained very different from what his oppressors laboured to render him and his detractors would fain make him appear. Their ancient virtues, industry and thrift, temperance and continence, and their consequent well-ordered and affectionate family life, the reverence of children for their parents, and their tender help to the poor—all those loveable traits, which contributed so largely to save the people from utter destruction in the bitter days of the Middle Ages, have happily not yet departed from them.

But the nature of the writer with whom I am at present dealing is cast in a sterner mould. He can see naught in the Jews but what is blameworthy. He places them on a par with the Gipsies. Gipsies they possibly would have become had it not been for the saving effect of their faith, their Bible, and their literature. But unfortunately Mr. Goldwin Smith, instead of preparing himself for writing on the Jewish question by a diligent perusal of the works of Zunz, Graetz, Kayserling, and others, drew his inspiration from some of the anti-Semitic pamphlets which have flooded Germany, fastened on some expression hastily jotted down by a traveller in his diary, or treated as sober fact the glowing fancies of an enthusiast.

He might also perhaps have paused ere he quoted approvingly the remark of M. Renan, that the Jew wished to enjoy the advantages of nationality without being a member of the nation or bearing his share of national burdens. One need scarcely expose the unhistorical character of this statement, as it is sufficiently well known that the Jews have never set up a league in defiance of national law, nor refused to pay taxes, nor refrained from entering military service when permitted to do so.

The expulsion of the Jews in 1290 is justified by the Professor by the statement that the English people had never invited the Jews to England. I fail to perceive how this plea extenuates the guilt of the banishment, seeing that as "the King's chattels" they had been specially assured of royal protection; and, as Mr. J. R. Green proves in his *History of the English People*, they had, at all events, in the earlier period of their settlement been beneficial to the nation at large. Nor does a word of sympathy escape the writer for the Jews of Spain, who endured the sore pang of banishment rather than abandon their faith.

The Professor is altogether at fault when he deals with contemporaneous history. With his characteristic love of paradox he lays down the startling proposition that the number of Jews in any country

31

is nearly in an inverse ratio to national well-being. I may at once refer to the instance of the country just named, and inquire whether it is not notorious that Spain even to this day suffers from the loss of the intelligence, mechanical skill, and general resources of its Jewish subjects. Hence, those statesmen most solicitous for its welfare are now promoting the re-introduction of the Hebrew element into the Peninsula. It is quite true that our people abound in Hungary. But we have yet to learn that the Transleithan monarchy is in a state of wretchedness caused by its Jewish inhabitants. On the contrary, Franz von Loher states that, without them, landed property would be entirely depreciated in value and industry paralysed. Ireland, unhappily, cannot be described as one of the soundest and healthiest of communities, yet it numbers very few Jews—fewer than Scotland. Holland is passed over in discreet silence; yet in this prosperous and well-ordered country the Jews bear as large a proportion to the general population as in Germany. These instances will surely suffice to show that the proposition laid down by Mr. Goldwin Smith is a glaring illustration of the logical fallacy, *non causa pro causa*.

I have yet to advert to the Judeophobia existing among certain sections of the population of Germany. Professor G. Smith traces this antipathy to the re-awakening of national life. Professor Mommsen, who assuredly speaks with greater authority on this theme, brands it as "a monster bred of national feeling run wild." The sentiment is probably due to a variety of causes. When cherished by the agnostic or atheist, it may probably be attributed to the fact that Judaism is the archetype of the religious principle which he abhors. Thus the Jew of Germany has, in our day, to bear the brunt not only of the *odium theologicum*, but also of the *odium anti-theologicum*. But there is also the economic cause. The bureaucrat of Germany whose salary is a mere pittance; the *Junker* who regards commerce and industry with disdain, and who eats up his patrimony in the morning of life; the small trader who, through lack of energy and industry, misses his chance—all these are filled with envy at the Jew, who by his self-denying thrift when young, his inexhaustible energy, his capacity for work, and his commercial skill, achieves success, and is enabled in the evening of life to live on a scale of luxury which to them is unattainable. Now, I will readily admit that the Jews of Germany (and possibly of other countries) are not free from a certain love of ostentation and fondness for superfluous finery. Yet purse-pride and money-arrogance are characteristics of the *parvenu* of every creed. It takes time for the gold fresh from the fiery furnace of success to quiet down to the sober beauty of *vieil or*. It would, however, be a monstrous injustice to assert that it is only in the race for wealth that the Jew seeks to compete with his Christian neighbour. The most rabid Judeophobe will readily admit that there is hardly one small town in Germany without its Jewish physician, and that there is no university which has not more than its due proportion of professorial chairs occupied by Hebrews. Nor can he deny the services rendered by that high-minded politician

Lasker, the value of the contributions of Traube to medical science, the importance of the studies of Benfey, one of Germany's best Sanskrit scholars, and the profound learning of such men as Bernays, Steinthal, and Lazarus. The solution of the Jewish question in Germany may then with safety be left to be worked out by the intelligence and good sense of the men of light and leading among the great Teutonic nation. The Christian, finding that the Jew has gained his position by his superior diligence, skill, and energy, will, instead of sneering at work and trade, seek to labour with equal diligence, equal skill, and equal energy, and while competing with him in every field, commercial, professional, and political, will yet live with him (as is happily the case in England, France, Austria, and Holland) on terms of amity and good fellow-citizenship. And the time is probably not far distant when Germany will regard the Jew-baiting as a hideous nightmare, which, during a period of political dentition, disturbed her for a brief while.

But it is impossible to speak with equal hopefulness concerning the anti-Jewish agitation which during the past seven months has been raging in Russia. Adverting to the persecutions which the hapless Jews endured in England and Spain during the Middle Ages, Mr. Goldwin Smith says complacently, "All these horrors now belong completely to the past." Would that it were so! Some few scanty notices have occasionally appeared in the public press respecting certain outrages perpetrated upon the Jews of Southern Russia. But I am certain that the general public has but the dimmest conception, if any, of the magnitude and intensity of the barbarities recently inflicted by an infuriated mob upon an unoffending population. I would fain not dwell at length upon, and yet cannot pass over in silence, the heart-rending atrocities enacted, between April and July last, in Kieff, Elizabethgrad, Ekaterinoslaw, Alexanderowsk, and numerous other towns and villages, when defenceless men were killed or dangerously wounded, tender women outraged by vile ruffians, infants flung from the casements into the streets below. In Kieff twenty-two married women and three maidens were dishonoured by savage troops; ten women died from the effects of fright and outrage; four men were killed. At Smiela twelve men were killed, and twenty-two wounded. In Elizabethgrad whole streets of houses in the Jewish quarter were literally razed to the ground, all the Jewish residences were sacked, all the shops plundered; and these scenes were repeated throughout a great part of the towns of Southern Russia where Jews reside. But a few weeks since the riots were renewed in Balbirishok, in the government of Suwolk. During these one men was killed and twenty seriously wounded; the synagogue and school were demolished; shops destroyed and pillaged. In fact, the various riots were accompanied by murders, foul, strange, and unnatural, by an utter disregard for sex and age, by such abominable acts of lust and lawlessness that I am justified in regarding them as a counterpart of the Bulgarian atrocities. Nor can these barbarous persecutions be considered as only local outbreaks. The Hebrews resident in Western Russia have also suffered from the wholesale burning of their houses and property, the work of incendiaries. In Minsk nearly eight thousand inhabitants have lost their all. In Koretz thirty people perished in the flames, and eight hundred families have been rendered homeless. The extent of misery caused by these disasters cannot easily be gauged. Newspapers and private correspondents tell us of the misery endured by many thousands of families during the summer months in consequence of the want of food, clothing, and shelter. What, then, will be their sufferings during the rigours of a Russian winter? Authentic information has been received from an eye-witness, now in London, that at a short distance from the Russian fontier, in Austrian Brody, ten thousand refugees are now, as I write, huddled in cellars and in the snow-covered streets, imploring to be sent to more hospitable lands. The Jews of Great Britain and other countries have, as a matter of course, bestirred themselves to relieve the immediate necessities of the victims; but all efforts are insignificant in the face of such gigantic evils, though in this work they have been and are still being humanely aided by their Christian brethren. This, however, is but a mere temporary palliative. The condition of the Jews of Russia is still grave in the extreme, as they are in continual apprehension of a recurrence of these outrages. We will not, we cannot, but believe that the Russian Government regards these riots with disapproval. Indeed, in many instances the ringleaders have been punished, and Commissions have been appointed to inquire into the origin of the outbreaks, which those best acquainted with the subject believe to be due to the restrictive laws and legislative disabilities that make the Jews as Pariahs and targets for every manner of insult and injury.

As might have been anticipated, a portion of the Russian press has defended these persecutions on the ground that the Jews ply trades injurious to the rest of the population. The value of this defence might easily be tested by a reference to statistics. It is well known that in many of the provinces of Central Russia Jews are not allowed to settle. Yet it will be found that, for example, among the Mujiks in the government of Saratow, where there are only sixty-four Jews among a population of 1,725,478, there is no less wretchedness, no less dram-drinking, than in the provinces of Grodno and Mohilew, where the Jews form respectively thirteen and fifteen percent of the entire population. It is quite contrary to fact to state that the Jews of Russia are exclusively pedlars, hawkers, and money-lenders. Among five hundred refugees from Brody who recently passed through Liverpool on their way to the United States, there was not a single money-lender. The majority of them were blacksmiths, bricklayers, masons, joiners, saddlers, tinkers, locksmiths, plumbers, painters, shoemakers, tailors, and agricultural labourers; about twenty percent were petty traders, and ten percent broken-down shopkeepers and merchants who had lost their all. Near Gulaipol there is a Jewish agricultural colony comprising about five hundred families; and though these poor tillers of the soil could surely not be charged with exploitation, yet they were not allowed to escape unscathed. At Kischinew (the principal town of Bessarabia) there is a flourishing trade school, where Hebrew lads are trained to be carpenters, blacksmiths, machinists, and cabinet-makers. Russia has its Brassey in the Israelite Poliakoff, the well-known railway contractor; its Titus Salt in the Jew Brodsky, the largest cultivator of the beetroot and the largest sugar refiner. Such men add to the wealth of the country, and stimulate industrial energy.

I do not mean to assert that the Jews of Russia are immaculate, that instances do not occur in which they seek to evade the restrictive laws which hamper them on all sides. In 1846, when stringent ukases [laws] had been issued against them, Sir Moses Montefiore went to St. Petersburg and besought the Emperor Nicholas to extend to them the Imperial protection. "They shall have it, if they resemble you," was the Czar's characteristic reply. Can it be expected that a people exposed to every kind of degradation for centuries can grow in a day or even in a generation into a community of Montefiores?

The wretched condition of the Jewish population of Russia, numbering above three million souls, and the inability of their brethren here and throughout Europe to help them efficiently, is a striking commentary on the powerful political influence with which the Jews of Europe are credited in certain quarters. We can only appeal to the sense of justice and humanity which we hope animates the Russian Government, and without which it can never aspire to maintain a position in the concert of civilised States. We can only implore the Czar the abrogate every restrictive measure by which his loyal Jewish subjects are hampered, to repeal every oppressive law which interferes with the freedom of domicile and hinders them from earning an honest subsistence. We can but call upon our own countrymen to influence public opinion in Russia. The Russian people are powerfully swayed by the utterances of free England. Only a few weeks since, the *Novoe Vremya* reproduced Mr. Goldwin Smith's view of the Jewish question, and pointed out exultingly that England shared its anti-Jewish proclivities. I am certain that every right-minded Englishman will indignantly repudiate such an assertion. Among the noblest qualities of England is her intense love of fair play, the generosity with which she has ever championed the cause of the persecuted and oppressed of every race and creed. And this may be averred without exaggeration, that no community has ever stood in greater need of sympathy and justice than the poor, down-trodden, panic-stricken, helpless Jews of Russia.

TESTIMONIALS FROM THE NEIGHBORS OF JEWISH FARMERS IN RUSSIA

by Arnold White

[The question of Jewish economic life is brought into clear focus by these statements from non-Jewish farmers concerning the ability of Jews to work in agriculture. The statements are clear evidence of the depth of the belief that Jews were unsuited to occupations other than commerce and finance, and Arnold White offered them as proof that Jews could work on the land and with machinery.

White gathered these statements, which were appended to an 1892 article entitled "The Truth about the Russian Jews," while on an eight-month mission to Russia at the behest of Baron de Hirsch. De Hirsch, a German financier and philanthropist, founded the Jewish Colonization Association, which attempted large-scale settlement of Eastern European Jews in Argentina, Brazil, the United States, and Canada. He believed that Jews were well suited to agriculture and sent White to examine the few Jewish farms in Russia. He considered the creation of a Jewish state a fantasy, and refused to aid the Zionist movement.]

"Testimonials from the Neighbors of Jewish Farmers in Russia" by Arnold White, first published in *The Contemporary Review*, 61 (May 1892), 706-08. This selection is the last part of an article entitled "The Truth About the Russian Jews."

The following are recent testimonials of responsible Russian proprietors and others to the agricultural capacity of the Russian Jews:

(1) Living on my estate in the district of Cherson for twenty-five years, close to the Jewish colony of Novopoltawka, I can testify that for all this time I have been content with their conduct as neighbours, and that there has never been a quarrel or misunderstanding between us. I can also testify that the majority of the inhabitants of this colony occupy themselves personally with agriculture, and have procured of

late years the best machines for agricultural purposes, for which they have also plenty of horses and cattle.—(Signed) Proprietaire honorary hereditary citizen, PETRE PETROWIEZ ZURITZIN.

(2) 1892, February 18.—I certify that my neighbours, the Jewish colonists of Novopoltawka, grow successfully different kinds of corn, as well as carry on all the usual occupations of an agricultural life, as for example, gardening, rearing of cattle, horses, &c.—(Signed) Proprietaire in the district of Cherson, NICOLAS PAWLOFF LOUGOWSKI.

(3) [Certificate.] The farm of Kaspar Nicolaewski offers to certify that the Jewish colonists of "Efengar" and "Dobroie," in the district of Cherson, are hired every year, by the above-mentioned farm, as labourers, to sow the winter and spring wheat, and the work in certain fields is confided to them alone, tilling, sowing, &c., and they acquit themselves very well as skilled agriculturists. Further, full of resources for supporting themselves and their families, they do in winter all that there is to be done. They cut fuel, put the sheafs in ricks, carry straw and fodder, drive and convey goods from the station to the farm; in a word, there is not any field work that they do not carry out honestly and carefully during all the year, for more than twenty years.—The 20th February, 1892. J. BOUTOWIEZ, landed proprietor.

(4) January, 1892. We, the undersigned German village agriculturists and Russian peasants, neighbours to the Jewish colonies of the rural department "Grafski," in the Government of Ekaterinoslaw, seeing the request of the provost of the rural (Schultz) colonies of Grafski, of Trondolonbouwka, Beer Ziroulski, of Netzaiewka, Leiba Schnukal de Grafski Beer Komissaruk, of Selenaia Pole Aisik Schwidler, of Nadejnaia Peisach Swirski, and of Sladkowodnaia, Isaac Gueberowiez delivers this to the effect to testify that the Jews of the above-mentioned colonies occupy themselves with agriculture with energy, cultivate their lands on the same footing as the peasant proprietors of the same class; are in character moral, temperate and honest. In support of which we add our names.—(Signed) D. SCHMIDT and G. SCHMIDT, proprietors; AIXENTI BURIAK, T. SATZERKLIANY, peasants of the village of Federowka; A. BONDARENKO, proprietor; KOSTENKO ANTONE G. BORETZ, peasant of the village of Ganzolo; I. KOCH, proprietor of Renfield and the Starosta of Renfield Frei.

Truly the Jewish agriculturists of the colonies of Grasskaia, Nadejnaia, Sladkowodnaia and Telenaia Pole, in the department of Grafski, work with their own hands as agriculturists, and cultivate the ground which has been granted to them by Government on an equal footing with their Greek, German and Russian neighbours. In proof of this I add the administrative seal, February 6th, 1892.—(Signed) the Chief of the District (Zemski Naczalnik) WLADIMIR MICHAILOWIEZ KOROSTOWEZEFF.

(5) [Certificate.] Ministry of the Interior—Government of Ekaterinoslaw, District of Alexandrowsk, Administration of the Commune of Temirof, No. 72.—Delivered by the Administration of the Commune of Temirof to attest the fact that the agricultural Jews in the neighbouring colonies of Priontnaia, Roskoschnaio, Bogadarowka and Gorkaia, in the Department "Priontinski," in the district of Alexandrowski, occupy themselves really with agriculture, and cultivate with their own hands the lots of arable land with the same diligence as our own rural population; each one possesses enough good utensils and instruments, and cattle for work and for breeding, as well as horses; they lead a quiet and irreproachable life. In proof of which we sign with the seal of administration.—(Signed) for the Starosta, A. PARCHOMENKO, clerk.

(6) [Certificate.] The 24th January, 1892.—We, the undersigned, neighbouring proprietors of the Jewish colonies of Novo-Slatopol, Weselaia and Mejeritz, in the department Slatopolsk, in the district Alexandrowsk, in the Government of Ekaterinoslaw, offer to certify that to our knowledge the Jewish agriculturists of the said colonies occupy themselves with agriculture with great energy, and yield nothing in field work to the peasant farmers of the same class. They have a fairly good number of agricultural instruments, and of cattle for labour and breeding: as to moral character, they live an irreproachable life. In witness of this we sign ourselves. [Here follow the signatures of the Russian proprietors.]

THE
JEW-BAITING
ON THE
CONTINENT

by Emil Reich

[Emil Reich was a well-known historian and lecturer on many subjects; he was once called a "universal specialist." Born in Hungary, he lived in the United States and France before settling in England in 1893.

In this 1896 article Reich puts a different stamp on anti-Semitism than most observers. He believed that the movement was both social and political. The social aspect, he wrote, was directed against the "New Jew"—the acculturated Jew who did not convert to Christianity. He felt that this sort of Jew was hated in large measure because he was a social upstart, which, Reich believed, he was.

The political basis of anti-Semitism was of a different stripe. Reich saw the political immaturity of some European states as the root of political anti-Semitism. For Reich, anti-Semitism was not a racial issue; nor did he disapprove of all the effects that anti-Semitism might have on European society and politics.]

"The Jew-Baiting on the Continent" by Emil Reich, first published in *Nineteenth Century*, 40 (Sept. 1896), 422-38.

Jew-baiting is no novel phenomenon in history. Ever since the dispersion of the Jews amongst the nations, rulers or classes of men, both heathen and Christian have practised that sport extensively. In former times, it is true, they did it in very rough fashion, and untold numbers of Jews were massacred all over Europe by crowds hounded on by that peculiar hatred which all nations have felt for the chosen people of God. Nowadays the persecution of Jews is more in conformity with our polished manners. Now, instead of the club and the hatchet, is used the poison of calumny, and the scandal of accusations, denunciations, and aspersions of crimes opprobrious and ignoble. Formerly there were persecutions *pur et simple*. No one cared to find another name for it. Now there is *anti-Semitism*. A new word was needed, and it were folly to regard that new word as a mere catchword of ephemeral value, and as hiding under its novel garb only an old and stale fact. Words, like men, have their successes, and in success there always is a certain measure of truth. The word anti-Semitism does mean something novel. It is not altogether the old persecution of the Jews, or rather it is not the persecution of that kind of Jews which was set upon by people in previous centuries. It is, I take it, the persecution of the reformed Jew, of the emancipated Jew, of the Jew who is a doctor, a professor, a banker, a playwright, a journalist, a lawyer—in one word, of the gentleman Jew. The Stoeckers and Ahlwardts, and Luegers, and Drumonts, and likewise all other leaders of the anti-Semitic movement on the continent, do not really hate the small Jew, the orthodox Jew, the petty trader in foreign garb and of strange manners. With regard to him, the meanest of anti-Semites has the great satisfaction of despising him. Nobody really wants to destroy the subject of his disdain. To look down upon a whole class of people, to feel oneself superior to them—is not this a satisfaction far too exquisite to be lost to the disdainer by the extermination of the disdainee? How true, if brutally so, was that Hungarian countess who used to hear the reports of her young Jewish steward in her bedroom early in the morning, lying on her bed in a state of nature! When being asked how she could so forget herself, she replied, with an astonished mien, "To be ashamed of Moses?" (meaning the steward) "Why, Moses is no man! He is only a Jew." No, it is not the Jew proper, the old-style and forbidding Jew whom the anti-Semites are after. What they aim at is the Jew who has practically abandoned the law and ritual of Judaism; and the appearance of that sort of Jews in large numbers being a novel phenomenon, their persecutors necessarily adopted a new party-name.

The new name is thus fully justified; it actually means a novel thing. This has been largely lost sight of by the writers on anti-Semitism. Both Jews and Christians have, as a rule, insisted on the obsolete traits of anti-Semitism. They have in tones of indignation or broad learning essayed to show that modern Jew-baiters are using old and worn-out armoury; that their accusations of Jewish rites have long been refuted; that the whole movement is a preposterous relapse into medieval obscurantism. It is well known that the late Emperor Frederick the Third, as well as Professor Theodor Mommsen, have publicly declared German anti-Semitism to be a stain on the honour of Germany. The sovereign as well as the scholar regarded any perse-cution of the Jews as attempts at reviving the worst and long outgrown diseases of a low and despicable stage of civilisation. Yet, with utmost deference to the noble Emperor and to the great historian, I beg to differ. Modern anti-Semitism is not a mere revival of medieval obscurantism. It has a *raison d'etre* of its own; and it is inconceivable how a scholar endowed with the fine historic instincts of Mommsen could be misled by some of the maneuvres of anti-Semitism into misconstruing the real purport of that movement. For the anti-

Semites have indeed had recourse to measures used by the lowest sort of Jew-baiters in long bygone times. They have revived the old calumny that Jews need the blood of Christians for the preparation of their Passover bread. Of the numerous trials to that effect in recent times, the most gigantic was that of the alleged murder of Esther Solymossy by the Jews of Tisza-Eszlar, a village in Central Hungary, in 1881. In that ghastly case the young son of the Jewish butcher of the village declared before the judge, and in presence of his father, that he had seen through the keyhole of the synagogue how his father, together with a number of other Jews, were slaughtering Esther, and letting her blood run into a receptacle used for religious rites. The trial lasted for nearly two years, and kept all Hungary, nay Europe, in a state of ever-growing intense excitement. The Jews were acquitted in all the three instances permitted by Hungarian law; but I must add, and from personal knowledge too, that the number of persons other than Jews believing in the innocence of the Tisza-Eszlar Jews was, and probably still is, exceedingly small, although the innocence of the Jews was established beyond the shadow of a doubt. Nor need that astonish any one. Popular rage wants its victim. The Hungarians, for reasons to be mentioned hereafter, were enraged against the gentlemen Jews. They wanted their victim; and what could satisfy them more than to cast the unspeakable ignominy of ritual child-murder on the subjects of their hatred? A few years later, in 1891, at Xanten, a small place in Westphalia, a child five years old was found dead in a barn with its throat cut. The barn being near the shop of a Jewish butcher, Buschhoff, he was accused of murdering the child in order to provide blood for Jewish rites. No clue to the actual murderer was found, and Buschhoff was put on trial. After two weeks' hearing of the case, during which time the whole of learned Germany was completely absorbed in and frantically excited over the guilt of the Jew, the public prosecutor himself asked for the prisoner's acquittal, claiming that the accused had proved an *alibi* for every minute of the day of the murder. Buschhoff was of course acquitted by the jury. I do not entertain the slightest doubt that the majority of Germans did not acquit Buschhoff at all. In vain did learned Christian Hebraists, such as Francis Delitzsch, publish ponderous treatises on the absolute lack of foundation in all these stories of ritual murder by Jews: the trials for such murders were steadily increasing. After Tisza-Eszlar in 1881 came the trials at Dohilew and at Grodno, in Poland, in 1886; the trials at Constantinople, Caiffa, Budapest, Pressburg, in 1887; at Saloniki, Samacoff, Kaschau, Pressburg, in 1888; at Varna, Kustendji, Aleppo, Pressburg, in 1889; at Damascus, Beyrout, in 1890; at Xanten, Philippopoli, Smyrna, Budapest, Corfu, in 1891; at Malta, Rahova, Posen, Kolin, in 1893, &c. &c.

This apparent resuscitation of past methods of persecuting Jews has given much colour to the view that modern anti-Semitism is but an incomprehensible revival of medieval fanaticism in the midst of our enlightened century, or one more type of "degeneration," atavism, social psychopathy, &c. However, none of these explanations will hold water. In anti-Semitism we are bound to recognise a social and political phenomenon growing out of the present constitution of the continent with inevitable necessity; and since this constitution is certainly not identical with the frame and tenor of society in the Middle Ages, or any other previous period, anti-Semitism too is largely an historic phenomenon of its own. To scoff at it, to indulge in bleak indignation over it, to minimise its various aspects by regarding it as a passing fad of the masses—any such attitude will at once preclude us from rightly comprehending it. It is passing strange to note how utterly incapable contemporary historians and philosophers have been to assign anti-Semitism its adequate significance in modern history.

On the continent the number of treatises, essays, pamphlets, and articles in journals published on anti-Semitism is legion. Some of the greatest of continental sociologists, economists, historians, and philosophers have pronounced upon that movement, and vainly tried to account for it. In the seventies, when anti-Semitism was in its first stages, they did not, with one single exception (the late Professor Treitschke), even surmise the coming growth of the movement. In the eighties, when all Germany and Austria-Hungary were drenched by anti-Semitism, they offered a most amusing variety and divergence of opinions as to its causes and cure. But ought not historians and historic economists proper to have given us a satisfactory explanation of this remarkable contemporary phenomenon? If history is not meant to help us, by the comprehension of the past, to a fair understanding of the present, if not also of the future, what then *is* History meaning? Yet our modern continental historians have so far not proved much more able in unlocking the present with the keys of the past. I am not overstating the case by attributing this peculiar inefficiency of history to the neglect of that powerful method of comparison which in other fields of inquiries has yielded such surprising results. What we want is comparative history. Organic beings cannot be understood by any other process of thought. Let us try that method in the study of anti-Semitism.

II

I premise a few words about the contentions and allegations of continental anti-Semites. These are simple enough. In their opinion all the evils in society, commerce, and more or less in any other sphere of life come from the Jews. The Jews oppress the labourer, corrupt the capitalist, bribe officials, contaminate the press, mislead justice, and, by marrying Christians, deteriorate the blood of the Aryans. The Jews as Semites—that is, as a race totally distinct from that of the Aryans—cannot but be antagonistic to the latter. The Aryan, and chiefly the Teutonic branch thereof, is an idealist born; the Semite is an unmitigated materialist. The Aryan, and more especially the German, is frank, slow, and unselfish; the Semite is cunning, shrewd, and selfish to the core. In short, the Aryan is all white by nature; the Semite is all black, also by nature. There is no compatibility between these two races, and to insist on the removal of the Jews from the communities of Aryans is only to obey nature's own imperative demand. The Jew has no fatherland, or rather, as Schopenhauer has put it, the fatherland of the Jew is the other Jews. They are a state within a state, as another great German philosopher, Fichte, has said long ago; and, adds that same thinker, the Jewish question could be radically solved only by cutting off each Jew's head, and putting in its stead another head in which not a single Jewish idea is to be found. The Jews cause financial paralysis by congesting all funds at the exchanges where they dominate. They likewise cause mental consumption by sullying the intellectual atmosphere, through the press, with its perfidious and mendacious misrepresentations of things political and social. They are moreover the chief promoters of Socialism, the two founders of which, Karl Marx and Ferdinand Lassalle, were Jews, as are its chief leaders at present. Nor must it be forgotten that the Jews, by supplanting the small trader and the small landowner, have, like locusts, devastated and depopulated the "flat land," or the country proper, and thereby only increased those plague-boils called large cities, which, according to Prince Bismarck, ought to be razed to the ground one and all, and at an early convenience too. The Jew is, in the beautifully inane words of Richard Wagner, "the plastic demon of man's decadence." He is purely negative, uncreative, imitative, and destructive. In music Jews have done nothing but bastard matters, and Aryan taste naturally revolts from such tone-hebraisms as Mendelssohn's violin-concerto, or his music to *Midsummer Night's Dream*; let alone Meyerbeer or Goldmarck, whose music is sheer talmudistic *yodlers*. In literature Jews are only successful in a kind of verbal bartering, and dexterous dazing of the reader. Heine, it is true, was a Jew; but it is equally certain that he ought not to have been one; and then he is far too witty to be a true German writer. And as to Spinoza, he proves nothing. Having been declared a nuisance by nearly all professors of philosophy, how can we expect him to be more accommodating for the professors of anti-Semitism? The fame of so many Jewish writers is owing only to a concerted mutual admiration society of theirs, rendered very efficient by their preponderance in the international press. Last, and yet first, the Jews have all the gold and other money in their hands. They are rich, all of them. There is really no poor Jew; and the Russian Jews were a mere farce palmed off on innocent Europe by the late Baron Hirsch, who, after fleecing the Turks—since which time they are so barefaced—posed as a founder of hospitals and other diseased objects. The Jews have the Mammon; and more particularly the Rothschilds have it. They own all governments. All ministers are in the pay of the Vienna or Frankfort house of the famous bankers. All posts are in their gift and patronage. They really run Europe. And if the Christian people of Europe will not pull themselves together ere long, then history will be reversed, and the Ghetto, wherein in former times Jews were locked up, will come to be the panel for Christians, kept under lock by their superiors, the Semites.

This is the sum total of the countless anti-Semitic writings published on the continent during the last eighteen or twenty years. To these theories practical responses were not missing either. Jewish merchants were boycotted, and annoyed in all imaginable manners. In the parliaments, in the press, from the pulpits of Catholic and Protestant preachers alike, Jews were and are being exposed to all the opprobrium and scandal that their opponents can muster. In vain did some Christian and a host of Jewish writers and journalists exhort the anti-Semites. The current of hatred went on increasing in bulk and rapidity, and finally reached a definite political organisation. Both at Berlin and at Vienna the anti-Semites, not content with the social taboo they had succeeded in spreading against the Jew, formed into parliamentary parties, with a programme and working staff. Their number steadily increased; their example was imitated in the various diets and councils of the provinces and towns of Germany and Austria proper and quite recently, as is well known, the anti-Semites gained such an overwhelming majority in the municipal council of Vienna as to enforce in the face of opposition on the part of the Austrian Government the appointment of Lueger, their leader, as temporary vice-mayor, and in due time as Mayor of Vienna. In consolidating themselves into numerous and thus influential parliamentary parties, the anti-Semites have become a real power in the state-life of Germany and Austria. In France they have not yet reached that stage; but it is nowise impossible there too. In Italy there is little anti-Semitism. Not on account of the small number of Jews though; for numbers do not have much influence in that matter. In France there are scarcely over 70,000 Jews; yet anti-Semitism rages there just as wildly as in Germany, where there are 600,000, and in Austria with its 1,500,000 Jews. In fact no one can at present conceal from himself that anti-Semitism is, in one way or another, a fixture of the political and social life of the continent. The Jews will no doubt survive it. Have they not survived all the attacks and onslaughts levelled at them by all the nations of Europe, and for nearly a score of centuries? Nor is it, to my mind, difficult to see why they survive all attacks. They never seriously resist. Since the reign of the Emperor Hadrian, when the Jews, broadly speaking, for the last time offered real and obstinate resistance to their assailants, they have, as a body, never seriously essayed to combat those that attacked them. They suffer and endure; they moan and wail; they bandy wit or sarcasms at their oppressors; but they never show real fight. The Protestants, whether in France or Germany, in Austria or Hungary, have, at the risk of millions of lives, fought their oppressors on hundreds of battlefields or in innumerable party strifes. Having shown tangible resistance, they were in some countries crushed out altogether, in others reduced to an insignificant minority. Not so the Jews, and least of all the modern Jews. They go complaining to everybody and write in the *Revue des Etudes juives*, or in similar learned periodicals, long-winded articles where, paragraph by paragraph, and especially by means of footnotes, it is proved that the Jews are really not *mechants*; that they are good, law-abiding, and quiet citizens; that one Jew, in 1801, provided food for French prisoners at his own expense, and that another in 1806 actually died in the interest of a French patriotic cause; and that in law, medicine, mathematics and other sciences, Jews like Stahl, Lassalle, Jacobi, Lombroso, &c. &c. have contributed to the stock of knowledge no inconsiderable share. That is to say, to the men who brandish real swords over their heads, they answer by showing them drawn revolvers indeed, but drawn on paper. The Jews harp on their undying tenacity and indestructibility. So may the gipsies do. Neither Jew nor gipsy ever resists; hence both indefinitely survive. Do not the German Jews, especially the better class among them, more than merit their treatment at the hands of the anti-Semites for enduring without any serious revolt the shame of being refused the rank of officers in the German army, although by law they are fully entitled to it? People who can stand that will stand anything. Where is the body of Jews in Germany that has publicly declared, and then manfully acted up to its determination to get access to the ranks of officers by means of agitation unrelenting and uncompromising? Had Catholics in Prussia been excluded from what by the constitution of Germany is their right, they would certainly not have rested until they could have forced the Protestant majority to admit them to the honour of officers in the army. The Jews in Germany have never made the faintest attempt, beyond incidental woeful reproaches in Parliament, and very funny remarks on the Prussian lieutenant in feuilletons. It has been said, every country has the Jews it merits. Truly, every aggregate of Jews has the anti-Semites it deserves. That a certain class of people is hated by other classes: nothing occurs more frequently in history. All real history is full of violent party struggles, and all parties cordially hated and fiercely fought one another. But here is a novelty. Here is a well-hated class, so gorgeously hated that many an ignored class might well envy them such solid hatred. They are fought in public and private, by means fair and foul, systematically and at random, from above and from below. What splendid occasion for people ambitious for greatness! But here is the worm. The Jews never coalesced into parties openly fighting their opponents. The individual Jew is virile enough. In no one case has the individual gentleman Jew refused or shirked a duel. All the more strange is their absolute passive resistance as a body. The modern Jews are, in history, the only class of people that, being openly attacked, recoil from openly fighting their assailants. And this is the historic novelty.

Or rather, not quite novel. For there has been indeed, and there still is, another class of people equally hated as the Jews by immense numbers of civilised men, and who have likewise never resisted attacks in an open and recklessly bold manner. Hence, having been not only persecuted and chased, but positively exterminated and declared to be non-existent, they yet exist, and will continue to exist for many more centuries. It is by comparing the case of the Jews to the case of their historic parallel that we will get at the right point of view wherefrom to judge and analyse the anti-Semitic movement on the continent. This other class of people is the Jesuits. They, like the Jews, are openly hated, and have been exposed to attacks and aggressions of a formidable character, and for the last hundred and fifty years. Their order was solemnly abolished by Pope Clement the Fourteenth in 1773. But their lease on life has been renewed and again renewed, and they still continue to wield very considerable power. And all this they achieved *because* they never offered open resistance. The famous phrase of their General Ricci, "Sint ut sunt, aut non sint," indicates an iron firmness and obstinacy which the Jesuits really never possessed. Had they acted according to their general's dictum, they would have long ceased to exist. They acted, however, otherwise.

III

Of the numerous orders of monks founded by the Catholic Church some have, at times and by certain people, been ridiculed or hated. The Franciscan friars of the thirteenth and the Capuchins of the sixteenth were objects of strong antipathies in many a country. However, the Jesuits, and they alone, have been and largely still are the best-hated organ of the Roman Church. Their name alone of all names of monastic orders has given rise to a new adjective, "Jesuitic"; and this testimony of language is sufficient to prove the intense animosity arrayed against them. It is in adjectives where nations store up their likes and dislikes. This general and lasting hatred—can it be explained by racial antipathies? The members of the order of Jesuits are of all races and nationalities. Can it be accounted for by a peculiar mental or emotional temper innate in such people as become Jesuits? They are of all possible tempers and emotional calibre. It remains only to ascribe that general hatred of Jesuits to the fact, instinctively or consciously present to all their enemies, that they are essentially strangers—strangers in every country, in any kind of commonwealth, under all circumstances. They have neither nationality nor race, neither family nor other social ties. They are outside all communities, and thus absolute strangers. By their system of education as founded by Loyola, their disciple necessarily becomes a being attached to no single person or groups of persons, to no particular or collective interest other than that of his order. He is the ideal stranger. Callous to the world of emotions engendered by the ordinary affiliations of human life, he becomes as it were extra-human, and so, in a sense, superhuman. But while this estrangement makes him unsympathetic, it also renders him more powerful. No wiser word ever fell from the lips of John Selden than the remark that they who want to rule people make themselves as different from them as possible. The stranger, by the very isolation in which he stands to the people around him, acquires a superiority over them. Their foibles are not his; and therefore where they are weak, he is strong. Their virtues are not his; and therefore where they recoil, he will boldly push onward. Their perils are not his; and therefore where they succumb, he will survive. But chief of all, where they are agitated by passion and blinded by violent desires, he is cool and collected. In all history strangers have exercised an enormous influence. As so many other chapters of history, this too has not yet been written. There is no history of strangers. Historians, from patriotic motives and from ignorance, have never dwelt upon that point. Yet pause a moment to weigh the influence of strangers in England, from King William the First, the Norman, to King William the Third, the Dutchman; or from Anselm, of Aosta in Piedmont, Archbishop of Canterbury, to Panizzi, the Italian, the creator librarian of the British Museum; in France, from Alcuin of York to Cardinal Mazarin the Italian, and Napoleon the Corsican; in Austria, from Rudolf of Habsburg in Switzerland, to Eugen, Prince of Savoy, Van Swieten the Dutchman, Count Beust the Saxon, and Count Andrassy the Hungarian; in Russia, from the first Ruriks from Sweden to Catharine the Great, the German Princess &c. It need not astound us that in countries where over fifty percent of the population are strangers, or the first generation of strangers, as for instance in the United States, the most marvellous progress has been made in all matters requiring push, enterprise, and feverish activity. The backwardness of Latin America has been ascribed to their Latin race, which is alleged to be a race unfit for the struggle of life, as witness the ancient Romans. It has also been ascribed to the Catholic religion, which is alleged to be an inferior equipment to Protestantism, as witness Catholic France. The simple truth is, Latin America has a very much smaller influx of stangers. Where the United States receive hundreds of thousands, Latin America receives a few thousands. This characteristic energy of the stranger is so true that it also applies to what we might call relative strangers—that is, the constantly increasing rural element in our large towns. Within less than three generations the population of London, Manchester, or Paris, Bordeaux, is entirely changed. The Londoner proper is supplanted by the man coming from the country with the keener energies of a stranger. Nearly all leading men of the French Revolution were provincials that had come to Paris hungry for money, glory, or blood. They were to the *Parisien* proper, strangers. So it was in ancient Babylon; so in Athens; so in Rome.

The Jesuits, then, and the Jews are the great types of the stranger. Being clearly distinguishable—one by their costume and organisation, the other by certain physical features and social habits—they cannot submerge in the mass of the strangers generally. When, therefore, circumstances prepare an attack on either of them, they are a clear aim, and the simplest know where to hit. Having arrived at this, the only correct standpoint, we need not trouble ourselves with ethnologic or historic researches in order to reconstrue the Jew and his mental or moral features. If we steadily keep in mind that he is, generally speaking, not only a stranger, but also that he has been so these fifteen or sixteen hundred years and in all countries, his innermost *esse* will become quite clear to us. He has the energy, aggressiveness, shrewdness, and frequently the recklessness of the stranger, but with threefold intensity. Being constantly on the alert either against danger or for rapid advance in fortune, he must needs be sober and temperate, and particularly keen in judging men and events. Being severed from broader interests of large aggregates of men, such as town, county, or nation, his emotions feed chiefly on family sentiments, and he becomes the most feeling of fathers as he is the most devoted of sons. Up to recent times he had only to gain by a change of *regime*; hence he readily enlisted with revolutionists. And finally, whenever he is received into society, he is practically an upstart, a *parvenu*; and hence he manifests all the objectionable qualities of that class of strangers. Upstarts, whether individuals or nations (witness the Prussians), are ostentatious, self-centered, vain, and boastful. These qualities are inevitable in upstarts. It is equally inevitable that good society resents these qualities very keenly. Good society is in reality a state of its own; the laws, officers, and procedure of which are even more finely developed than in states proper. In classical antiquity society proper did not exist. Laws were given by the public assemblies both on matters treated in modern parliaments, and on matters now left to the sway of fashion and other social powers. Hence the Jews in their antique *Diaspora* could not commit the specific crime that they are perpetrating at present. For there is little doubt that the main and most general cause of the dislike for Jews at present is their lack of social tact. The laws of society are unwritten, because everybody knows them. They form an organised whole covering the smallest detail, the minutest eventuality. No man can conform to them unless he has been in the habit of so doing from childhood onward. In consequence of the more or less complete emancipation of the Jews on the continent in the course of the last hundred years, a very large number of Jews have, by entering liberal professions, received access into society. In the years 1876-81 the Jewish students at the Berlin *Gymnasien* (colleges) formed no less than 17 percent of the total. In 1887 the Jews furnished 10 percent of the students at Prussian universities, although they formed only 1 1/3 percent of the population of Prussia. Nearly 10 percent of the judges in Prussia are Jews; and at the highest law court of the German Empire, at Leipsic, there are ten Jewish judges among a total of seventy-nine. In the twenty-one universities of Germany there were, in 1888, one hundred and four Jews as regular professors, that is, 8 percent of the total; and of the *Privatdocenten*, or tutors and prospective professors, the Jews formed 18 percent. In the University of Vienna there were in 1885-86 two thousand and odd Jewish to three thousand and odd Christian students. In Hungary and Italy, and also in France, the statistics show similar results.

From the above facts it will be seen that the Jews of the continent have been given access to professions and social preferments which had been closed to them for centuries. The stranger was given a chance of blending with a native. How did the stranger use his privilege: Did he really assimilate himself with the world into which he was admitted? Did he appropriate both the faults and virtues of his new profession? The most favourable critic of the Jews cannot assert that. And how could the Jews have done so? I have already hinted at the fact that the Jews in modern times never fought for their emancipation as did the Protestants or other sects. They got it indeed, but without fighting for it. The ideas of the French Revolution had such a profound influence on the peoples of Europe that governments were fairly ashamed of the bondage in which Jews were held by them. So these governments hastened to liberate the Jew. Had the Jews been going through all the anguish and terrors of religious wars, had they acquired their citizenship by efforts as immense as were those of other oppressed religious sects, they would have come out of the struggle diminished in numbers indeed, but worthier of their privilege. As it was, the Jews were not only upstarts, but upstarts by dint of sheer good luck; that is, the worst of upstarts. In countries like Hungary for instance, where the liberal professions were, up to 1867, exclusively in the hands of the nobility, the sudden influx of Jewish lawyers, judges, and writers could not but be most injurious to the interests of the hitherto privileged class. For a nobleman to be obliged to treat as his peer the son of the Jew whom his father had kept as "village-Jew" was a most tantalising position. What made it absolutely unbearable was the lack of all social tact on the part of the *novi-homines.* In the ballroom, in the "casino," or club of the town, in the street, the newly emancipated Jew displayed a familiarity and forwardness with the men and women of the old Hungarian society, that, as it was in the worst taste, so it was most bitterly resented. Duels among Jews and Christians began to increase at a terrible rate. To no avail. That initial vice mentioned above went on cankering the whole relation. I am fully aware of the fact that the Jews constantly harp on the principles of "humanity," "civilisation," "enlightenment," throwing them wholesale into the face of whosoever wants to exclude them from social or legal equality. This modern humanity, this modern civilisation, this modern enlightenment, however, was it won by the Jews? Was it not won by Christian peoples labouring and fighting for it in the blood of their bodies and in the distress of their souls? This world of Europe is a sword and rifle begotten world. He who has kept outside that secular fight has no claim to the benefits thereof. If the fighters generously admit him within their ranks, let him practise many virtues, but foremost of all let him practise the virtue of modesty. And here is the heavy and unanswerable indictment against the emancipated and reformed Jew: he is profoundly immodest. The old orthodox Jew is perverse and uncouth if you please, but he is a character. There is system and logic, and even poetry, in his weird consistency of forbidding exclusiveness. If properly roused he, and he alone, may still show fight—real, honest, fatal fight. He is absurd perhaps, but true. There is a grandeur in his stintedness, and fascination in his self-inflicted isolation. The greatest of Jewish luminaries in science or philosophy have nearly always come from among the orthodox Jews. He is not immodest or forward, for he does not crave for Christian society. He is an erratic block on the surface of Europe. But the reformed Jew, he who abandons the ritual of his fathers without adopting the creed of the Christians, he who is ashamed of meeting his lowly and still orthodox relative, and arrogantly struts on the boulevards and other public places of great capitals, he is downright absurd and worthy of the lash of society. And thus far modern anti-Semitism is quite right. It was and is a just and legitimate reaction against the preposterous arrogance of the New Jew. Nor has this reaction been without its beneficial effect on many of these New Jews. No inconsiderable number of the fiercest anti-Semites have arisen from among Jews. Thus to the funds for the "mission" of Stoecker, the arch-Jew-baiter of Berlin, Jewish bankers of that town contributed very largely. A still larger number of New Israelites have taken the lesson of anti-Semitism to heart, and have seriously tried to blend with the nation whose members they are. But much, very much, remains to be done, and unless Christianity will be embraced by the reformed Jew, he will, it is to be feared, never quite assimilate himself with the Christian.

In studying these causes and these effects of what might be called social anti-Semitism, many differ with its promoters as to some of the means they have employed in propagating it. But there is another and more serious species or aspect of anti-Semitism—the political—and as the former is vested in a socially intolerable failing of the New Jew, so this is arising from a politically poor constitution of the nations of the continent.

IV

The study of movements in the past, similar to that of political anti-Semitism in our time, reveals the fact that nations either unripe for, or decadent from, parliamentary government show their inferiority especially in the incapacity of producing real political issues of parliamentary struggle. Their parties take up "platforms" which in times of high parliamentary development would have been left to the regulation of the home or the drawing-room. Instead of rallying around men and principles of truly political drift and weight, they try to hush up their inaptitude by falling foul of relatively harmless classes or institutions. This generally happens when, after long wars, a period of peace is setting in. The excitement of war having subsided, people long for new modes of excitement. The evils of war have been shown up by many a well-intentioned writer. The evils of peace have scarcely been pointed out. Yet they are almost as glaring as the former. No sooner had the Romans, by the middle of the second century B.C., conquered the Mediterranean world than they began to interslaughter themselves; and agrarians, socialists, and religious reformers were calling upon the citizens to remedy the "terrible diseases" of the commonwealth. It was exactly the same after 1763. Europe, sick of three immense and useless wars—that of the Spanish succession (1701-13), the Austrian succession (1740-48), and the Seven Years' War (1756-63)—Europe wanted peace but could not stand it. Political life was just beginning to grow, first in the heads of thinkers and writers, then in the bosoms of the bourgeois classes, and this new life wanted issues, aims, centres of struggle. Having absolutely no parliamentary issue proper in that they had no parliaments, the *Zeitgeist* forthwith created a surrogate which was sufficient to animate the masses and the governments.

This surrogate was the fight against the Jesuits. In all Catholic countries of Europe a deluge of pamphlets and skits, popular books, and elaborate treatises was poured forth containing all imaginable accusations and denunciations of the Order of Jesus. The Jesuits were the root of all evil. They had clandestinely caused by their intrigues all the late wars. They were the perdition of the youth whom they taught, of the nobility whom they confessed, and of the kings and princes generally whom they ruled. The accusations levelled against them in the seventeenth century were mere sops and child's play beside the fearful insinuations now raised against them.

By this time we are pretty fairly informed about the truth of all these fearful incriminations. In common fairness we cannot any longer write history and hold the Jesuits guilty of one hundredth of the crimes imputed to them at about the middle of the last century. We do know that they then abused their power indeed, but far less—nay, infinitely less—than from 1550 to 1650, and that on the whole they were not much more harmful than any other of the then ruling classes. That they were and are hateful on account of their very constitution as absolute strangers, this much we may and do grant. That they were or are the root of all evil is untrue, and preposterous to hold. No parliamentary fight will kill *and* exterminate them. They must be met by means over which parliaments are powerless: by a change in the minds of the people.

The parliamentary fight against the Jews at present is precisely on the lines and has the same origin as had the fight against the Jesuits in the last century. After the gigantic wars of the French Republic and Napoleon the First, Europe was held in a state of siege from 1815 to 1848—in some countries as late as 1860 and 1867. During that long torpor the various nations were constantly clamouring, if in subdued tones for parliamentary government. In reality, however, they were not ripe for it at all. It was only a timid imitation of the theories of the French Revolution. They cried for modes of government which they had long unlearned to practise, and of which they had no clear idea. The revolutions of 1848 affrighted the rulers; and fearing lest all Europe should break out in a second and still more formidable French Revolution, they slowly consented to grant parliamentary governments, and at the end of the sixties nearly all continental countries had been granted parliaments of their own. After the wars of 1864, 1866, and 1870-71, peace settled down on Europe. The various parliaments were opened, and the necessity was felt to create parties. This is easily and naturally done in countries of long parliamentary habits and wants. In the New Parliaments, however, this was the chief stumbling-block. Parties arose indeed, but they were so unnatural, so far-fetched, that they had scarcely any vitality in them at all. The "fractions" of the German Reichstag rose and fell and changed like fractions of coloured glass in a kaleidoscope. Their number sometimes reached twenty. Likewise in the Reichstag at Vienna. And now it was that men endowed with considerable insight into the needs of the time began to work at the formation of a new nucleus of party-crystallisation. As had been done a century ago by the Jesuit baiters, so now those clever agitators, feeling that the politically untrained masses in Germany and Austria would never get enthusiastic over purely political issues, substituted for it one of the ready-made social antipathies. Society indeed was, all over the continent, in a stage of maturity infinitely superior to that of the parliamentary state. Society had material enough for party organisation, and among these none was surer of general acceptance than the hatred of the New Jews arising from circumstances related above. Here then was a nucleus of a party endowed with enduring vitality.

And now followed with necessity, as in the case of the Jesuits, the string of accusations, all the more exaggerated the less they were founded on truth. The Jews are the root of all evil; they corrupt the administration; they are murderers of children; they enslave the labourer and bribe all governments, &c. In reality the Jews have, either in commerce or in other walks of life, not done more harm than many another class that had, and abused the chance of power. In reality Jews are, *as a rule*, very far from rich, and any one of the rich monastic orders is far richer than they. In reality Jews have a particular and almost craven horror of blood, and have never murdered children for ritual needs; several Popes have declared this blood accusation to be the most absurd of allegations, and in no single modern case have Jews been convicted for such a crime by a court of law or a jury. Yet nothing will convince or can convince the anti-Semites, and for the simple reason that their existence as a strong political party depends on the belief in those alleged atrocities. And if all the Jews of Germany and Austria suddenly left Europe altogether, the anti-Semites, far from ceasing their agitations, would continue to exist as heretofore. They would fight the "Semitic" element in Christians generally or in Turks, Russians, or—Englishmen. This is no mere assumption. For so far have things anti-Semitic come to develop that the word "Semite," again, and precisely as the word "Jesuit," is used in a general sense, and quite irrespective of Jews. The large portion of Frenchmen who cordially hate the English have, in an elaborate book written by one Louis Martin, given utterance to their firm belief that the English are

Jews. The anti-Semites of Vienna carry on a crusade against the Jews and the Hungarians at the same time.

The political aspect of anti-Semitism on the continent is thus an unmistakable symptom of the poorly developed political instincts of most of the continental nations. Should they ever reach political manhood, they will drop anti-Semitism as too barren a means of great political work. The Hungarians, for instance, whose political life dates back to centuries before the French Revolution, have soon dropped anti-Semitism altogether. They do have real political issues to work on. They do not need surrogates. Most of the other nations on the continent, however, still need it as a first schooling in public business. And this is the redeeming feature even in political anti-Semitism. It indicates that Germans and Austrians are beginning to wake up from their inertia in matters public and political. It is a prelude to something better. The New Jews will not benefit by that. They will continue to practise their policy of abstention. They will not crystallise into parliamentary parties, and their most likely fate is to get swamped by the orthodox Jews. The sooner this will happen the better. In this well-knit and plastic Europe of ours we do not need hybrid, colourless cosmopolites like the New Jews. And if anti-Semitism had done nothing but bring the great question of nationality into still stronger relief, it has well deserved of Europe.

THE
ZIONIST
CONGRESS

by Theodor Herzl

[This article, published in 1897, was both a report on the First Zionist Congress held at Basle, Switzerland, and a reply to the critics of Zionism. Herzl defended the concept of a Jewish nation with a barbed pen and, in a somewhat more thoughtful style, wrote that the Basle Congress proved Zionism to be a practical solution to the Jewish Question.

The article also provides insight into Herzl's view of the Jewish people, particularly Russian Jewry, and his own role in the salvation of his newly discovered Jewish nation. Herzl was compelled by the rise of anti-Semitism, especially the 1894 Dreyfus trial, which he witnessed as a reporter for Vienna's Neue Freie Presse, *to the conclusion that the only hope for the mass of European Jewry was a national home outside of Europe and "secured by public right."]*

"The Zionist Congress" by Theodor Herzl, first published in *Contemporary Review*, 72 (Oct. 1897), 587-600.

The three closing days of August saw a congress at Basle concerning the significance of which friends and foes alike seem already pretty well agreed. It was the Congress of Zionists. Zionists! Until then that word was almost unknown to the public at large. Zionism virtually made its bow to the Gentile world at Basle, and disclosed for the first time what its aims and its needs were.

It requires only a superficial acquaintance with public life to know that every champion of a political idea is inevitably doomed to misunderstanding, to accusation, and to calumny. Let the subject only be one of general interest, and every one will feel himself called upon to pronounce his final and indisputable opinion concerning it. Nor will the inability to grasp its ultimate significance prove in any way a deterrent; on the contrary, the opinion will be volunteered with all the more readiness and positiveness. For the dispassionate observer of mundane things, truly a source of ever fresh diversion!

In undertaking the solution of a great problem, it is necessary, above all things, to allow your opponents the utmost freedom of opinion and expression. In that way their most stenuous efforts, their most mischievous strivings, will be robbed of their sting, and prove, to say the least, refreshing. I can only say that since the moment when I took up the gauntlet on behalf of my poor brethren, and rubbed shoulders with much suffering—with more, alas! than I had at first guessed—the very bitterest opposition of my foes has provided the only source of relaxation for me. That was the humour of it.

Otherwise the situation is sad enough. Our movement is assuredly born of necessity—of the necessity of the Jews throughout the world. But, before I go further, it shall be my task to define the nature of this Zionism, for the benefit of the reader who is unacquainted with its elementary principles.

It was in my work, "The Jewish State," which appeared a year and a half ago, that I first formulated what the Congress at Basle virtually adopted as an axiom. In the terms of that definition: "Zionism has for its object the creation of a home, secured by public rights, for those Jews who either cannot or will not be assimilated in the country of their adoption." When I glance at that familiar passage, which I have uttered over and over again and as often defended, and recall the bitter struggles which it has given rise to within the ranks of the Jews themselves—when I see how, as it issues from out the pale of the Ghetto, it is pounced upon, worried, and even dragged through the gutter—I wonder at the blindness of human passion. One can scarcely believe that a demand so modest, which threatens or endangers the rights of no man, could arouse such a wild storm of feeling. But the fact is there all the same, and I know only one adequate explanation of it: the Jewish question is still the same living force in the mind of man as it was of old. In this year of grace humanity is just as little able to view the matter through the calm, dispassionate glass of reason as it was throughout the whole of the eighteen centuries following upon the Captivity, when our conquered forefathers were scattered over the face of the earth. And yet there are many who venture to assert that a Jewish question does not exist. Ah! would that it were so. The Jewish question is a living reality, and those to whom that question has come home morally or physically will look in vain for freedom from their pain. That is the position of most Jews today, albeit it is just as remote from my intention now as ever it was to raise a feeling of false sentiment on behalf of my persecuted brethren. I wish simply to establish the fact that we suffer. Max Nordau gave utterance to that truth at the Congress in words, the lofty anguish and sonorous force of which it would be difficult to match. He said: "This is the moral Jewish misery, which is more bitter than the physical, because it befalls men who are differently situated, prouder, and possessed of finer feelings."

It is candidly admitted that we Jews hold the moral sufferings of our people as paramount, although in many countries our brethren are the victims of bloody persecution and maltreatment, and find themselves robbed of the common right to earn or to claim security for their property. But there are other racial minorities and individuals throughout the world who have to endure cruelty and hardship of every kind, for we are still far from that ideal condition of things when the right of every human being to pass his earthly life in peace and happiness shall be respected. We do not ask that the Jews' lot shall be better than that of other races. We simply want to see removed that odious privilege which forces us to fill an exceptional position in the world because of the accident of birth. "Each according to his works," is a motto which actuates the Jew equally with the Gentile. To us there are no other means to obtain that legitimate end than the creation of a lasting home for the Jewish race based on the solid foundation of legal rights.

But is this not apparently begging the question, which is: Does a Jewish nation still exist? Those to whom a nation means nothing more nor less than an accumulated mass of humanity living together in territorial unity, have naturally answered that question in the negative. These sagacious thinkers have overlooked the necessity of considering the term "nationality" from a purely abstract point of view. Also they have entirely forgotten that an exception must be made of the special case of the Jews. I consider the nation to be a historical group of human beings of evident kinship held together by their common enemy. Look at the history of nations and tell me, has there ever been an exception to this rule? Accepting this historical definition of a nation as our standard, then it will be difficult to deny to the Jew his right to national consideration. It is not too much to say that the Jews are a race of quite exceptional tenacity of existence. Eighteen long centuries have flown by and wrought no change in their aspirations; eighteen centuries of unexampled suffering. But they have outlived it all and preserved intact the consciousness of state and the sense of territorial possession.

That is the position which I took up when I wrote my "Jewish State." Today such a method of reasoning is no longer necessary. In the place of logical inference and historical proof, we have a new and living fact of very special force and significance—the Basle Congress. At that Congress, the Jews demonstrated in word and deed their unshakeable nationality. Naturally, even that will be disputed. Everything that we do or say will be disputed. Facts so obvious have perhaps seldom been denied with such vehemence as in our case. Black is called white and straight crooked, yes is no.

The Gentile has never yet disputed our nationality. It is true that, while admitting this fact, he does not act consistently with his view. No unbiased critic, however, has as yet had anything to say against the facts. That *role* has been reserved for the Jew. The Jew it is who has gone head down against the cause. And why? We have to deal here with a state of nervous apprehension. He is filled with a mistaken fear, and under the influence of that fear he goes too far. It might perhaps be better if our opponents were to content themselves with declaring that they personally no longer belong to the Jewish nation, whenever such a declaration appears to be necessary in a particular case. A confession of that kind would win respect for the confessor whose character was deserving of it, and whose motives were above suspicion. But to deny a whole nation's existence, to blot it out utterly from the world, because one does not wish to belong to it, is an excess of caution, nay, it is more; it is, to say the least, an immodesty in argument. Mr. A. or Mrs. B. is not a Jew. Excellent! (In certain cases very excellent for us.) But there can still be a Jewish nation in spite of that.

But this does not by any means exhaust the list of curious freaks which the Jewish opponents of the Jewish national idea have treated us to. And here I am reminded of an anecdote from the Ghetto, one of those anecdotes which Heinrich Heine found so diverting. Two Jews appear before the magistrate. The plaintiff demands compensation for a pot which, having been lent to the defendant, was returned by the latter broken. The defendant submitted three points for his defence: "Firstly, he did not lend me any pot at all; secondly, the pot was already broken when he gave it to me; and, thirdly, I have returned it to him whole." The comparison is odious, not to say burlesque. But we have the spirit of burlesque developed to a far higher degree when we hear individual Jews say: Firstly, the Jews do not form a community; secondly, Judaism has a mission to fulfill in the world; thirdly, they alone are patriots who only think of the country of their birth.

Firstly: The Jews do not form a community. Good. Then in that case the denier has no right to put up his own individual opinion as a standard for others. It can have just as little or as much authority over the rest as the speaker himself.

Secondly: Judaism has a mission. Then a community does in reality exist; for Judaism, whose *Diaspora* is here expressly admitted, can only be contained in the persons of those who proclaim it. But Judaism in its essence is independent of its supporters; it has long since formed an inseparable unit of the ethical principles and the imperishable records of human culture. To say that therefore the Jews have felt themselves called upon to play the schoolmaster to the world is to go from facts. The Jew who would presume to take that standpoint would be guilty of the grossest and most ridiculous coxcombry. There may be individuals actuated by this conceit; the great mass of the Jews are free from it. What we want and what we strive for is to go shoulder to shoulder with the rest of the nations in the realisation of a millennium of peace and happiness for the whole world. That dream is great enough.

Thirdly: The patriotic objection. We Jews have the firm conviction that in drawing off in a legitimate manner a superfluous and unhappy population from the countries where their presence has aroused much discontent, we are doing our mother-country a great and lasting service. In many countries it would mean nothing more nor less than the establishment of peace among the citizens. Shall we call that unpatriotic?

For some countries Zionism will have a preventive value. Today there are two oases in the anti-Semite world, England and Hungary. In Hungary, however, the question of prohibiting further emigration of poor Galician and Russian Jews into the country has been under lively discussion. And who knows whether tomorrow England will not be anti-Semitic—should the influx of unhappy Russian Jews into the East-end [of London] continue, and the Jewish palaces around Hyde Park go on simultaneously increasing in the same striking degree? The necessity for drawing off the pauper elements from England and Hungary cannot be gainsaid. Doubtless many, perhaps all, who feel their position secure, are one with us in our proposals to "channel and drain" the great masses of the proletariat. Not a word, however, must be breathed of a "State secured by public rights"—it would be such a reflection upon the patriotism of those who would willingly remain behind! Who in all reason could ever find anything mischievous in the demand for a guarantee of public rights when such mighty issues are at sake? Today countless numbers of human beings are consistent and unconditional supporters of the Zionist movement, but only under the one condition that this fundamental law of our national existence shall not be yielded up. Let that fundamental law once be lost sight of, and for the time being at least, the leaders would sacrifice all authority, while the masses in whom the sense of national consciousness has been aroused would in a twinkling be scattered into countless atoms again. Nothing was more instructive at the Basle Congress than the vigour— I might almost say violence—with which the representatives of the great Jewish strata of population resisted any attempt to limit the guarantees for a State based on public rights. The executive appointed to draw up a programme had proposed "a legally secured home." The delegates, however, were not satisfied, and clamoured for an alteration to "secured on the basis of international rights." It was only by adopting the intermediary expression "public rights" that an agreement was arrived at. What the Jews desire is not to acquire more tracts of land, but a country for the Jewish people, and to emphasise that desire in terms as plain as possible without wounding certain legitimate and sovereign susceptibilities. We can acquire land any day in our private right everywhere. But that is not the point with Zionists. In our case we have nothing to do with private rights. What the Zionists are alone directing their attention to is the "public rights" idea. In that they hope to find a remedy for the old evil. Were I to express myself paradoxically, I should say that a country belonging to the Jews on the basis of public rights, even though down to the very last parcel it was the legally secured property of non-Jews would mean the final solution of the Jewish question.

On the other hand, the increase in Jewish possessions based on private right has given rise to anti-Semitism everywhere. Therein lies the kernel of the whole question. It has been often asserted that the Zionism which I represent is nothing more than what Baron Hirsch and others have already attempted—viz., to transform the Jewish proletariat into agriculturists. I venture, notwithstanding, to think that they are not identical. Hirsch and the "Lovers of Zion" took up the question from the standpoint of private rights. We, the political Zionists, on the contrary, wish to attack the question from the "public right" standpoint. That is the difference.

If I am not greatly deceived, there is just as little of the element of exaggerated self-importance in our movement as there is of illegal intention. It is simply an attempt to do adequate justice to a great question, and our public proceedings have shown already that we intend to do nothing against established right and morality. We have held a gathering at Basle before the whole world, and there we saw the national consciousness and the popular will break forth, at times like a convulsive upheaval. To Basle came Jews of all countries, of all tongues, of all parties, and of all forms of religious confession. There were more than two hundred representatives of the Jewish people— most of them delegates for hundred[s] and thousands. Men from Rumania alone brought over fifty thousand signatures of those who had sent them there. There surely was never such a motley assembly of opinions in such a narrow space before. On the other hand, there would certainly have been more conflict of opinion in any other deliberative assembly than there was in this. We saw people brought together who were the direct antipodes of each other in their philo-sophic and religious views and in their political and economical professions, and who, knowing that, did not attempt to hide the fact. In short, they formed the parties which are to be found in every nation, and which promote, rather than hinder, the welfare of a people. But in Basle all differences were set aside, as if an arrangement had been entered into by which in the great moment that the nation arose, no one should any longer be Socialist, Liberal or Conservative, Free-thinker or Orthodox, but simply a Jew. All of us who went to Basle to consult as to the solution of the Jewish question were surprised, nay, overpowered, when we saw, as it were, a thing spring into being over our heads with a fullness and power we had little guessed—unanimity in Judaism. We were far too deeply moved to be able at the time to do full justice to it. The Basle Rabbi, who was not a member of the Congress, but who attended as an onlooker, asked leave to speak during the closing meeting, in order to confess solemnly that he had been a decided opponent of Zionism, but that he had become a convert. Even the calm listeners, the strangers and also the onlookers, who had come there with the intention to mock, were, as we learned later, deeply moved by this particular incident. And what was it for us; what did we feel and experience in the moment when the new-born nation first saw the light of day? Aged men, with white beards, sobbed freely, and to the eyes of youth came the light of a new earnestness.

But I will not speak here of our feelings. A Jewish gentleman has seen fit to publish in the *Times* a few premature remarks concerning the Basle Congress. Had he been in Basle, he might probably have spared himself these foolish observations. Among other things he contended that the Congress was not a real national assembly, owing to the fact that certain benevolent corporations and boards of deputies were not represented on it. They were not there? We did not invite them. What have we to do with boards of deputies, benevolent institutions, and the hundred and one Jewish Pickwick clubs? Our good friend of the *Times'* columns has simply failed to understand our movement. He does not know what the resurrection of the nation is. He has not seen that we have already begun to place Judaism upon a new basis without sending round the hat, and without any banquets. But even if we are not exactly displeased with these communities, we are certainly far from allowing ourselves to be influenced by them. Zionism has in view another kind of community for Judaism, a new and greater one, and a single one. Also another system of representation.

There is a certain form of West European superciliousness which is dearly fond of treating the Jews of other countries as backward creatures indeed. He is always a barbarian who does not happen to be understood. Thus we have people representing the East European Jew as a sort of Caliban. What a mistake! For my part I am bound to confess that the presence of the Jews from Russia was the greatest event of the Congress. For some time I had been in correspondence with many Russian Jews and had received some visits which had proved interesting. Notwithstanding this I did not venture to draw my conclusions as to the conditions of the masses from these specimens of modern culture. I accepted alone as truth the reports concerning the physical efficiency and love of work of the lower Jewish strata in Russia. It was, in fact, impossible to do otherwise, as sufficient evidence appeared to be forthcoming—the reports being confirmed by every witness who had seen the Jewish mechanics and agricultural labourers at work in the "Colonies," or philanthropic experimental stations, as they are called. The efficiency of these mechanics and unskilled labourers forms one of the bases of our plan. They will have the task of introducing the first work of civilisation into a waste land. They are selected to make the land arable, and they will do so, although we have never conceived of any other arrangement than that they should have our intellectual help and guidance. In that Congress at Basle we saw a Russian Judaism arise, having a degree of culture that we had not anticipated. From Russia they were nearly seventy strong, and we can say without fear of contradiction that they represented the views and feelings of the five million Jews of Russia. Truly a humiliation for us who had believed that in culture we were superior to them! All these professors, medical men, lawyers, engineers, manufacturers, and businessmen, have attained a level of education which is certainly not inferior to that of Western Europe. They speak, on the average, two or three modern languages, and that all must possess ability in their calling can be easily guessed from the bitterness of the struggle for existence in Russia. They intentionally held themselves somewhat in the background of discussion at the Congress, because the purposes and aims of Zionism are not sufficiently known throughout the world. It is possible for the mistake to arise, or to be disseminated by malicious enemies, that there was a tendency at the Basle Congress to break through the existing order of things. The Jews from Russia, therefore, felt themselves called upon to observe a certain reserve, for reasons easy to comprehend, until all uncertainty in this respect had been removed. Every speaker, no matter from what country, grasped the situation and made allowance for it. We may fairly assume that today Government and public opinion in Russia alike are perfectly clear as to the aims of Zionism. The Russian papers have, as a fact, treated the Congress with consideration.

But if our Russian Zionists only took a modest part in the discussion, we certainly learned to know and respect them in private conversation. To express in one word the deep impression they made, I would say that they possess that internal unity which has long since been lost among most of the European Jews. They feel themselves to be national Jews, but free from the narrow and intolerant national conceit which, in view of the present condition of the Jews, would indeed be difficult to comprehend. They are troubled by no thought of assimilation; their existence is simple and unbroken. It is the force of their whole being that they bring as an answer to the point which some pitiful cavillers have seen fit to raise—whether national Judaism will not have as its inevitable result the severance of a people from modern culture? No! These people are on the right track, without the need of much reasoning and, perhaps, without having noticed the slightest obstacle in the way. They assimilate with no other nation, but they endeavor to learn and acquire everything that is good in other peoples. In that way their work will be complete—it will be sincere and genuine. And they are Ghetto Jews beyond doubt—the only Ghetto Jews that our time can show. It is in studying them that we have understood the strength and the spirit of endurance of our forefathers, in the time of their greatest trial. Our history came before us in these human figures with a fullness and vividness all its own. I could not but recall how, in the initial stages of the movement, I was frequently told: You will only win the Russian Jews for the cause. Were any one to say that to me today, I would reply: That is sufficient!

It is in no sense of the word a mere East European movement. Zionism has its followers throughout the world, and, as the Biblical expression has it, "they came from all the four ends of the earth."

And now let us ask ourselves, What have we accomplished in this assembly of the scattered? Did we only come together to weep, to hold speeches, to listen? I believe that in Basle we have also done something else.

Perhaps, in the course of time, when mankind shall be able to view our movement through the vista of history, unbiased by the passions and the mockery attending its inception—perhaps then men will admit the logic of our action. Our only course was to make our nationality apparent, if we would secure a home based on international rights. Let a nation only be there, and it will create for itself the plot of ground which it requires. I believe that whenever a group of human beings in the past has been compelled to find a settlement for itself the process has been the same. We do the same, but in the mould of the present; therein lies the whole difference. We adapt our movement to the economic exigencies and the methods of communication of our time. We never lose sight of the fact that, though our idea be an old and simple one, we can and must carry it out in a modern form. The news of our movement is no longer spread through the medium of wandering shepherds or storm-tossed fishermen; it dashes across the seas and the continents along the electric wire, and rustles through the thousand and one leaves of the world's press. Reports of assemblies, interviews, chats and caricatures scatter our ideas broadcast. And so it will be, as soon as we have passed the stage of counsel and reached the time for action. On the day that we have gained the land which we want, we shall, as it were in a moment, provide it with culture, with railroads, telegraphs, telephones, factories, machines, and, above all, with those social reforms for which today every civilised being clamours with the same hot eagerness as he does for rapidity of communication, for the cultivation of the arts and sciences, and for the comforts of life. Let only human beings be there, and everything else will be there. The task is to set these beings in motion. Up to the present our movement has shown this vital force, and it will continue to show it more and more. The acquired velocity must increase, and with the added force of attraction of the collective masses.

There are times when I have wished myself out of the movement, not only because of the worries which others have caused me, but from reasons of curiosity, for I have the idea that our movement, viewed from outside, must present a remarkable spectacle. I imagine it must be of exceptional interest to modern students of constitutional law. Whether it succeeds or not, it is a modern experiment, a contribution to an insufficiently explored field—the psychology of the masses—and shows the evolution of the popular will in the direction of law and order. Is it not one of those moments affording compensation for care and toil in the lively enjoyment of human stupidity, when our movement, impregnated as it is with a longing for legal rights, is mistaken for a revolutionary one?

We have to deal with enormous difficulties, and many of our activities will naturally arise as these difficulties are faced. This is not the time when everything can be determined. The Mont Cenis Tunnel was bored from both sides, and until the last moment, when light met light, there was always a doubt whether here and there the same level had been maintained. But we shall yet remain undaunted. The public opinion of the whole world must assist us in the settlement of our difficulties. We open up a new thoroughfare for human well-being.

The diplomatic difficulties are manifold. In the first place, it must be recognised that we shall solve a portion of the Eastern Question when we make a treaty with his Majesty the Sultan with the consent of the Powers. The appearance of the European civilised Jews in the Orient would undoubtedly provide a protection for the Christians settling, or about to settle, there, just as it would signify an improvement in all the conditions prevailing in the Ottoman Empire. What! many will exclaim—shall we strengthen a *regime* under which the unforgotten cruelties of late years could be renewed? Whoever raises such an objection does not, I take it, know the Turks. They are characterised by an inborn indolence and good nature which, it is true, often degenerate into violent excesses. Country and people are becoming more and more impoverished, and that which one might consider as an outbreak of fanaticism may be traceable, perhaps, when viewed more clearly, to a wild expression of rage at their own rotten internal situation. In fact, it is just the Mussulmans—at least, those now in Turkey—who are very tolerant towards the religious confessions of others. I know that these words will clash with many prejudices in England. But I have taken my statement from my own observations, made during my Eastern tour, and from many trustworthy reports. Turkey has fallen upon bad times, and with the *naïveté* of children the Turks would sooner make others responsible than themselves. Help this simple people to a higher well-being; bring them under the disciplinary influences of modern life; help them in a peaceful way, and introduce reform into their hopeless administration, and one would see a future free from any such excesses.

It would therefore appear to be to the interest of Turkey to come to an arrangement with the Jews. But what are the interests which other Governments would have in assisting the realisation of a legally guaranteed Jewish home? The interest would vary with each country, but it is present in some form or other everywhere. It would mean the drawing off of an unhappy and detested element of population which is reduced more and more to a condition of despair, and which, scattered over the face of the earth, and in a state of unrest, must perforce identify itself with the most extreme parties everywhere. Governments and all friends of the existing order of things cannot bring themselves to believe that, by helping us in the solution we propose, they could give peace to an element which has been driven to revolution and rendered dangerous through its dispersion. That a mighty conservative people, like the Jews, have always been driven into the ranks of revolutionists is the most lamentable feature in the tragedy of our race. Zionism would mean an end to all that. We should see results accrue for the general condition of mankind, the full benefits of which we cannot even guess.

There are, of course, a great number of existing political difficulties to be overcome, but these, given the necessary goodwill, might be surmounted. The question of the holy shrines is in itself serious enough. Roman reports, circulated in the press after the Basle Congress, asserted that his Holiness the Pope had the intention of opposing Zionism. The great statesman who now sits in St. Peter's chair is probably as yet imperfectly instructed with regard to the facts of our movement. When have Zionists had the remotest thought or even spoken of gaining possession of places rendered sacred by the faiths of the whole of monotheistic humanity? In the same sense that the Roman law conceived of a state of things *extra commercium*, we are of opinion that these shrines have lost for all time the quality belonging to any one earthly Power. Under no consideration whatever would the mad attempt be made to alter anything in the present conditions, which after all may not be very satisfactory to Christian feeling, without the united consent of Christendom.

The Zionist movement has above all—and here we have to thank the Basle Congress—won for itself the most complete publicity. What we say and do is under the control of, and subject to, discussion by public opinion. We do not shirk daylight, we invite it.

In a recent article in a Prussian paper, the tone of which was not exactly friendly, the belief was expressed that Jesus Christ could only arise from the midst of a weak people like the Jews, because His super-human figure would have given to any other race to which He might have belonged a preponderance over the whole of humanity. One might ponder for days and days over a thought so remarkable. But that would lead us too far from our present purpose. It might not, however, be inappropriate to add another thought to it. The possession of the places where He once trod would also raise any other people than the Jews to such an exceptional position in Christendom that one cannot really comprehend how the remaining nations could ever give their sanction.

How would it be, however, if in spite of all—if after public opinion has been fully set right, the Powers have been won for our side, and important advantages have been assured to Turkey—the Government of the Sultan should refuse to come to terms? The answer is simple. We must await the end of the latent crisis in the Orient. A people can wait. It outlasts men and governments. And things have reached such a point in the East that the coming hour of disintegration can be calculated watch in hand.

As matters are at present, the Jews have not the slightest interest in sending even a single colonist to Palestine. Those already there may remain. There are Jewish beggars enough in the Holy Land, who can and must be turned into mechanics and peasants. They are certain of the good-will of the Turkish Government—the more so as we have declared with no uncertain voice that under the present conditions we do not wish to see further immigration. The Basle Congress gave expression to the desirability of retaining the existing Jewish agri-cultural colonies, which have yielded such excellent results, but declared that no fresh settlement should be created until adequate legal guarantees were secured. We will not found any unprotected colonies, which may increase the value of the land without any political equivalent, and at the same time place them at the mercy of any change in Government policy or any revolution in the present friendly attitude of the population. Let Turkey be willing, and she will be

64

helped. Large funds for the purpose are already there. On some points it may be that the administrators of this fund will hold another opinion than mine—that has just as little to do with them as with me. They are, for the rest, men whom I respect. They will be called upon to collaborate when the time for action comes. The possibility of their refusal need not be taken into serious consideration. They are of tried excellence and philanthropy, and besides they would have to fear every ragged Jew who came to them with haggard eyes. We have now given the matter such a turn, however, that it is no longer subject to the favour or the disfavour of philanthropists. The nation has the power to self-help when only the will is awakened.

Many and various were the proposals at the Basle Congress concerning the national fund and other financial schemes. The proposal of Professor Schapira of Heidelberg University to form a national fund was accepted. Subscriptions were announced then and there. The very first duty, however, of the Bureau established by the Congress will be to work out a scheme for forming a public administration and accountant's department, for no one intends to risk his reputation in any secret money transaction. The various bank and financial projects were treated with the same caution, and public reference to them was under no consideration permitted. For practical reasons, we shall give all due encouragement to enterprise, but only to those private undertakings for which we may safely answer to the Jewish people, and concerning which we can presume with some certainty that they will promote the people's cause. We know too well how our opponents are lying in wait to see a vulnerable point in this respect. In the initial stages of the movement, when the idea was considered as one impossible of execution, we were called fools. The more its practicability becomes apparent, all the more will they suspect us of being business men. The men at the head of the movement have never been in business, neither are they, nor have been, professional politicians. We appeal to our peers, the artists and philosophers, to save us from such suspicions. They are able to read the inner meaning of our words and will stand bail for our opinions.

From the desk of our study we have arisen, as the tumult around the Jews became too harsh. We went out to our people because it is in distress, and without guidance cannot help itself. But when we, who above all love the moulding of dreams and the contemplation of the course of earthly events, are compelled in meetings to say always the same, always the same; when we feel that the truths which are dearest of all to us are reduced to commonplaces in our own mouths; there arises in us the longing for that more peaceful world. The task is now to go on to the end. And when we shall have succeeded in bringing our nation to the goal for which we strive, we shall once more put to shame the base imaginings of our foes. What may be our intentions there concerning ourselves? The future will see our people governing itself as best it can and will. I doubt not there will be speculators and politicians there—certainly not less, I trust not more, than elsewhere.

And we ourselves have only the one wish: to return whence we came—
to the desk.

ZOLA, THE DREYFUS CASE, AND THE ANTI-JEWISH CRUSADE IN FRANCE

[In 1894 Captain Alfred Dreyfus, a Jew on the French General Staff, was accused of treason. He was convicted on the basis of secret, forged documents, and sentenced to life imprisonment. His brother Mathieu and a small group of others protested the conviction with little success until 1896, when Colonel Picquart, the new chief of French counterespionage, found evidence that a Major Esterhazy was the actual culprit. Picquart, ordered by the Army to suppress the information, did not. Instead, he gave it to the vice-president of the French Senate. Soon support for Dreyfus began to build, and French society violently split on the issue. Pressure from the pro-Dreyfus side forced a trial of Esterhazy, and similar pressure from the anti-Dreyfusards led to his acquittal. Emile Zola, France's world renowned novelist, then wrote his famous J'Accuse, wherein he directly accused French government and military leaders of a monstrous injustice against Dreyfus. Zola was tried for libel and found guilty. His trial caused international attention to focus on France and further inflamed the passions of Frenchmen.

Throughout this era Dreyfus' Jewish identity was a major factor, and anti-Semitism increased in intensity until, as this 1898 report shows, some believed that Frenchmen were about to rise up and massacre the Jews of France. This article is actually a series of interviews with three of the major figures in the Dreyfus Case and an explanation of the anti-Semitism which surrounded it.]

"Zola, the Dreyfus Case, and the Anti-Jewish Crusade in France," first published in *The American Monthly Review of Reviews*, 17 (March 1898), 309-20.

I. THREATS OF A NEW ST. BARTHOLOMEW IN FRANCE

In correspondence cabled from Paris to New York, Count Esterhazy is quoted as having said to an interviewer on February 14: "If

Dreyfus were ever to set foot in France again there would be one hundred thousand corpses of Jews on the soil. If Zola is acquitted there will be a revolution in Paris. The people will put me at their head in a massacre of the Jews."

Unquestionably Major Esterhazy has been the hero of the mob since his acquittal by the military court that was charged with investigating the grave accusation that he was the real culprit in the matters which have been laid at the door of Dreyfus. And in spite of his boastful exaggeration, Esterhazy is probably right in his assertion that the vindication of Dreyfus by Zola would be the signal for a fearful outbreak against the Jews.

On August 24, 1572, on the ringing of the tocsin in the tower of the Church of St. Germain l'Auxerrois in Paris, began a massacre of Protestants which has left a permanent bloodstain on French history. Before the slaughter had ceased a multitude, variously estimated at thirty thousand and one hundred thousand, had been massacred. From that day St. Bartholomew has become synonymous with cold-blooded widespread conspiracy to massacre. Lest the world should forget its significance, the Supreme Pontiff struck a medal in honor of the extermination of the heretics, sang a *Te Deum* in praise of the massacre, and proclaimed a year of jubilee.

And now it appears, upon the testimony of the leaders of the opposing camps in France, the world is once more threatened with a St. Bartholomew massacre. The victims this time will be the Jews, not the Huguenots. That is a detail. Huguenot and Jew alike are human.

" 'Twere long and needless here to tell" how the immediate cause of the prevalent irritation came to threaten civilization with so prodigious a crime. A moment's reflection, aided by the events of the last fortnight, serves to show that the Dreyfus case is but a triviality compared with the prodigious tumult of passion and prejudice that rages throughout the republic.

The Dreyfus case is but as a dead dog tossed hither and thither by the surging billows of a great ground swell arising no one exactly knows how, or whence, or why. The dead dog did not and could not rouse so great a commotion.

A few words will suffice to dispose of this dead dog. Alfred Dreyfus, an Alsatian Jew holding a commission in the French army and having access to the secrets of a somewhat leaky War Office, was suspected of having communicated information to a foreign power. He was arrested and tried by a court-martial sitting in secret, found guilty, and sentenced to degradation and penal servitude for life. He is now a close prisoner in an iron cage on the Devil's Isle, in the French colony of Cayenne. His wife, with influential friends who believe in his innocence, have never ceased to agitate for a revision of his sentence. The agitation, gaining strength from the absence of any authentic record of the evidence on which the court-martial had acted, succeeded at last in convincing M. Scheurer-Kestner, a Vice-President of the Senate, that Dreyfus had been wrongfully convicted. Then the matter was brought forward in the Chamber. Members refused to reopen the case. Repeated demands for a retrial were countered by a declaration that the matter was judicially decided, and that a regard for the honor of the army rendered it impossible to discuss the matter on its merits.

By way of vindicating Dreyfus, a charge was brought against another officer, one Esterhazy, which was promptly disposed of as baseless by a military tribunal. Popular excitement grew day by day as the struggle went on. The fact that Dreyfus was a Jew afforded the anti-Semitic leaders an opportunity of inflaming popular passion against the Jews, who were represented as attacking the honor of the army in the interest of a Jewish traitor. So successful were they in their campaign that in a few weeks they have brought everything into question. Scenes of outrageous violence disgraced the tribune of the Chamber, where deputies bespattered with blood and ink showed that the temperature had risen to a point far beyond relief by mere articulate utterance. In Paris the troops were called out to maintain order in the streets at the point of the bayonet. In the provinces and in Algeria order was not maintained. Savage attacks upon the persons and property of the Jews occurred in various places—which were hailed with savage glee as a foretaste of the things to come. The question of the guilt or innocence of a single Jew is becoming merged in the problem of the fate of the race and of the republic.

In France it is always the unexpected which happens. Therefore those who shrug their shoulders and ridicule the absurdity of the notion that France, France of the Third Republic, could possibly reproduce the sanguinary horrors of St. Bartholomew a century after the French Revolution, will do well not to be too cocksure. Meanwhile, let them listen for a moment to the voice—the potent voice—of M. Drumont, whose paper day by day sounds like a tocsin peal, the summons to the new St. Bartholomew.

II. M. DRUMONT, WHO RINGS THE TOCSIN

An Interview By Valerian Gribayedoff

(In order to obtain an authentic word and pen picture of the leader of the anti-Semites, Mr. Gribayedoff, whose work has long been familiar to the readers of this *Review*, was commissioned to wait upon Mr. Drumont and obtain from him a direct and authentic statement of his views as to the present position and future prospects of the anti-Semitic movement in France. The date of the interview was January 23.)

By this time it must have become clear, even to the least observant or the most skeptical that the Dreyfus-Esterhazy affair was but an acute symptom of a condition in France which has been a long while assuming form and consistency. The hasty and evidently ill-founded accusation brought against Major Walsin Esterhazy, Catholic, by

Matthien Dreyfus, Jew, has acted as a spark applied to a powder train, causing an explosion of anti-Semitic feeling all over the country as well as in Algeria. As I pen these lines I hear the cries out in the streets of: *"A bas les Juifs! A bas les Juifs!"* [down with the Jews] broken now and again by the clatter of the cavalry horses' hoofs on the asphalt, and the measured tread of the Municipal Guards on their way from one post of duty to the other. Thus it has been going on from day to day. Dreyfus is forgotten, Esterhazy is forgotten, Scheurer-Kestner is forgotten, even Zola, the most aggressive of the so-called "Dreyfusards," is little mentioned for the nonce. The one cry which resounds from north to south and from east to west, the rallying cry of thousands and hundreds of thousands of French citizens, is *"A bas les Juifs!"*

This cry sums up the situation. Rightly or wrongly, the question of opposing "Israel's encroachments" has become the one burning issue. Upon the anti-Semitic platform stand the most diversified elements—Ultramontanes, Freethinkers, Radicals, even, as it now proves, a considerable fraction of the Protestant population. They may be totally at variance with one another in matters of religion, politics, and economics, but they are firmly of a mind on one proposition, and that is that "the Jew must go!" Numerically the Jew forms one-five-hundredth part of the population of France. By fair or foul means, more particularly by the latter, say the anti-Semites, he has secured possession of a quarter of the personal property of the country— twenty milliards of francs out of eighty. (The figures are taken from the Philo-Semitic *Matin*.) He controls the markets, and owns the executive, the legislature, and the judiciary. He would like to secure control of the army, but this will prove the rock against which his ambitions will be dashed to pieces! So sayeth the anti-Semite!

To the average Anglo-Saxon mind anti-Semitism is of course incomprehensible, as a psychological condition or phenomenon out of keeping with the spirit of the age and of modern institutions. Nevertheless, the question in general has become so hopelessly confused in certain English and American periodicals with the judicial intricacies of the Dreyfus case, that it seems next to impossible for the reader to separate the one subject from the other. As a step in this direction it may be appropriate to present the anti-Semitic version of the case in the words of the man who is universally credited with having created this peculiar sentiment among his fellow-countrymen, but who is satisfied with the honor, as he often says himself, of having crystallized it and given it its present direction, the sentiment itself being the natural outcome of the prevailing conditions. I refer of course to Edouard Drumont, author of *La France Juive* and editor of *La Libre Parole*.

Edouard Drumont lives in a quaint out-of-the-way corner of Paris, a narrow thoroughfare that runs into the Rue de l'Universite, a few minutes' walk from the Eiffel Tower. The stranger might fancy himself here in one of the side streets of some sleepy provincial town were it not for the distant hum of the city's traffic. There is such a forlorn and abandoned look about the whole place. A white-haired woman opens the front door of the musty and rather uninviting edifice in answer to my bell, and ushers me into a conventional French parlor. M. Drumont is at home. Although all Paris is in a ferment this gray Sunday afternoon, although infantry and cavalry occupy the leading thoroughfares, and the garden of the Tuilleries has been turned into a military encampment prepared for every emergency, Drumont sits at home, engrossed in the preparation of the next day's editorial, not a soul in the place but himself and the aged housekeeper. A curious contrast, indeed, the calm, the almost deathlike stillness of this household, and the turmoil and excitement its occupant's vigorous pen has created at this moment within the bosom of the huge metropolis.

Presently the door opens and Drumont enters. The great high-priest of anti-Semitism looks his part to a T—which is that of a *fin-de-siecle* Peter the Hermit. He wears a black velvet coat and a loose black necktie, and a shock of raven black hair falls down to a level with his collar and gives his head an almost leonine appearance. Despite a slight stoop—due no doubt to sedentary occupations and the consumption of midnight oil—the first characteristic that impresses the observer is the man's superlative strength, both physical and intellectual. The short neck and broad shoulders can only belong to a Hercules, the keen penetrating eye, the aquiline nose, the heavy jaw, partly hidden by a scrubby beard, and the firm mouth are indications of an iron will and of superior intellectual force, without which qualities no apostle can stamp his views upon a community, be his mission good or bad. He possesses to an unusual degree that gift for polemics, the delight of every true Parisian newspaper reader, combined with rare power of analysis and a remarkable clearness of expression. He is a fluent and vigorous speaker, moreover. He emphasizes his remarks with frequent gestures, ofttimes raising his hands above his head like a diver, and bringing them down with one sweep to a level with his knees. His first remark after I had explained the object of my visit was as follows:

"*Mon Dieu, Monsieur.* What use is there of my saying anything for the benefit of the English-speaking peoples? As far as I can judge from the English press, the Jewish side of the story is the only one that seems to pass current on the other side of the channel. The Jews must be influential enough over there also, since they are able to control all the channels of news and of publicity, and to impose their way of thinking on the public. Yet even England has little reason to congratulate herself on her alliance with the race of Shem. The Jew Disraeli rendered her a poor service when he left her the legacy of Russia's hatred and suspicion. Nor has she profited very much by the Jameson raid organized by the Jews, Lionel Phillips, Alfred Beit, Joel, Barnato, and the rest of them, when as usual the Aryan acted as the Semite's catspaw and received cold lead for his pains."

"But to come to France," I remarked. "How do you think this trouble is going to end?"

"Ah," came the reply, with a shrug of the shoulders, "what shall I answer? It seems a serious statement to make, but to tell the truth, as things are, I see no way out of the present awful situation excepting by a general revolution, which will sweep away our present masters and replace them with some form of one-man power—not necessarily an emperor or a king, but some kind of dictator, a strong, patriotic man who will put an end to Jewish supremacy and clean out our Augean stables of vice and corruption!''

Having got this far, the speaker's heavy frame leaned over, and swaying his arms in characteristic fashion, he plunged earnestly into the subject, scarcely stopping for breath.

"*Que voulez vous, Monsieur?* When a malady is as far advanced as ours, heroic remedies alone avail. Let us glance back a little. Before 1789 there was no need of anti-Semitism, and none existed. Why? Because at that period France possessed a stable, well-organized government. The Jew was properly considered an enemy of Aryan and Christian society, and without being abused or ill-treated he was kept in his place, and was subjected to certain necessary restrictions which rendered him harmless. Whatever its faults may have been, the *ancien regime* had at least the economic interests of the masses at heart and protected them against encroachments. Public thieves and plunderers invariably received their due. The finances of the government were well administered. But with the revolution of 1789 everything changed. From a regularly constituted homogeneous society, France, as one writer has expressed it, broke up into a heterogeneous mass of atoms. With the shattering of the old idols, with the repudiation of the old ideals, with the disappearance of the traditions, French society lost all cohesion; and when the Jew came upon the scene, *les mains libres*, enfranchised, untrammeled by restrictive legislation—the Jew, with his marvelous cohesion, his thorough organization, his racial solidarity —the Jew with his mind disciplined, his wits sharpened by ages of battling against mankind—the Jew, I say, was bound to become the master.

"And he has become so with a vengeance. Look at the situation at present. Does he not control everything in France? We French had a few breathing-spells from his exactions at various intervals earlier in the century. Things were not quite so bad while some of the monarchs reigned over us, but since 1870 we have been absolutely at the mercy of the Jews. The fall of the empire was the signal for immediate operations on their part. They did not even have the decency to wait until peace had been concluded, but then and there, while France was struggling in the throes of a cruel war, the Jew Cremreux and his clique rushed through a law conferring the franchise, not on the brave Arab population of Algeria that had sent its sons to defend this country's soil side by side with its own children, but on the Algerian Jew—that vilest of beings, usurer, middleman, parasite, the object of undying contempt and loathing on the part of his Mohammedan neighbor and former master. Naturally the consequences of this monstrous act were easy to foresee. The Arabs resented the indignity of being discriminated against in this flagrant manner by rising in revolt, and the troops we might otherwise have used against the Prussian invader had to be employed in crushing the Algerian rebellion.

The speaker having paused for breath, I ventured to suggest that a rigid and impartial application of existing laws against usury, monopoly, disloyal competition, and the other misdeeds laid to the door of Israel might suffice to eliminate abuses and evils of which the anti-Semites complain.

"No, a thousand times no," returned M. Drumont with energy. "The existing laws would never meet the requirements of the situation. What we demand is special legislation, such as existed to some extent before 1789, that will make it impossible for the Jew to despoil us further. The Jewish money-kings who rule this country must be rendered harmless, their shameless financial maneuvers, their monopoly of the country's wealth must end, the tentacles of the monster must be severed. If their immoral sources of revenue are cut off the Jews may begin to listen to Dr. Herzl's sensible advice, and decide to return to Palestine *en masse.*"

"Do you anticipate any legislation of the kind in the near future?"

"I certainly expect nothing from the present government. As I said at first, there seems no salvation for France excepting in an uprising of the people. Remember that with all their acumen and judgment in financial and business matters, with all their foresight in everything appertaining to the accumulation of wealth, the Jews are singularly blind to the realities of their own social and political situation. They have ever been thus from the commencement of their history—an obstinate, stiff-necked people, who would never yield unless compelled to by the most bitter experience. Never was this mental blindness more apparent than it is today. Half the Jews you meet will tell you even at this hour that anti-Semitism is a transitory mania, confined to a weak but loud-mouthed minority. They have been beaten all along the line in this Dreyfus case: their methods and maneuvers to saddle the crime on an innocent man have been exposed and held up to public reprobation, and yet they are working away as hard as ever to attain their damnable purposes. They are buying up newspapers and disseminating lying statements all over the country. They are hiring anarchists to break up our meetings and assault the participants. Nothing seems to open their eyes to the danger threatening their own race. It has grown to be a veritable mania with them, this determination to ride rough-shod over the feelings, desires, and convictions of the Aryan community, justifying but once more the ancient saying that whom the gods destroy they first make mad.

"It is this blindness which would cause them to fight tooth and nail any attempt to introduce the special legislation I alluded to just now, even though their only hope of salvation lies therein. For, after all, it is better to have one's wings clipped than to be killed outright—which is the fate that awaits a large number on the great day of reckoning—*la grande lessive!* For my own part, as a humanitarian, I would much rather this day never came, and that, instead, our evils were abolished by an evolutionary process. That is why I am really acting as a friend to the Jews when I advocate the introduction of laws placing them on a different footing from the rest of us and withdrawing from them certain rights of citizenship. They never should have been admitted into the great French family anyhow. They are as different from us as night is from day. Their ideals, their methods of thought, their whole mental make-up, are different from ours. They have formed part of the body politic for over a hundred years, and yet they have never understood us—they have never succeeded in comprehending the national genius of France, they have never desired to become assimilated with us. On the contrary, they have done everything in their power to lower our standards and degrade our civilization. Our present condition of decadence, with its filth, its vice, its pornography, can be traced directly to Jewish sources. Not content with robbing us of our worldly goods, they have attacked the ramparts of our virtues, our morality, and our religion. But the day of reckoning will come!"

This was said with much warmth and energy and in a tone of unmistakable conviction.

"But, M. Drumont," I remarked, "there are Jews enough in England, and a million of them in the United States, and yet in neither country can it be said that anti-Semitism exists in the same way that it does in France?"

"Ah, that is altogether a different proposition," answered the speaker, raising his eyebrows and throwing his head back. "But you must not compare our people with the Anglo-Saxons. The Englishman, for example, is fitted much better by nature to cope with the Jew than the Frenchman. He is cold-blooded, prudent, long-sighted and a born 'shopkeeper'—I used the word in the less offensive sense, of course. But what renders him unassailable even more than this are his admirable political institutions, the slow and solid work of successive ages. England has for centuries enjoyed a degree of liberty unknown to us in France. Her citizens are adults, politically speaking, while ours are the veriest children. That is why the English can hold their own against the onset of the Jewish hordes, while our people succumb. See how quickly the people of the United States disposed of the Chinese question. It did not need a bloody revolution to settle that. The Jew would fare the same way both in the United States and in England if he proved too dangerous. He knows it himself, and not having been blinded over there by a hundred years of battening on the public wealth, as in France, he is comparatively innocuous. It is not in the temperament of the French to resist encroachments and oppression by sober systematic action. You could not even organize a successful boycott against the Jews here. The Frenchman will mildy stand every form of injustice and tyranny up to a certain point, but once beyond that, he will suddenly arise and sweep everything before him. French history is full of these examples. The Jews are preparing things for just such another; they are sowing the wind and will reap the whirlwind."

M. Drumont talked on for a while in this strain, until I asked the concluding question on my list, which was whether he had any reply to make to the charge that his opposition to the Jews was based on religious grounds, and that his campaign was backed by the Ultramontanes, the Jesuits, and certain dignitaries of the Roman Catholic Church.

"Take this down word for word," he exclaimed, drawing himself up at full height. "These statements are pure inventions on the part of the Jews. I am a Christian and a Catholic, it is true. It is in my blood to be so, for I was born a Catholic and am descendant from Catholic stock. But what can this have to do with my anti-Semitic sentiments, I ask you? Anti-Semitism is an economic, not a religious war. In our ranks you will find men of every religious belief, also atheists and agnostics. As to the Church dignitaries or the Jesuits being interested in our movement, I know absolutely nothing about that. I have no personal acquaintanceship, no relations with any cardinal, bishop, or Jesuit. I never see any, and, in fact, the higher clergy are rather inimical toward the movement. They are the servants of the Jews as much as our magistrates and politicians. If we have any friends among the hierarchy it is in the lower ranks. The poor village *cure*—who receives a miserable pittance from the government and is treated like a lackey in return—being in touch with the masses and understanding their needs and their troubles, naturally wishes us success. No, we are not clericals; and for my own part I would even hail the separation of Church and State as a salutory reform."

Thus ended the interview. M. Drumont accompanied me to the door, and as a parting admonition added earnestly: "Whatever you say, do not forget to lay stress on the blindness of the Jews in this crisis—that is the most dramatic element of the situation—it is almost pathetic!"

Paris, January 24, 1898.

III. DR. NORDAU ON THE JEWS AND THEIR FEARS

An Interview by Robert H. Sherard

(No Parisian Jew is so famous as Dr. Max Nordau. His books have made the tour of the world, and he has last year added to his other achievements the exploit of acting as Aaron to Dr. Herzl's Moses in that Zionist movement which has cheered Europe with the vision of a new Exodus. In order to obtain from so influential and well-known a leader of the Semites a calm judgment upon the question as to the peril with which his race is threatened, the *Review* commissioned Mr. R. H. Sherard to procure from Dr. Nordau a statement of his views on the subject.)

By no one in Paris is a more alarmist view of the present anti-

Semitic agitation in France taken than by Dr. Max Nordau. Received by him in the little study of his modest apartment in the Avenue de Villiers, he said, in answer to my inquiry whether anything was to be feared from the present state of things: "We are quite simply marching in France toward a new St. Bartholomew's Eve, to a massacre which will only be limited by the number of Jews whom the Catholics can find to knock on the head. I believe, and most emphatically, that the slightest relaxation in the present display of force on the part of the government would lead to a general slaughter of the Jews throughout the country. This massacre would only be limited by this: that it is not in France, as in other Latin or Ligurian countries, an easy matter, as it is in the Slavonic and Teutonic countries, to distinguish the Jew from the Christian. For instance, the type of the southern Frenchman is most pronouncedly a Jewish one. So that the rioters might hesitate in striking down as a Jew a man who might be only a southern Frenchman."

"But have not the Jews, on the whole, been favored in France?"

"Certainly not! In France, as in every other country, the history of the Jews is a record of blood and suffering. At the time of the Crusades, the gallant knights, sallying forth for the Holy Land, practiced their swords and killing powers on the Jews. In 1306 there were massacres of the Jews all over France. Then followed their expulsion *en masse* by Philippe le Bel. For centuries afterward they were not allowed to live in any other part of France but the Ghetto of Bordeaux."

"But the Revolution emancipated your race?"

"Yes, after a hard struggle on the part of Abbe Gregoire against the uncompromising resistance of such *grands seigneurs* as Rohan and La Rochefoucauld. But how could the Revolution refuse this emancipation, under the implacable logic of the declaration of the rights of man? Were not the Jews men? Were they not, as such, entitled to the rights of man? Then Napoleon I: 'tis true that he favored the Jews. He was a man of great imagination, who would have been a great novelist if he had not been a great conqueror, and the spectacle of this ancient race scattered over the face of the earth fascinated his imagination. Then he had dreams like those of Alexander the Great, dreams of Oriental conquest, the dominion of the East, where, as part of his policy, would be the reconstitution of the kingdom of Judah, just as it was one of his favorite political dreams with regard to Europe to reconstitute the kingdom of Poland. Napoleon was indeed a friend of the Jews. He admitted them to officers' rank in the army; he allowed them to participate in the benefits of the Legion of Honor while refusing permission to any Jews to settle in the Eastern provinces of the French empire. Since then the Jews have enjoyed in France the equal rights to citizenship to which they are entitled as men. It remained for the Catholic Church at the end of the nineteenth century to direct the reaction against us to incite the mob to rid the face of the earth of our accursed race by violence and slaughter."

"Do you seriously charge the Catholic Church with being at the bottom of this anti-Semitic agitation?"

"Most seriously. God forbid that I, who in my person and in my family have suffered persecution all my life, should wish in my turn to persecute any one by directing against him false accusations, but I can come to no other conclusion in face of the evidence than that all this outburst was prompted and is being fomented by Rome. . . . I do not believe that the Pope in person has had anything to do with it. To begin with the Pope is eighty-six, a very old man. Then, again, as the Latin proverb has it, *Manima non curat praetor* [one can not force the hand of the man in power]; and so small is the number of Jews in France—we do not exceed seventy thousand professing Jews all told—that he must look upon us with the disdain that small matters inspire the priest. But that the Church is the guilty factor is shown by the two recent articles which have appeared in the official organ of the Vatican, *L'Osservatore Romano*. The first of these articles, which may be said to have given the signal of the outburst of anti-Semitic fury in France, was published about a fortnight ago.

This first article was directed against Zionism, and the argument of it was that the Jews must always be outcasts—a scattered and homeless race, so that the prophecy may be verified, and that we may forever bear this curse for that we crucified Christ. The second article appeared about five days ago. Its argument was that we Jews have no right to complain of the outburst of hatred and violence everywhere against us, for it is our fault and our fault alone. We have corrupted Christianity, it said. Breaking forth from our ghettos, we have spread hateful doctrines of liberalism, and have spread the pestilential paradoxes of free thought. As long as we remained in our ghettos the Church protected us—by burning us in *auto-da-fes*," added Dr. Nordau, with a bitter laugh. "We have burst open our ghettos and we must take the consequences. See what the consequences have been already. The massacre of Algiers, the violence in every corner of France. You may say that so far only very few Jews have been attacked. As many as could be found have been attacked, nor was it any different during the night of St. Bartholomew. The murderous could not kill more Protestants than they could find. As I have said, our protection will be mainly in the fact that as we cannot be forced to wear a distinctive sign to mark us out of the mob, and that as the facial type of southern Frenchmen is almost identical with our own, the murderers will hesitate to strike for fear of killing a brother. In the meanwhile the energetic attitude of the government inspires us with some confidence. But the extermination of the Jews has already begun and the Church can wait *patiens qua aeterna* [eternally], until the wicked work of which she gave the signal has accomplished itself."

Dr. Nordau was not less emphatic in his declaration of the absolute innocence of Alfred Dreyfus. "It is mathematically proved," he said, and added: "It has never been pretended that Dreyfus acted as a traitor toward any other country but Germany." That is well understood. From the very beginning of the *affaire* Dreyfus the German Government published in the semi-official organs of the empire denials that the empire had had dealings with Dreyfus. It repeated this statement in a more explicit and official manner five months ago by publishing in the *Koelnische Zeitung* and next in the *Nord Deutsche Allgemeine Zeitung*, which is the official journal of Berlin, the most categorical denial that Germany had had any dealings whatsoever with Dreyfus. Then came Von Bulow's declaration on his word of honor as a gentleman, made on the 24th of this month before the committee of ways and means of the German Reichstag, that neither directly nor indirectly had Germany had any traffickings of any nature whatever with Dreyfus. Is not that mathematical proof? I may add of my own knowledge that the proofs of Dreyfus' innocence in the form of irrefutable documents are in the possession of one of the highest officials in the French republic, who will produce them when the times comes."

IV. M. ZOLA ON FRENCH ANTI-SEMITISM

An Interview by Robert H. Sherard

(During these past weeks of M. Zola's prominence in connection with the Dreyfus case, no journalist has been in closer relations with the great novelist than Mr. Robert H. Sherard. The interview with Zola secured by Mr. Sherard for this number of the *Review of Reviews* does not take so serious a view of the anti-Semitic movement as other observers have expressed. This interview of course occurred before M. Zola appeared in court himself on trial for the position he had taken in the Dreyfus matter.)

It has fallen to me twice within the last two months to discuss with my old friend, Emile Zola, the burning question of anti-Semitism in France. The report of our first conversation, which I contributed to the *Humanitarian*, was taken at a time when the agitation, though violent, had not outstepped the limits of newspaper polemics. At that time Zola was still speaking of it as the "imbecile anti-Semitism" with much contempt in his voice.

"I cannot believe," he said, "that France, the great, generous, enlightened nation, will tolerate a movement which, springing into being a century after the French Revolution and the declaration of the rights of man, throws us back into the dark night of the Middle Ages. The movement is an idiotic one, fostered by certain men who wish to derive from their connection with it a notoriety which they could not obtain in any other way. Formerly it was usual to direct the fury of the mob against the Church. The proletariat was invited every morning in those days—I am speaking of ten or twelve years ago—to breakfast off a priest. The present *plat du jour* is a Jew, as fat and prosperous a Jew as the pamphleteers can dish up. Yet, with all their shouting, these men cannot stir the people of France, with their love of justice and their good common sense, to do a single act which shows that all these pernicious teachings have had any effect upon them whatever. It must be rather disheartening to Drumont and all the rest of his school to see that after all their efforts to incite the mob against the Jews not a single pane of glass in the windows of any Jew in France has been broken. That is why I speak of this anti-Semitic movement in France as an imbecile one, imbecile because impotent."

This conversation took place, it must be observed, before any attacks had actually been made upon the Jews. The agitation had even then attained sufficient dimensions to fill M. Zola with alarm. He said:

"I have to admit regretfully that the movement has taken a great hold in France, but I do not admit that the people really understand its significance. It is merely accepted by the mass of the people as the newest form of socialism. The Jews have been made to represent in the eyes of the ignorant the have-alls, the capitalists, against whom the demagogues have always directed the furies of the proletariat. Instead of crying as they used to cry ten years ago, 'Down with the capitalists,' the people are now taught to cry, 'Down with the Jews,' the leaders of the anti-Semitic campaign acting largely in the interests of the Catholic party, having induced them into the belief that all the capitalists are Jews, that it is the Jewish money which employs all the labor of France, that the whole nation is a vassal to the purse of the Rothschilds, and such-like absurdities. Absurdities, yes; which, however, the people have come to believe. So that the cry of 'Down with the Jews' from the mass of the French people means nothing but down with the capitalists. Anti-Semitism as it exists today in France is a hypocritical form of socialism. It is a lie, of course, that all Jews are capitalists, that all Jews have no love for anything but the acquisition of wealth by the labor of others, and nobody knows this better than the leaders of this campaign. And nobody better than the leaders of this campaign know that if the Jews do show wonderful superiority in the matter of money-getting, it is because we trained them to this in an apprenticeship of eighteen hundred years."

At the time of his first talk he was much inclined to plume himself upon the fact that in the whole of France the campaign had only resulted in calumny. The attacks in the press had not resulted in any actual violence; nevertheless, he saw that it was thitherward tending:

"I have been surprised to notice the apparent development that it is taking. Surprised, indeed. The very initiation of the movement stupefied me—that there should be a return to fanaticism, an attempt to light up a religious war in this epoch of ours, one hundred years after the revolution, in the heart of our great Paris, in the days of democracy, of universal toleration, at the very time when there is an immense movement being made everywhere toward equality, justice, and fraternity. A handful of madmen, cunning or idiotic, come and shout in our ears every morning, 'Let us kill the Jews. Let us devour the Jews. Let us massacre them. Let us exterminate them. Let us get back to the days of the gibbet and stake.' Is it not inconceivable? Could anything be more foolish? Could anything be more abominable?"

Questioned about the popular report as to the syndicate of Jews alleged to have been formed for the purpose of saving Dreyfus from the penalty which he had incurred, Zola asserted that the syndicate was a myth:

"There is no syndicate of Jews to free Dreyfus. There is no syndicate of Jews, the world over, for any purpose. That they are helpful to each other, that among members of no other religious faith is there such great solidarity, that a Jew can always count on the assistance of his fellows, is a fact, and the primary cause of this, as I have just pointed out, is that they were bound together by centuries of common suffering. Their solidarity, their helpfulness to each other, are very fine traits in their character. Who can make a grievance of that against them? Naturally, these attacks on the race, if I may use that expression, will only serve to bind them more closely together."

The origin of the whole business was jealousy, and M. Zola regretfully compared the different methods in which the Jews were treated in England and France:

"In the world of business, the Jews are disliked because they are, for the reason I have indicated, much more skillful in matters of finance than the Christians. When I was writing my book *L'Argent*, I used to go to the bourse [stock exchange] every day to try and get some comprehension of that part of society, and I remember being told by a Catholic banker that the Christians could not compete with the Jews in money matters. 'Ah! Monsieur,' he said, 'they are much stronger than we are. They will always get the better of us.' If that were true it would be very humiliating for the Christians. But I don't believe that it is true. I believe that with work and intelligence our bankers could do just as well as the Jewish bankers. Indeed, I know many bankers who are not Jews who are fully as successful in their undertakings, and who show as much acumen and judgment in their enterprises as their Jewish rivals."

The second occasion on which I saw Monsieur Zola in this connection was on the day before the list of the witnesses to be called in his defense was published. He was in a state of great mental agitation, and the impression that his manner produced upon me, who have so long regarded him with sincere admiration and affection, was decidedly a painful one. He was almost hysterical in his affirmations of Dreyfus' innocence, in his protestations that the government well knew that he was innocent and had been wrongfully convicted.

There was a pathetic ring about the cries of *"C'est monstreux! monstreux!"* with which he qualified their action in detaining in prison a man whom "everybody, everybody, I tell you, knows to be innocent." He had tears in his eyes as he read out to me a passage from Renan's "Life of Christ," which, he said, had been sent him by an anonymous friend "for Maitre Labori," and so exactly described what the government had done with reference to Dreyfus, and what were likely to be the consequences entailed upon it by its malfeasance, that one might think that Renan had written in a prophetic spirit. Then there was wild laughing, and altogether the effect produced upon me was that the strain of all these events, the magnitude of the struggle in which he had embarked, perhaps without well weighing the consequences, had been too much for him, and that he was suffering from a nervous collapse, which might account for the extreme violence and what may, perhaps, be described as the want of logic in the letter of accusation on which his prosecution is being based. I was much distressed and disturbed until, two days later, calling on him again I found him calm, composed, cold, the old Zola whom I had known for so many years, a hard-headed, level, logical man, in whom watchful and affectionate eyes could not detect a single trace of the nervous collapse which had frightened me on the previous occasion.

"The explanation of recent outbreaks and acts of violence against the Jews is a very simple one," he said. "I told you when we spoke on this subject some weeks ago that the leaders of the movement with very wicked hypocrisy and deception have induced the people, the Have-Nots, to believe that the word Jew is synonymous with capitalist, and are directing the discontent of the poor against the Jews as representing the moneyed classes. Jew now means to the unthinking proletariat, capitalist, monopolist, sweater, blood-sucker, and what we see today is about another phase of the struggle which has gone on ever since. Property was between those who have and those who have not. The people believe that all the Jews are rich, and rich by evil practices, and instead of shouting as they used to do, 'Down with capital!' they shout, 'Down with the Jews!' It is idiotic! It is wicked! I have, however, absolute confidence in the common sense of the French nation. It will open its eyes sooner or later and see through the fraud that has been imposed upon it. It will see that it is false that all the Jews are rich, that the word Jew means capitalist; it will see that there are poor Jews, hard-working Jews, whose struggle for their daily bread is as keen as that of the poorest among them."

Even now that Jewish blood has been shed, Emile Zola continues to speak with contempt of the movement, and he smiled with real amusement when I related to him the substance of the conversation I had had that afternoon with Max Nordau. He certainly did not share the doctor's gloomy anticipations. "Not that there can be any doubt," he remarked, "that at the bottom of the present agitation the Catholic clubs, joining themselves for the nonce to the professional agitators of anti-Semitism, are doing all they can to foster the agitation, and that a due share of the responsibility for what has occurred or may occur rests upon them. But the fact remains that the people are only acting as at present because they have been duped in the way I have stated. This is not an attack on the Jews as a race or as members of another religion. The French people are far too sensible, even in their lowest strata, to listen to any such war-cry. The *Droits de l'Homme* is a universally accepted creed. The outbreak is only, so far as the people are concerned, an outbreak of the poor against the rich. That is the only explanation of it. And I repeat, as soon as the people understand that they have been duped, all this will subside."

With regard to his present position Zola is supremely confident. "I had to act as I have done, otherwise matters might have been allowed to drop, and that was what, as a firm believer in the innocence of Dreyfus, I could not allow. Later on people will say, 'The government meant to grant a fresh trial, and there was no need for Zola to be so violent.' That is what Louis XVI said when the Revolution broke out—that there had been no need for the people to act with violence, that he had intended all along to grant them the liberties they desired. If I had done nothing people would have said, 'Now the affair is finished; Esterhazy has been acquitted. Let us say nothing more about it.' I had to keep the agitation going, because nobody with any sense of justice and of humanity can rest until this fearful error has been rectified. With regard to the criminal prosecution [against Zola], the penalties imposed by the law are not very heavy, and as to the other suits that are brought against me, I know that it is not the wish of the government to drive me to extremes. From a pecuniary point of view I am indifferent to consequences, and supposing that an attempt to ruin me were successful, which can hardly be, I have had offers of support from numerous friends, and did this week receive such an offer from a correspondent in Switzerland. I have no knowledge and no care what effect my act will have on the sale of my books. I have never in my books sought after anything but the truth. My life shall be as my books, an ardent quest for truth and for justice."

THE
JEW

[This 1913 review of two books, Werner Sombart's The Jews and Modern Capitalism *and Arthur Ruppin's* The Jews of Today, *reflects the racial approach to Jewish identity. The reviewer reported Sombart's belief that while history had played a role in making Jews into businessmen, the ultimate reason for Jewish influence in this area lay "in the Jewish religion and the Jewish character." Sombart's thesis that Jews invented modern capitalism added to the widely held belief that Jews were arch-capitalists and preyed upon the non-Jew. His work was quoted by anti-Semites throughout the first half of the twentieth century.*

Ruppin's book is interesting because he foresaw a danger that assimilation would lead to the disappearance of Jewish identity. He saw Zionism as the best way to preserve the Jewish people.]

"The Jew," first published in *The Spectator*, 3 (July 19, 1913), 102-03.

(1) *The Jews and Modern Capitalism.* By Werner Sombart. Translated by M. Epstein. London: T. Fisher Unwin. (2) *The Jews of Today.* By Arthur Ruppin. Translated by Margery Bentwich, with an Introduction by Joseph Jacobs. London: G. Bell and Sons.

When Mr. Houston Stewart Chamberlain produced his *Foundations of the Nineteenth Century*, in which the Teuton is regarded as the motive power in the world's progress, sundry critics protested that it would not be very difficult to write the same kind of book on an exactly opposite thesis, and find the secret of civilization in the Latin or the Jew. It would, perhaps, be scarcely fair to say that Professor Sombart had written this book, but he has come within measurable distance of it. The distinguished author of *Der moderne Kapitalismus* is an acute social observer and one of the most brilliant of the historical school of economists. In the present work he discusses the relation between the Jew and modern capitalism, and provides incidentally an illuminating analysis of the latter term. Like all exponents of a novel thesis, he is inclined to overprove his point and unnecessarily extend his argument. His historical section is, generally speaking, uncritical, and he relies too much on secondary authorities. He scents the Jew in unlikely quarters—Columbus, for example, and John Law of Lauriston, who was a decent son of the Lothians and no connexion of the tribe of Levi. Much, too, that he claims as Jewish is found as clearly among the Gentiles—in Puritanism, for example, as has been demonstrated by Max Weber and others. Yet the book is in a high degree stimulating and original, and with its main argument there will be pretty general agreement.

Professor Sombart begins with a necessary *caveat*. In a specialized study where only one set of conditions is considered, Jewish influence may appear greater than it actually was. On the other hand, since he is dealing with direct influence only, the Jewish contribution must be partially underestimated, so that these defects will neutralize each other. His first historical point is that the shifting of the economic centre from Southern to Northern Europe was due to the emigration of the Jews consequent on their expulsion from Spain and Portugal. For this he adduces good evidence from the records of the Dutch and German cities. It is too much, perhaps, to say that Cromwell protected the Jews solely from economic reasons; though opposed to the Fifth Monarchy men, he shared in their belief that the conversion of Israel was the first duty of the Saints. To the Jews we owe the framework of modern capitalism, for they invented our commercial machinery, founded trade on a truly international basis, and contributed largely to the creation of the modern state as we know it. We find them from the first specializing in international activities, controlling, for example, the imports of foreign articles of luxury, developing colonial producing grounds, and eager to take up industries like cotton and indigo, which represented new methods. They also obtained supremacy in all the countries from which it was possible to draw large supplies of ready money. They were interested in all colonial enterprises in every quarter of the globe. In North America, according to the author, they kept the New England colonies solvent by bringing in the precious metals from their West Indian and South American trade. He goes further, and argues that it was Jewish influence which made the United States what they are. "For what we call Americanism is nothing else, if we may say so, than the Jewish spirit distilled." The Jews, too, invented the whole system of public credit, which they democratized by forcing the big creditors—the rulers—from their monopoly and bringing into their place a number of miscellaneous creditors. The whole of Professor Sombart's historical chapter is interesting and original, though the argument is often a trifle finedrawn.

He is on stronger ground when he traces the Jewish influence on the machinery of commerce. He shows conclusively that to the Jew we owe the system of securities, what he neatly calls "the standardization of personal indebtedness." The Bill of Exchange, the cornerstone of modern business, is Jewish in origin; so are stocks and shares, banknotes, and public bonds. The Jews of the Middle Ages, when kings were troublesome, had to adopt some device to conceal the fact that they were the recipients of money or goods, so they invented the "bearer" security. That is why the Jews when plundered speedily grew rich again; they never lost their "all," or anything like it. The Stock Exchange, too, is Jewish by descent. Even in industries they were pioneers, especially when industries became commercialized and the technical side was separated from the financial. The Jews throughout modern history have been the chief capitalistic undertakers, and Professor Sombart passes to the consideration of the exact meaning of this term. During the Middle Ages trade was a stereotyped thing, and the activity of the trader was circumscribed by convention and sometimes by law, both as to profits and methods and as to locality. Advertising and other modern business devices were regarded as unworthy of the dignity of the stately merchant. People believed in a "just price" as something governed by religious and ethical rather than economic principles. Into this decorous world came the Jew, bound by none of its rules and desirous of making as large a profit as the market allowed him. He had no rank or style or dignity to keep up, and he was ready to attract customers by every means which his ingenuity suggested. He advertised, he cut prices, he disregarded etiquette, he invented new and cheaper processes, he introduced new articles of cheaper material, he sought small profits over large areas, and generally played the deuce with old-fashioned ways. He realized that "small profits with a frequent turnover of your capital pays incomparably better than big profits and a slow turnover." These are modern business methods, the foundation of capitalism, and the Jew may fairly be regarded as their introducer, though he is frequently beaten nowadays at his own game by his Gentile competitor.

Professor Sombart's last question is as to the reason of this development. Why should the Jew be specially fitted for capitalist undertakings? There are several obvious historical reasons. The Jews were scattered over a wide area, and yet clannish, so that they were specially adapted for international trade. "In the first instance, their linguistic ability enabled them to be of service to crowned heads as interpreters; thus they were sent as intermediaries on special negotiations to foreign courts. Soon they were put in charge of their employer's fortunes, at the same time being honoured through his graciousness in allowing them to become his creditors. From this point it was no long step to the control of the State finances, and in later years of the Stock Exchange." It is the old story of Joseph in Egypt. Again, they were aliens in every commonwealth in which they settled, and had no chance to engage in politics or the professions, so that money-making remained the only outlet for their activity. Then from the start they had wealth, and became money-lenders, and money-lending contains the root idea of modern capitalism. "In money-lending all conception of quality vanishes, and only the quantitative aspect matters. In money-lending the contract becomes the principal element of business. . . . In money-lending there is no thought of producing only for one's needs. . . . In money-lending the possibility is for the first time illustrated that you can earn without sweating; that you may get others to work for you without recourse to force." But Professor Sombart finds certain ultimate reasons in the Jewish religion and the Jewish character. The Jewish religion is essentially rationalist and intellectual, establishing a legally regulated relationship between God and His people. It has no mysteries or spirituality in the ordinary sense of the word. Getting rich to a Christian always savours of sin; to the Jew it is a high and positive virtue. Usury was allowed so far as Gentiles were concerned, and the Jewish usurer knew no qualms. "In the evening of his days he gazed upon his well-filled caskets and coffers, overflowing with sequins of which he had relieved the miserable Christians and Mohammedans. It was a sight which warmed his heart, for every penny was almost like a sacrifice which he had brought to his Heavenly Father." His religion, too, enjoined frugality and temperance, an admirable basis for money-making. There was in his character, too, a largely developed intellectuality and elasticity. He carried no baggage of prejudices and could adapt himself to the ways of any country. Israel remained a nomadic people, and could therefore look at any problem on its merits by the light of their keen rationalism, for they had no old modes of thought to bias them. Capitalism is only the triumphant application of pure reason to the business of buying and selling.

Dr. Ruppin's book is concerned with a different problem. He takes the Jewish characteristics for granted, and inquires as to how far the race is being assimilated into modern European culture, and whether in such an event it is likely to retain its racial features. He comes to the conclusion that such assimilation is progressing rapidly, and that there is a real danger of the disappearance of the specific Jewish spirit. This is especially marked in the case of religion, for the modern Jew is deeply impregnated with scepticism. The author's own solution is Zionism, for which he argues with much force and eloquence. Mr. Joseph Jacobs, who contributes an introduction, takes a less gloomy view, maintaining that it is historically proven that the Jew can assimilate the best of a foreign culture and yet retain his race characteristics. He thinks that if Russia reformed her ways and admitted Jews to citizenship the danger would largely be removed, for Russian Jews would then take a position in their native country, and be no longer thrust artificially into contact with alien societies at a low stage of culture which makes assimilation unavoidable. Dr. Ruppin's work is an interesting commentary on Professor Sombart's. If Jewish characteristics built up our capitalistic world, then it would seem that this very world is now destroying those characteristics.

PART
II

SHATTERED SOLUTIONS: 1914-1932

World War I changed the face of Europe and dramatically affected Jewish life both in Europe and the Middle East. When the war began, Europe had three empires, the Russian, the German, and the Austro-Hungarian, which together held the vast majority of European Jewry, and the Ottoman Empire ruled Palestine—the object of the Zionist dream. After the war all of these empires were gone. Defeated Germany became a republic, and her ally, Austria-Hungary, was divided into several states. Russia ceased to exist, and in her stead rose the new Union of Soviet Socialist Republics. In the Middle East Britain came to rule Palestine as a mandate of the new League of Nations. Combined, these changes had an enormous impact on Jewish life and the Jewish Question.

Several events during the war foreshadowed the new dimensions of Jewish life and politics that would follow. The fighting in Eastern Europe, unlike that in the West, was mobile, and the Jews, confined to the pale of settlement in Western Russia and living in the northeast of Austria-Hungary, suffered mightily as the battle raged through their homes for three years. The misery of Jewish life in Eastern Europe was compounded by war, and while some forgot politics in their effort to stay alive, the belief in a need for a change from the pre-war status quo lingered and grew.

Ideological change in the West also laid part of the framework for the post-war era. The length and lethality of the war had come as a shock to Europeans, and they searched for a moral purpose that would justify their sacrifices. During 1917 this search seemingly came to an end as the "new" diplomacy of morality replaced the "old" diplomacy of acquisition. No longer, many hoped, would secret treaties for territorial gain be the reason for war. Instead, statesmen began to speak of the war in terms of a great moral crusade which would herald a new age of peace and justice.

People looked at the causes of the war and determined that one of the basic reasons for the conflict was that various nationalities had bridled under the domination of others in the multi-national empires of Russia, Austria-Hungary, and the Ottomans. After all, they reasoned, the war had begun when a Serbian nationalist had assassinated the Austrian Archduke. Thus, national self-determination, the right of nationalities to decide their own destinies, was not only moral, it was an important aspect of international peace. Woodrow Wilson had said during the war that self-determination was a principle which "statesmen will henceforth ignore at their peril."

This attitude was not forgotten at the war's end. Poland was reconstituted as a national state, Rumania was enlarged, Austria and Hungary emerged as separate states, Czechoslovakia and Yugoslavia were created as homes for Serbs, Croats, Slovenes, and Czechs, and the Turks lost control over the non-Turkish parts of their empire. Jews lived in all of these Eastern European states, and it remained to be seen how they and other national minorities would fare under the new regimes.

All, however, was not left to chance. The peacemakers of 1919 realized that the new boundaries left pockets of Germans in Poland, Poles in Germany, and other national minorities. They also realized, largely due to Jewish efforts before and at the Peace Conference, that Jews needed protection and some guarantee that they would neither be denied civil rights nor at least some rights to maintain their religion, language, and culture.

The end result of these beliefs was a series of Minorities Treaties with the Eastern European states. These treaties made the League of Nations the guarantor of certain basic civil and cultural rights. The treaties dealt with Jews and all other "racial, religious, and linguistic" minorities. Here lay a possibility that Jewish life would finally be able to flourish without pogroms and legal disabilites. Two countries which would play a central role in the Jewish history of the inter-war years were not signatories to the agreements. The Powers saw no need to make Germany sign a treaty to protect minorities, and the Soviet Union, with its 2,500,000 Jews, was not a participant at the Conference. Thus neither German nor Soviet Jews had any legal right to appeal to the League of Nations.

But the failures of the system surpassed these two initial ones. Poland and Rumania were two states most proud of their national sovereignty, and resented the treaties which, they believed, infringed upon that sovereignty. Poland's three million Jews suffered greatly during the 1920-21 Polish-Soviet war, and were later subjected to a form of economic anti-Semitism which attempted to close them out of Polish economic life. Even after these regulations were lifted in 1926, Jewish economic life never recovered. Throughout this period Polish nationalism and anti-Semitism continued to grow, and after 1933 Polish anti-Semitism became open and violent. Along with Rumania, whose long history of anti-Semitism continued during the inter-war years, Poland was a center of European anti-Semitism. The League of Nations was powerless to act simply because it had no means to force a state to comply with a Minorities Treaty.

Jewish life in the Soviet Union was a mixture of improvement and new forms of persecution. Jews were saved from pogroms, for the Bolsheviks launched a campaign against anti-Semitism, but the Russian hatred of Jewry was not put to rest. After Stalin gained power, anti-Semitism resurfaced.

Economically, Soviet Jews were, at first, in terrible trouble. Many of their trades were considered superfluous, and many Jews were forced into unemployment. The Soviets did not, however, prohibit Jews from entering new trades which came into being with the crash program of industrialization; they encouraged Jewish participation both in heavy industry and agriculture. Jews who had been artisans, peddlers, and tailors became members of the proletariat.

Nevertheless, all was not well for Soviet Jewry. The new government of 1917 launched a massive assault on Jewish religion and culture. A Jewish section of the Communist Party sought to destroy Judaism, and while Yiddish theater and publishing did flourish for a brief time, they were devoid of any Jewish content. Zionism, like Judaism, was denounced, and the Hebrew language was forbidden as its tool. The attack on Jewish life seemed to be a great success: the Jewish community began to lose its identity.

In defeated Germany anti-Semitism did not die, but neither was it a dominant political factor until the 1930s. In general, German anti-Semitism rose and fell with the economy. In hard times anti-Semitic parties gained strength, and they tended to fade when the economy improved. They never lost all support, and when the depression struck in 1929, the Nazi party found many adherents to its anti-Semitic program.

The war, of course, also affected the Zionist dream. In November of 1917 the British Government issued the Balfour Declaration, which promised British support for a Jewish national home in Palestine. This document, secured by the efforts of Chaim Weizmann and others, was another result of the belief in national self-determination. Again humanitarian considerations were mixed with the pragmatic. Balfour believed, and others agreed, that Jews were a talented people who would use their abilities to aid a state if allowed, but in the face of persecution would use their talents for revolution which would disrupt the peace. The Jews demanded an outlet for their national ambitions, and Palestine was to provide that release.

The Palestine Mandate, like the Minorities Treaties, did not yield unqualified blessings for the Jews. Britain exercised her control of the area with little effective League supervision, and she had great difficulty in determining a policy for governing Palestine. Riots in 1921 and 1929 showed both the British and the Zionists that the road to a Jewish national home was not an easy one, and the British re-examined their pledge to the Jews. Palestine offered the dream of a Jewish homeland, but it was a dream unfulfilled.

The essays in this section reflect the duality of the period in Jewish life. The Minorities Treaties, the Palestine Mandate, and the end of the Czarist regime in Russia promised a new life for European Jewry, but anti-Semitism continued as an ever-present reality in Europe. The seeds of crisis were sown during this period of hope.

JEWISH HOPES AT THE PEACE TABLE

by Julian Mack

[The possibilities of a restored Zion and national rights for Eastern European Jewry were not met with unrelieved support by the Jews of America or Western Europe. In this 1919 article Julian Mack, an American jurist, Zionist, and philanthropist, powerfully addressed the issues that divided the American Jewish community. Some feared, Mack wrote, that to support Jewish national rights in Eastern Europe would weaken the civil equality of American Jews, and that support for Zionism would cause the patriotism of American Jewry to be questioned. Mack believed that the Eastern European states were unions of nationalities, and that Jews living in them needed national status to be truly equal. As regards Palestine, he believed that American Jews needed to have no political tie to a Jewish commonwealth. Mack felt that a Jew who feared to speak out for Jewish rights would "abdicate his manhood."]

"Jewish Hopes at the Peace Table," by Julian Mack, first published in *The Menorah Journal*, 5 (Feb. 1919), 1-7.

No one can positively foretell what the Peace Conference is going to do with reference to "Jewish Rights." But we have our hopes, our aspirations and our aims, and we know that these have met with the most sympathetic response and approval at the hands of all of the allied powers. So we feel certain that when the representatives of the Jews of these allied countries appear before the American representatives at the Peace Conference, or before the Peace Conference itself, if that privilege is granted to them, their requests will be addressed to sympathetic ears, and they will find a readiness never before equalled in the history of the world to devise ways and means by which at last the rights that are due to the Jew shall be accorded to him. And in this cause, we American Jews are pursuing no selfish purposes. We ask nothing for ourselves. All that any Jew can ask has been accorded to us as to every other citizen in this free land of western civilization. We go to speak for the people from whom we have sprung, for the stock of which we are a part, for our brethren in Eastern and in Central Europe who heretofore have been denied all of the rights, not merely that a people may request and expect, but that every human individual is entitled to.

The Jews of America have cheerfully and splendidly responded to the appeal to relieve the material wants of their afflicted brethren in the War Zone. New York Jewry alone has just raised five million dollars, as it did a year ago, and the rest of the country's Jewish population, with the assistance and help of many non-Jews, has raised an additional five to ten million dollars the past two years for this purpose. That money, it need hardly be said, is essential. It was necessary, in dealing with the afflicted Jews in the Eastern war region, that a Jewish War Relief Fund should be created, because in most of those lands, unlike our wonderful country, and that of our western allies, the Jew was never accorded full and equal rights; not even a proportionate share in the world's philanthropic offerings. The cry of the widow and the orphan and the homeless and the hungry always meets with a splendid answer from every Jew, and it is not surprising that American Jewry met the demand made upon it for this material aid as it always has met and always will meet similar demands.

WHAT RIGHTS DO WE HOPE TO ATTAIN?

In the same week that the noble record of the last great relief fund was being written in letters of gold, there was a still more important event that marked an epoch in the history of the Jews. That was the assembling of the first American Jewish Congress. There were gathered together four hundred men and women; three hundred of them elected democratically from every section of the country by their fellow Jews; the remaining hundred appointed as representatives by the national Jewish Organizations. Two or three organizations, not entirely negligible in the number of their membership, or in their religious zeal, were absent. It is sad, it is pitiable that in these days of Jewish suffering, any Jews or Jewish organizations should so misunderstand the implications of this Congress, the problem of Palestine and the demands for Jewish rights in Europe; and it is still more pitiable that these misunderstandings should be due in part to fear— fear lest the patriotism of the American Jew may be suspected or assailed—a selfish fear that deters some American Jews from standing up and working in the light of day for the just demands of their brethren in the lands of oppression. I care not how honestly anti-Zionistic these dissenters may be, or how loyal their Americanism—so long as they participate in the utterly false representation that Zionism is antagonistic to full-fledged unalloyed Americanism, they are disloyal to their people and to their religion. And against their patriotism as American citizens, I am ready to measure and to compare before any impartial tribunal the sturdy, exclusive, unqualified Americanism of any true American Zionist. The aims and aspirations of the Zionists were never misunderstood by the non-Jew. The charge of lack of patriotism is not made by the non-Jews of any land against the Zionist; that charge comes only from some of our brethren deluded by their fears.

What then are we seeking at the Peace Congress? What "rights" does the American Jewish Congress hope to obtain by sending a delegation to Europe to work in co-operation with the world's Zionist Organization and with representatives of Jewish organizations from all of our co-belligerent lands? Two rights, to put it briefly: justice for the Jewish people as a whole through the re-establishment in Palestine of a national home for the Jew; justice for the Jew in all of those lands of eastern Europe and the newer countries that are to be recognized at the Peace Congress—justice for the Jew in those lands in which justice has heretofore been denied to him.

Are these worthy objects or unworthy? Should the Jew bow his head in shame for striving to secure them? Should the Jew attempt to hide these aims from the world? Should they excite fear on the part of any man and especially any Jew? Let us examine them, and see what they involve.

THE LESSON OF THE RUMANIAN FLAW

One of these two claims directly affects the larger number of Jews—the Jews of eastern and of central Europe. Rights have been asked for them before. At the Peace Congress of 1878, when the kingdom of Rumania was established, it was understood that citizenship had finally been secured for the Jew in Rumania. It was thought that the Powers had imposed this as an express condition to the creation of the Rumanian kingdom. It was believed that all Rumanian Jews—the ancestors of many of whom had been inhabitants of that land for centuries—would attain full and equal rights with their fellow Rumanians. The clause guaranteeing this was faultily worded. The Powers that entered into that treaty, limited as they were by the independent rights of each sovereign state, not having at their command what we sincerely hope the world will have henceforth, a League of Nations, felt themselves unable to compel Rumania to live up to the full measure of the obligation assumed by her not merely to the Rumanian Jews but to the signatory nations. Hence, but the smallest fraction of Rumanian Jewry attained to citizenship, while the vast majority for the past forty years have been condemned to the position of aliens in their motherland—men and women without a country. That is a condition of such rank injustice that the whole civilized world should blush with shame that it has been unable to correct it. That is a condition that will not be permitted to continue hereafter in Rumania if the Jews are able to obtain from the Powers the hoped for recognition of their rights—nor will it be permitted to begin in any of the new or enlarged states of Europe.

This is the first essential demand of the Jew for his brethren—equal civil, political, and religious rights in every land. But it is true that the resolutions of the Jewish Congress and the cry of the Jew in Eastern Europe go beyond this. He asks for equal civil, religious, political, and *national* rights in those countries. And it may properly be asked what do we mean by national rights.

WHY THE JEWS MUST HAVE NATIONAL RIGHTS IN CERTAIN LANDS

Are we not content here in America with absolute equality of the individual before the law? Do we ask any national rights for the American Jew, for the English Jew, for the French Jew? Then why ask it for the Czecho-Slovak, or the Rumanian, or the Polish, or the Jugo-Slavic Jew? Of course we ask no such rights in the countries of western civilization. Their entire make-up and political structure is totally unlike that of the countries of Eastern Europe. This country has grown up in the traditions of English liberty, of Anglo-Saxon freedom; no man wants to change it. This country of ours is unique in the history of the world. Here are gathered together representatives of fifty or more different stocks or peoples, all working together, all coalesced into one great people, the American nation. But let us not forget that history has developed differently in other lands. Let us not attempt illiberally to impose our American political conceptions upon the peoples of Eastern Europe. Let us rather look at their situation from their own point of view—observe how they treat the various peoples within their realm, and then let us ask for the Jews—always recognized in these countries of Eastern Europe as a distinct group—only the same rights that each of the other groups, called in Eastern countries nationalities, are there accorded. In other words, free and equal rights means free and equal rights according to the customs of the country in which they are demanded. In those countries that look only to the individual, we of course ask only free and equal civil, political, and religious individual rights. But in countries that are divided into groups, each of which has a separate language, independent schools, and a distinct culture, there surely equality of right demands that the Jews, there recognized as a distinct group, should have exactly the same group rights, there described as national rights, that each of the other groups has.

An expression of opinion on this point which is of great significance was made recently by a true friend of the Jew, although he was not speaking primarily of the Jewish problem—President Thomas G. Masaryk of the new Czecho-Slovak State. Dr. Masaryk is himself a Bohemian—a Czech. German Bohemia, he declared, is of course a part of the Czecho-Slovak State, its people are citizens of that State; but we have no thought of making Czechs out of the Germans; we recognize their minority group right; we recognize their right to their language, their schools, and their church, and in the Czecho-Slovak State that right of minority groups will always be respected and protected. He made the same declaration concerning the rights of the Jewish people in his country and in those countries of eastern Europe in which from time immemorial the Jewish people have been recognized as a separate and distinct group—countries where three or four, perhaps five distinct groups, not fifty as in this country, have always lived together, formed one state, but each with its own distinct and separate ideals, culture, literature, and education. And he fully recognized and declared that for the realization and protection of these minority rights, minority political representation in the councils and administration of the State and the municipalities was essential.

If the American Jew were animated by selfishness and fear, he would keep his hands off this problem and would let these groups of people in foreign lands struggle for themselves. But if the American Jew, true to his ancestry, true to himself as a man, is ready to stand up for the oppressed of every nationality, color, or creed in every part of the world, how can he remain silent when his own brethren in eastern Europe are in danger of being denied that equality which for all other groups in those lands is an unqualified right? He would have to abdicate his manhood, if he feared to stand for his own brethren, for the incontestable principle of the right of the Jewish people everywhere to equality of states, a principle with which the delegation of the American Jewish Congress found President Wilson, as it expects to find the leaders of the Allied Powers, fully sympathetic.

WHAT WE REALLY WANT IN PALESTINE

And now as to the second problem—Palestine. What is it that we want there, and what is it that some fear? The problem seems so simple to those who have been dealing with it for years that it is even difficult to explain. It is difficult certainly to comprehend the doubts and fears of the *antis*. We do not want an independent State for the Jewish people in Palestine *at this time*. And why not? Because at this time the Jews form only one-sixth of the population, and an independent State under such conditions would be both impractical and undesirable. We are entirely content that the land shall now be placed by the League of Nations under the trusteeship of Great Britain, with the obligation there to lay the foundations of and, by proper land and immigration laws and administration, to promote the development of the Jewish Commonwealth. Only when the Jews shall be in the majority will they be ready for the Jewish Commonwealth.

The age-long dream of the Jew, the prayer of the Orthodox, has been that the Jewish people may be re-established in Palestine. What this means is not that all Jews should be gathered there—the land would not hold them—or that any Jew shall be driven out of his home.

But simply that those Jews who for any reason have the pioneering spirit to refound their people—one of the glories of the world, shall be able to do so; that it shall be made possible again for this people to flower as a nation or a commonwealth, not merely for the benefit of the Jew but for the benefit of all humanity; a people which when gathered together in earlier days on this soil—not a majority of the Jews of the world but simply a nucleus—evolved and created those fundamental principles of religion, of ethics, of morals, of social justice, on which our entire civilization is based; a people scattered for two thousand years and yet having within itself the vital spark that preserved it throughout centuries of oppression the like of which the world has never seen. With such a past and with the demonstration they have made in the past thirty-five years through their sixty Palestinian colonies—oases in the deserts of Asia Minor—and that miracle, the re-creation of a dead language as the living tongue of the whole community, the Jewish people may be trusted, when gathered together again in their homeland, to bring forth the higher fruits for the benefit of all mankind.

THERE IS NOTHING UNAMERICAN IN OUR PROGRAM

In the light of these facts, should we American Jews, because of the splendid opportunities we have here in our own country or because we are afraid of being misunderstood, hold ourselves aloof from this eternal cry of our brethren for a regained Palestine? Should we stand apart and say to them—You are endangering us—this small group in America. Assuredly not, even if there were some danger of being misunderstood. But in fact, if there be any danger, it comes not from our thinking non-Jewish fellow-citizens, but from a few of our own Jewish brethren.

The restoration of a Jewish commonwealth in Palestine was merely a fond dream, a vision, up to a year ago. It was not in the political platform of any of the governments of the world. It was the cry of the downtrodden Jew. It was the hope of the prosperous Jew who heard and did not refuse to listen to that cry. All of this is changed since November 2, 1917, when the Government of Great Britain published the Balfour Declaration "that it viewed with favor the re-establishment of a national home for the Jewish people in Palestine." When the other allied nations seconded this declaration and the Pope gave it his endorsement and at last the leader of all humanity at this day, Woodrow Wilson, although he could not declare himself offi-cially, because we were not at war with Turkey, expressed his deepest sympathy with the Zionist aims and movement, it became more than probable that at this Peace Congress, with the establishment of the League of Nations, the age-long dream of the Jew would come true. And when President Wilson stated on March 2, 1919, to the delegates from the American Jewish Congress, "I am persuaded that the Allied Nations, with the fullest concurrence of our government and people, are agreed that in Palestine should be laid the foundation of a Jewish Commonwealth," all doubts were dispelled. The Jewish people, through a nucleus of them, will be re-established in Palestine as a Jewish Commonwealth under one of the great powers—most likely Great Britain, through whose arms Palestine has been wrested from the oppression of the Turk.

And when this national home for the Jewish people is established, what will be the relations of the American citizens of the Jewish stock, of English subjects, and of all the other Jews in the other countries of the world, to this Commonwealth? Politically, nothing. We are Americans politically and nothing but Americans. There is no dual nationality in any political sense; there can be none. We look to Palestine for nothing. We look to America for everything. But when our brethren, descendants of our ancestors, inheritors of the same traditions, the same civilization, the same culture, shall again bring forth the highest values for civilization, as we trust and hope they will, we of the kinship will be the spreaders of that civilization among the peoples of the world. Surely there is nothing selfish about that. Surely there is nothing harmful in this for us or for our American fellow-citizens. Surely in this program there is no cause for fear.

JEWISH NATIONALISM

by Philip Marshall Brown

[Jews were not the only people perplexed by questions concerning either the existence or the future of a Jewish nation. In this 1919 editorial in The American Journal of International Law, *Philip Marshall Brown, a professor of international law at Princeton, raised several important issues about Jewish nationalism and Zionism. He believed that a Jewish nation did exist, but that Palestine was too important for three religions to become the special province of one. He thought that the Jewish nation would have to remain a nation without territory, but that such a continued existence was contingent on the states of Eastern Europe allowing the freedom necessary for Jewish national survival. He did not believe that such freedom was present. Brown had, then, raised a basic issue of Jewish national survival in the twentieth century. Was there any practical way to guarantee the future of the Jewish nation?]*

"Jewish Nationalism" by Philip Marshall Brown, first published in *American Journal of International Law*, 13 (Oct. 1919), 755-58.

The principle of the "right of self-determination" has not yet been clearly defined or accompanied by guiding rules for its application. One result has been the discovery of "nations crowding to be born"—of the existence of national self-consciousness where unsuspected, and of confused racial situations, as in Hungary—where no practical rules could be devised to insure without discrimination this right of self-determination.

One of the most interesting nationalistic problems raised by this war is that of Jewish claims to Palestine. The Zionist movement of course has long favored the return of Jewish colonists to the home of the race. But this movement had no political significance until after the famous declaration on the subject by Mr. Balfour, British Secretary for Foreign Affairs, in November, 1918 [sic], following the occupation of Jerusalem by General Allenby's forces. This declaration was addressed to Lord Rothschild, the leading representative of Jews in

England, and read as follows:

> The Government views with favor the establishment
> of Palestine as a national home for the Jewish people, and
> will use their best endeavors to facilitate the achievement
> of this object, it being clearly understood that nothing will
> be done that may prejudice the civil or religious rights of
> existing non-Jewish communities in Palestine.

The effect of this declaration on the scattered members of the Jewish race was almost dramatic. To many it was the realization of Talmudic prophecies; to Zionists the achievement of their dearest hopes; and to all Jews a historic event appealing poignantly to their emotions.

The Zionists were quick to follow up this important declaration by the adoption of plans for the immediate penetration of Palestine under the aegis of British military occupation. A British Zionist Commission was organized with the consent and active cooperation of the Government to proceed to Palestine for purposes of investigation and counsel. A few foreign representatives were permitted to be added, one of whom, Mr. Walter Myer, was an American.

This commission reached Palestine early in April, 1918, and proceeded to play a most active role. Among other things, it concerned itself in the administration of relief to needy Jews, in organizing Jewish civic communities, in advising with the military authorities, in political negotiations of a varied character, and in investigating conditions generally. One of the most impressive acts of the commission was the laying of the foundation-stone of a Jewish university on a spur of the Mount of Olives. Instruction in this institution is to be entirely in Hebrew, and is to be open to all nationalities.

The commission was particularly preoccupied with political questions affecting the Moslems and the Christians, who had become greatly perturbed over the prospective establishment of a Jewish State. The Zionists endeavored to allay these fears by assurances to the effect that they did not seek political independence, but desired merely freedom for Jews to settle in Palestine under the protection of a liberal regime such as Great Britain would afford. They interpreted the words "national home" used by Balfour as having only a moral and ethical sense, and as having no political significance whatever. These efforts were apparently without success as the Moslems and Christians have made common cause in refusing to sell any more land to Jews and in generally antagonizing the plans of the Zionists.

Despite the protestations of some Zionists, there can be no doubt about the awakening of Jewish national self-consciousness as a result of the declaration by Balfour. The attempt to limit the meaning of "national home" has failed, and most Zionists now abdicate openly the foundation of a "Jewish State." The arguments in behalf of this scheme stress not so much the need of an asylum for oppressed Jews, as they do the need of a national rallying point. The heart of Zionism seems to be the preservation of the solidarity and integrity of the Jewish race. Its main objective is to arrest the process of assimilation of Jews throughout the world by reviving their sentiment of loyalty to the old home of their race.

As had been pointed out, the principle of the right of self-determination has not been so clearly defined as to indicate to what extent historic wrongs may be righted. It would not appear reasonable, however, to attempt to revive claims reverting eighteen hundred years ago. The dispersal of the Jews was so complete as to make it impossible for them to maintain even the nucleus of a national culture or preserve any real historic continuity. What militates more forcibly still against the demand for a Jewish State is the fact that Palestine has come to have a very special significance for Christians and Moslems as well as for the Jews. It is truly a "holy land" for them all; and no one sect or race can now claim with justice any special privileges.

It is this fact of the international significance of Palestine that makes it impossible to consider Jewish nationalistic claims on a par with the claims, say, of the Poles, the Czechs, or of the Albanians. The right of self-determination in these instances does not encounter the difficulties of a religious and of a historic character that it does in the case of the Jews. The problem is unique and can only be solved in some unique fashion. The solution, however, might not be as difficult as would now appear, provided all parties were willing to concede the international significance of Palestine. In this age of "internationalism" there could hardly be found a more suitable spot for the practical application of the idea of internationalism than in the land revered by the three great theistic religions which have exerted so profound an influence on the world.

If the Jewish race is determined to resist all assimilative tendencies and to preserve its integrity, and is not satisfied with the internationalization of Palestine, there would seem to be but one other alternative, namely, in a much larger spirit of tolerance and a more liberal attitude on the part of nations toward the foreigner within their gates. Modern ideas of sovereignty have been much affected by feudal notions to the effect that "a man was possessed by the land"; and has identified national jurisdiction with territory. Lorimer once pointed out that the idea of a nation without territory, as in the case of the Jews and the Gypsies, was not utterly unreasonable, provided they were permitted to preserve their peculiar institutions under a regime of the character such as has prevailed in Turkey, Persia, Siam, China, and elsewhere. Under the "exterritorial" or "personal" theory of sovereignty, great concessions might be made to the peoples of many nationalities who wished to preserve their own national and racial ideals, provided, of course, that these ideals in no way imperilled the morals and public security of the sovereign state granting these concessions.

It is doubtless too much to expect so liberal and tolerant an attitude among nations today. In spite of many internationalizing agencies, most nations today are still more or less chauvinistic, and, in a sense, bigoted in their jealous adherence to their own ways and ideas. But it is this very fact that makes the need for mutual toleration all the greater. Nowhere is this need more apparent than in the case of the Jew. He must either seek a "national home," or obtain a much greater measure of tolerance than has yet been accorded to his race or any other race, or he must reconcile himself to the gradual loss of his racial identity. These are the alternatives before him. The problem of the right of self-determination in the case of the Jew is by all odds the most baffling of the many nationalistic claims now clamoring for recognition. It is not strange that the Peace Conference in Paris has been unable to find a solution.

DISRAELI
ON THE
SECRET SOCIETIES
AND THE
JEWS

[In 1920 a pamphlet entitled "The Jewish Peril" was published in Britain. It was, in fact, the famous Protocols of the Learned Elders of Zion. *This work pretended to be the record of a meeting of the leaders of a secret Jewish conspiracy to destroy Christian civilization by the introduction of liberalism and socialism, and to establish Jewish world domination. Jews had played major roles in the liberal revolutions of 1848 and the Russian Revolution of November 1917, and although the* Protocols *were shown to be a forgery in 1921, the idea of a Jewish plot was not easily dismissed. Some, such as Henry Ford, firmly believed in the concept, while many discussed a perceived Jewish proclivity for revolution.*

This 1920 article was a part of that discussion. The author, using the writings of former British Prime Minister Benjamin Disraeli, of Jewish ancestry, raised the issue of the Jewish role in the secret societies of Europe. Why were the Jews so active in revolution and what should be done about it? He agreed with Disraeli that "the Christian States have the Jews they deserve." He also believed that the secret societies were a danger and should be watched, but that increased persecution of Jews would only intensify the activities of Jewish extremists. The specter of a Jewish plot, raised in the Protocols, *reflected a fear of the Jewish people, a people with no clearly defined place in a society increasingly structured in terms of nation, state, and race.]*

"Disraeli on the Secret Societies and the Jews," first published in *The Spectator*, 124 (12 June, 1920), 782-83.

It will be seen from the whole of Disraeli's writings, that he considers, like every Jewish politician, and probably quite rightly, that the Christian States have the Jews they deserve, and that it is persecution upon persecution and not the natural wickedness of the Jewish race that has made the Jew a revolutionary.

Persecution, in a word, although unjust, may have reduced the modern Jews to a state almost justifying malignant vengeance. They have become so odious and so hostile to mankind as to merit for their present conduct, no matter how occasioned, the obloquy and ill-treatment of the communities in which they dwell, and with which they are scarcely permitted to mingle. Let us examine this branch of the subject, which, though of more limited interest, is not without instruction. In all the great cities of Europe, and in some of the great cities of Asia, among the infamous classes therein existing, there will always be found Jews. They are not the only people who are usurers, gladiators, and followers of mean and scandalous occupations, nor are they anywhere a majority of such, but considering their general numbers, they contribute more than their proportion to the aggregate vile. In this they obey the law which regulates the destiny of all persecuted races; the infamous is the business of the dishonoured; and as infamous pursuits are generally illegal pursuits, the persecuted race which has most ability will be most successful in combating the law. The Jews have never been so degraded as the Greeks were throughout the Levant before their emancipation, and the degradation of the Greeks was produced by a period of persecution, which, both in amount and suffering, cannot compare with that which has been endured by the children of Israel. This peculiarity, however, attends the Jews under the most unfavourable circumstances: the other degraded races wear out and disappear; the Jew remains as determined, as expert, as persevering, as full of resource and resolution as ever. Viewed in this light, the degradation of the Jewish race is alone a striking evidence of its excellence, for none but one of the great races could have survived the trials which it has endured.

But though a material organization of the highest class may account for so strange a consequence, the persecuted Hebrew is supported by other means. He is sustained by a sublime religion. Obdurate, malignant, odious, and revolting as the lowest Jew appears to us, he is rarely demoralized. Beneath his own roof his heart opens to the influence of his beautiful Arabian traditions. All his ceremonies, his customs, and his festivals are still to celebrate the bounty of nature and the favour of Jehovah. The patriarchal feeling lingers about his hearth. A man, however fallen, who loves his home, is not wholly lost. The trumpet of Sinai still sounds in the Hebrew ear, and a Jew is never seen upon the scaffold, unless it be at an *auto-da-fe*. But having made this full admission of the Jewish race, we are not prepared to agree that this limited degeneracy is any justification of the prejudices and persecution which originated in barbarous or medieval superstitions."—(*Life of Lord George Bentinck*, Chap. XXIV).)

In other words, Disraeli asks us why we wonder that the Jew is what is he when we treat him as we do. We must confess, however, that the essential thing at the moment is not so much criticism of the past but the question whether conspiracies are in existence for the destruction of the civilized world, and whether a portion of the Jewish race are taking the lead in the great plot for world havoc.

We are inclined to think, as we have said before, that there are a great many Secret Societies now existing in Europe, and that in them the Jews are very often to the front. We think also that the power of these Secret Societies has been immensely exaggerated, but at the same time we think that these societies and the Jewish extremists ought to be very carefully watched, though not persecuted, by all Governments. Persecution will only intensify their action. Left alone, though observed, they will tend to become merely ritualistic. But watched they ought to be. We are very much afraid, however, that the matter is not being studied by our statesmen.

Though this is our view, we ought in fairness to note a curious fact which tends to prove the innocence of the Jews in the matter of the Secret Societies. At the time of the Dreyfus trial there was a great deal of talk of Jewish Secret Societies and of the Grand Orient Freemasons. The clerical papers in France were full of vague charges. We may be sure that persecutors of Captain Dreyfus would have been only too eager to have exposed these Hebrew conspirators in open court had they been able to produce evidence. Yet they entirely failed to do so— and this though the whole of the French Secret Police, still the most efficient in the world, was at the service of those who desired to bring to light and destroy an alleged Jewish conspiracy. In a word, it is very difficult to believe that if the Grand Orient Freemasons and Jews were then, as asserted, engaged in a conspiracy of the Anti-Christ order that it would have been impossible to bring evidence of their aims, objects and actions.

ZIONISM AND THE JEWISH PROBLEM

by John Punnett Peters

[John Punnett Peters, an American Biblical scholar, believed that Zionism was the cause of the modern Jewish problem. In this analysis, Peters found signs of exclusiveness in the Jewish religion, and tied this facet of Judaism to the modern Zionist movement which he thought raised the idea of a Jewish nation above the religion of Judaism. He saw Zionism as a dangerous movement that would cause even greater friction between Jews and non-Jews. He also disagreed with the idea that the Jews had a special claim to Palestine, and wrote that attempts to create a Jewish land there had already inflamed and would continue to inflame hatred against the Jew. For Peters, the solution to the Jewish problem was to abandon the concept of a Jewish nation. The article, first published in the Sewanee Review *in July 1921, proved to be very popular; it was reprinted in January 1926.]*

"Zionism and the Jewish Problem" by John Punnett Peters, first published in *Sewanee Review*, 29 (July 1921), 268-94; rpt. 34 (Jan. 1926), 62-88.

The Jewish problem has become within the last few months rather angrily acute both in England and in this country. It has long been a familiar problem on the continent of Europe, in Russia, Poland, Rumania, Germany, and even in France, as witness the Dreyfus case, and now we are experiencing it. The so-called protocols have been published in England and in this country by reputable papers, and high-toned publishers have issued the volumes of those who would warn the world of a Jewish peril. This has called forth from Jewish sources protests, and there have been recriminations and denunciations; but especially it is the Zionist Jews who have been engaged in this warfare, for the Jewish problem is principally the result of Zionism, and the attempt at the practical realization of political Zionism in the mandate under which England has taken Palestine has brought it to the fore.

On sentimental grounds there has long been a tendency among English-speaking people to sympathize with the Jewish religious dream of restoration to Palestine and consequent revival of the ancient glory of Jewry. Sympathy with this dream was elicited by the persistent hope and faith which through manifold vicissitudes and much suffering had enabled the Jew to maintain a separate existence awaiting its fulfilment. That vision of restored glory had kept alive a spirit of idealism in the souls of a people otherwise steeped in a crass and sordid materialism, and the glamor of it, like a jewel in the mire, appealed to the imagination. Affected by such sentiment, few have examined the Jewish claim to Palestine historically, or considered it in its relation to the similar sentimental claims of the great body of Occidental and Oriental Christians, of Mohammedan believers everywhere, or to the practical claims of the present inhabitants of Palestine.

Historically, the Hebrews acquired Palestine by the usual process. Lusting after the good things of others, the Hebrews invaded the country of the Canaanites, following the worldwide method pursued by countless numbers of other peoples, who, with greater or less cruelty, robbing and despoiling those who had industriously tilled the land and accumulated wealth, have possessed themselves of that land and that wealth. The record of the contest as handed down in Hebrew tradition is rather gruesome; not more so, however, than that of other similar conquests, and in point of fact less so than appears at first sight from the Old Testament record. The whole land was never fully possessed, even at the time of David. He, however, established a Hebrew kingdom in Palestine and put the Canaanites not already amalgamated under tribute, and ultimately by victorious raids and wars the neighboring peoples also, thus creating what may be called an empire, covering almost all of the territory from the borders of Egypt to the river Euphrates. David's empire laid the foundation of that dream, which has come down among orthodox Jews to this day, of the re-establishment of a great kingdom of Israel, possessing all David's conquests, with much more besides, and dominating the world. David's empire lasted for two generations. It began to disintegrate under Solomon, and under Solomon's son all the remaining tributaries threw off the Hebrew yoke, while the Hebrews themselves divided into two parts, the larger part, and the more advanced in culture and religion, constituting the Israelite kingdom; the smaller part, chiefly David's own tribe, the kingdom of Judah, occupying a tiny territory about Jerusalem, not so large as a fair-sized county in this country or in England.

This petty kingdom of Judah endured for 350 years, sometimes independent, sometimes a subordinate or tributary state, and then Jerusalem was destroyed and the better part of its nobles, priests and skilled artisans deported to Babylonia, while others fled to Egypt, leaving only a peasant population to possess a moiety of the territory of Judah immediately about the ruins of the ancient capital. Largely through the influence of Ezekiel and some fellow priests the exiles in Babylonia maintained their integrity, and half a century later such of their descendants as would, were permitted and helped by the Persian conqueror, Cyrus, to return from Babylonia to their homeland and rebuild Jerusalem and the Temple. Few took advantage of this opportunity. So they developed a theory that some day their God would transport them and their wealth together to a transformed Palestine, and continued in Babylonia to bewail and pity themselves as the *Galutha*, or Captivity, making amends for their failure to return by a visit or pilgrimage once in a lifetime, by money contributions, and by a painstaking application to and development of the theory of their religion, and especially of a law of exclusivism which should keep them separate from the people among whom they lived, until the Lord should intervene to carry them back in triumph to Jerusalem. This theory, their superior education, their greater wealth, and their material support enabled them to impress upon their compatriots in Palestine, until at last there was built up there a religious community, with the Temple as its centre, where priests might sacrifice and pray for their brethren throughout the world, all of whom were bound together by this holy law of separation from the peoples among whom they lived, counting Jerusalem as their future home, to which they should sometime be wafted from the four corners of the earth by the powers of the Lord, who would also make Palestine a land flowing with milk and honey, and establish there a king of David's line, to avenge them on all who had oppressed them and to establish a mighty dominion. This was Judaism, and with the establishment of this ideal came into being the people who called themselves Jews. Judea itself constituted under Persian rule a church rather than a state, autonomous, religiously and socially, although obligated to recognize the Persian suzerain in its sacrifices and its prayers, politically and economically a part of the Persian empire, ruled by Persian officials. Under this system Judaism grew and throve, Jerusalem became rich and prosperous, and Jews multiplied and waxed fat and influential in all parts of the empire.

But in Judaism there were at war two principles, the one the principle of rigid exclusivism, the development of a legalism which should completely mark off the Jew from all other peoples, prohibiting marriage with them and social intercourse. This had its centre in the Captivity, that is, among the Jews in Babylonia, but became dominant in Judea from the time of Ezra, forcing among other things the breach with Israel or the Samaritans. The other principle is that which we call the prophetic principle, which found expression in the prophets from Amos onward, and in its highest form in the great Prophet of the restoration [Isaiah], who set forth the view that Israel might not live for itself, that its dispersion among the Gentiles was for the beneficent purpose of revealing to the Gentile the glory and love of the one true God and uniting Jew and Gentile together in the service of that God. The former party looked to the re-establishment of David's kingdom and their triumph over the nations before whom they must now cringe. The latter looked to a kingdom of God upon earth the basis of which should be love and service, and in which Jew and Gentile should be united. The former party prevailed, but in the sacred book that was adopted as a guide of life for the Jews, both the Law and the Prophets were included, the former being given, however, much the higher place and counted the supreme authority.

Religious national exclusivism, it should be said, was not originally peculiar to the Jew. It was the property of practically all ancient religions, but under the influence, first of the Persian empire, then of the great Hellenizing movement resulting from the conquests of Alexander the Great, and finally of the establishment of the Roman Empire, this older conception of the separateness of peoples one from another, and the combination of their religion with their state in this separateness, was broken down, in some places altogether, in others in part. Only the Jew resisted with all his might this tendency, and developed his Law for that purpose.

From the separation of Christianity from Judaism dates, one may say, the orthodox Jewish faith, the four cornerstones of which are: (1) belief in one God; (2) belief in a Messiah who shall redeem God's chosen; (3) belief that the Jews are God's chosen people set apart and bound to keep themselves separate from all nations of the earth; and (4) the belief that God will ultimately gather his chosen people in Palestine, restore the Holy Temple, service, sacrifices and all, and the Jewish kingdom and priesthood. The former two principles or beliefs are not, the latter are, peculiar to the Jews. While here and there the Jews have followed false Messiahs, or established temporal states by force of arms, in which cases they have shown themselves intolerant and persecutors, yet in general it may be said that this Zionism, which has been the belief of the Jews through all the ages since Christianity has been dominant, has not, for many centuries certainly, directly endangered or embroiled the state by its endeavor to realize its expectation of a return to Palestine and the establishment there of a Jewish state. They have expected that this would be brought about, not by human agency, but by a direct intervention of God. While the Jewish Church and nation were in their minds one, the nation was in abeyance, the Church only functioned.

Because, however, of their point of view that they were a chosen people, separate and bound to keep themselves separate in blood and customs from all about them, the Jews constituted an unassimilable mass wherever they found themselves, and have been on that account equally obnoxious to Roman paganism, to Christianity and to Islam. For ordinary purposes their attitude has seemed to the rest of the world to be that of the famous grace: "God bless me and my wife, my son John and his wife, us four and no more." This position rendered persecution and religious-racial prejudice inevitable. The persecution which the Jews suffered was in some part religious, but chiefly political, economic and social. The Jew resisted with singular stubbornness, and the results were, on the whole, worse for the persecutor than for the persecuted. Jewish racial pride and religious intolerance were intensified, the latter displaying itself in bitter persecution, so far as their position permitted, of all apostates, the former in their almost pathetic boastfulness in the success of those of Jewish stock, even though renegades, as an evidence of the inherent superiority of the race. The Jews were bound more and more closely together, constituting an international religious-racial unit, inside which they developed singularly beautiful conditions of trust and mutual helpfulness, and an idealism in certain regards very noble. As the opportunity for physical achievement was denied them, mental qualities took their place, which made them in the ordinary competition of life, and in the business world particularly, more than a match for their oppressors. On the other hand, they developed certain offensive habits of servility and that trickery and chicane which such conditions will produce in any race, which have been the ground of much of the social objection which the Christian feels toward the Jew. But after all has been said which can be said to palliate or explain the persecution or oppression of the Jew through the Christian ages, the chief blame therefore must rest upon the Christian, because his was the position and consequent responsibility of power, and further because he professed principles which made his conduct the more damnable. The relation of Christian to Jew through the 1,600 years of Christian rule is not a pretty memory, and the Christian world suffed [sic] the inevitable in the degradation of its moral fibre, and in the destruction of some of the elements most desirable in the progress of civilization, culture and religion, of all which things Exhibit A is Spain, where Jewish persecution was carried to a terrible extreme.

It was toward the beginning of the last century that a new movement made itself felt in Judaism, as a consequence of that new movement in the Christian world which expressed itself in the French Revolution and the establishment of the American Republic, spreading everywhere new conceptions of liberty and freedom. With our own country in the lead there came for the Jew political emancipation, gradually extending from the west eastward, made effective as far as Vienna and Berlin by the middle of the last century. As a result of this political emancipation and a removal of the civic disabilities under which they had labored for so many centuries, some Jews began to lose the consciousness of being a separate political unit, and there arose in Judaism a movement to adapt the external character of Judaism to these new conditions. This was Reformed Judaism. It moved the ethical ideas of the Hebrew prophets into the foreground, as over against the ritual and the ceremonial of legalism. Its adherents sought to be true citizens of the country in which they found themselves, following in this the recommendations of the prophet Jeremiah to the Jews in Babylonia 2,500 years earlier. The essence of reformed Judaism was the disassociation of religion and nationality. It would separate Church and State, breaking all national and racial barriers, and making religion the life of the individual, according to the dictates of his own conscience. Israel would be the chosen people, not in the sense of possessing a tribal deity separating them from the rest of the world, and of looking for special privileges from that deity, but as especially gifted with the knowledge of the true God and therefore with the solemn obligation, imposed by their historical position, to spread the doctrine of divine unity and to exemplify the teachings of their religion by their conduct in life, not merely toward their fellow Jews but toward all men.

This new position and new opportunity of the Jew produced the inevitable reaction. The newly arrived always attain a self-consciousness which asserts itself in an aggressiveness and bumptiousness obnoxious to those who arrived before. This is true of both individuals and races. In the industrial and social world, where it is a phenomenon so common that it has found abundant expression in literature, it is answered by snubs and a species of ostracism; in the political world, by more overt action. Where it is a race or nation, and not an individual, raised or liberated, which expresses its self-consciousness at a new arrival, the expression becomes more obnoxious and the response more emphatic. If religious or racial differences mark off the newly arrived, religio-racial prejudice manifests itself, always most emphasized, of course, where these newly arrived constitute a large element of the population, in which case the old possessors are instinctively drawn together to battle for their place and their integrity. Unfortunately, just at this time the Germans also began to develop first a national and then a race consciousness, a development enormously accelerated by the victories of 1866 and 1870. The consequence was *Teutonism*, which ultimately resulted in a conception by the German of his race and its mission strikingly similar to that of the Jew. This new German race-pride and Jewish self-consciousness led to the Berlin *Judenhetze* of 1880-81 and the organization of anti-Semitism. This was not religious in its inception, the leaders being rather anti-religious Teutonists and Wagnerites. The dominant position of Germany insured the spread of anti-Semitism, as of the nationalistic race movement. It naturally manifested itself in its worst form in Russia, where the Jews were massed in great numbers, namely, in pogroms, for the same reason that race prejudice against the Negro manifests itself in the southern part of the United States in lynchings. The solid mass of the Jews seemed to constitute a political and economic menace, which the relatively ignorant and unprogressive Russians knew how to combat only by violence. In Russia, moreover, Judaism manifested itself in its crudest and most unmitigated form, not only in its practical application of the Golden Rule to the Jewish neighbor alone, but in its distinct doctrinal exception of the Gentile from the scope of that rule. On the other hand, in Russia as nowhere else, there were emancipated Jews who had broken loose from all religion, and rebelled against the whole social-economical system which had so oppressed them, anarchists and revolutionaries, often men and women of marked ability.

On the Russian side there was an ignorant and superstitious piety among the masses, easily inflamed to fury against enemies of the faith by a corrupt bureaucracy, which dreaded progress in Church or State. Hence the infamous May Laws and the pogroms, which began to scatter Jewish refugees from Russia throughout the world.

The effort to provide for the Jews coming out of Russia and the effort to protect from persecution the Jews remaining in Russia brought together Jews of East and West as never before. It was this effort which developed economic Zionism. What should be done with all these Jews coming out of Russia? They had been separated from the soil for centuries. They had lived within the pale and in ghettos. They were to a considerable extent parasitic. It was necessary to introduce them to industrialism and agriculture. The former they took to more or less naturally, the latter unwillingly, and yet the wisest Jewish leaders considered it of the first importance to bring back a part at least of the Jewish race to the soil.

Attempts of all sorts were made to establish Jewish agricultural colonies in this country and in South America. Proposals were made looking to the settlement of Jews in East Africa and in Egypt; and colonies were established in Palestine. This was an economic and philanthropic Zionism, a movement with which Jews everywhere sympathized and Christians of every sort. It did not seek to colonize Jews in Palestine with the idea of claiming Palestine as the homeland of the Jews, the chosen people who are entitled to dispossess all others, to take possession of that land and to rule the world; but it was felt by Jew and Christian alike to be a proper thing to colonize refugees from persecution in a land which had for them both historical and sacred associations. There seemed something infinitely touching and lovely in bringing them back in that way. As in the old days of the release from the Babylonian captivity, there were few who actually returned to Palestine. The great bulk of the Jews brought out of Russia sought homes in Europe or the Americas, and especially in our own country.

This contact of the Jews of the East and West strengthened the feeling of race solidarity, and even agnostic Jews who had abandoned Judaism began to realize anew the bond of race kinship. Numerous societies of one sort and another sprang up here and there seeking to solve the new problems which arose, to remold Judaism or to secure the rights of Jews, and thus prepared the way for the third and present phase of Zionism, racial-national or political Zionism. This was a further development of race self-consciousness, connecting itself naturally with the general movement of racial rehabilitation which made itself felt toward the close of the last century throughout the world, beginning in Germany with Teutonism. It was with Teutonism that racial Zionism had its closest affinities. The leader of this new racial or political movement was Herzl, a journalist of Vienna. A Jew by race, not by religion, finding himself socially at a disadvantage, he came to believe that he and others similarly situated were hampered in the fulfillment of their aspirations by racial prejudice on the part of the

Christian majority. Convinced that even though the Jew were to become Christian, he would be regarded as a Jew because his race had no national home, he reached the conclusion that the only method of breaking down prejudice was to reunite those who were Jews by race only, as well as those who were Jews by religion, in one great nationality, securing for them a homeland somewhere. This homeland would, in his opinion, exalt their honor and procure respect in whatever foreign country they might live, precisely as Germans or Italians or Frenchmen living in England and America, though aliens in those countries, are respected because they have the protection of a national homeland. Herzl displayed a remarkable ability in urging his claim. It appealed to the self-consciousness of a great number of racial Jews who, like himself, were galled by a prejudice against them which they did not know how to overcome and against which, therefore, they welcomed any quick-cure panacea, and he achieved speedy success. The first Zionist congress was held in 1897, and from that time the movement developed rapidly. It fell in with the dominant racial movement which was sweeping the world. It expressed that something which appealed to men who, become conscious of power and strength, found themselves hampered in taking the places they believed were theirs; it harmonized with the philanthropic appeal to aid oppressed Jews and give them a home; and it touched a sentiment rooted in ancestral tradition which powerfully appealed to all religious Jews, and which many of those who had practically cast off Jewish orthodoxy could not escape from.

Not being Jews by religion, Herzl and his first followers were ready to establish this Zion anywhere where land could be obtained, and entered into negotiations with the English government for a tract of land in East Africa. But the sentimental appeal of Palestine was so strong that the idea of any other country had shortly to be abandoned, and before Herzl's death in 1904 this general principle was adopted by the Zionist Congress: "The object of Zionism is to establish for the Jewish people a publicly and legally assured home in Palestine." The Zionism here referred to is a definitely organized international movement governed by a congress and a committee. Its purpose is to strengthen and develop race-consciousness among the Jewish *nation*, for so they designate all people of Jewish race in all nations throughout the world, binding them together by a revival of their ancient language, a study of their literature and a community of interests, and to provide as a homeland for this Jewish *nation*, Palestine, to which their ancient traditions look. This is to be the heart and centre of Judaism throughout the world, and, wherever the Jew may live or have his being, it is hoped to infuse him from this centre with the national life and the national intelligence.

The great and evident danger of this movement is the development of a race allegiance paramount to the national, and it was a sense of this danger which led a body of prominent Jewish citizens of this country to present to President Wilson, by Congressman Julius Kahn, for transmission to the Peace Conference at Paris on March 4, 1919, a protest "against such a political segregation of the Jews in Palestine or elsewhere"; first, "because the Jews are dedicated heart and soul to the welfare of the countries in which they dwell under free conditions. All Jews repudiate every suspicion of a double allegiance, but to our minds it is necessarily implied in and cannot by any logic be eliminated from the establishment of a sovereign state for the Jews in Palestine." The second objection is to the unfortunate effect such "political segregation of Jews would have on the millions of Jews who would be unable to migrate to Palestine from those states where a strong prejudice already exists against them." The establishment of a Jewish State will manifestly increase that prejudice and serve in such states "as a new justification for additional repressive legislation." The multitudes who remain would be subjected to greater discrimination or persecution than before. The third objection is to the serious danger of sanguinary conflicts with the present inhabitants of the land and their co-religionists which the proposed establishment of such a state is sure to involve. The fourth objection is that "the re-establishment in Palestine of a distinctively Jewish state" is "utterly opposed to the principles of democracy which it is the avowed purpose of the World's Peace Conference to establish." The fifth objection, which has been keenly felt also by orthodox Jews, is that it would substitute a merely national bond for "the bond of common religious priniples and experiences."

Supplementing objections two and three,—it may be observed that Palestine has been for a longer time in possession of the Moslems than it ever was in possession of the Jew or of the Hebrew race. The present inhabitants of the land claim its possession with as good a right as the inhabitants of any country in the world; and not only that, Palestine is a holy country to the Moslem and to the Christian as much as to the Jew. Christians have occupied it and fought and bled for the possession of its holy sites, and the Christian has left far more marks of occupation and cultivation on the land than did the Jew. In normal times tens of thousands of pilgrims of both religions visit its religious sites every year. The Christians especially have invested immense funds in the land for religious and educational purposes in connection with those holy sites and the pilgrims who visit them, and the number of Christian and Moslem dead who lie buried within sight of Jerusalem, in the hope of bettering their chance in the hereafter, is greater than the number of Jews whose graves cover the slopes of Olivet. For every Jew who has a sentimental claim to Palestine as the land of his forefathers and of his faith, there are hundreds of Christians and Moslems who with some similar sentiment make a like claim upon the land. To plant a Zionist State there is to run great risk of religious turmoil, and to invite grave perils to those who make such settlement.

While the dominant control of the Zionist party is at present in the hands of those who are not religious but merely racial Jews, and while the movement is in itself political, the glamor of it has appealed to considerable numbers of the religious Jews, both orthodox and reformed, and the number affected by that appeal seems to be on the increase, as a result of the "Zionist Mandate" accepted by England from the Peace Conference. One can understand, without approving, the appeal which a Zionist State makes to the Jew who believes he is one of a race chosen by God, marked off from the rest of the world as a peculiar people, to whom God gave the land of Canaan as his people's possession and Jerusalem as their holy city, appointing the Temple as the place of His dwelling in their midst, where they are to offer sacrifices to Him, and whence He is sometime to manifest Himself in glory, subduing their enemies and making them dominant over them. It is difficult to comprehend how a Zionist State can appeal to those more modern Jews who believe in Judaism as a religious, ethical force only, for Zionism would make religion dependent on locality, creating a holy city, which in the common experience of all religions everywhere has always resulted in the creation of an unholy community; and in point of fact, such Jews are in general opposed to Zionism. The establishment of a Zionist State on the old orthodox basis—and the orthodox Jews in the end are in vast majority, and it is they largely, and not the agnostics and the theoretical Zionists, who are returning and who will return to Palestine—is to run the risk of a revival on an enormous scale of the old hostile attitude of the Jew against the world and the world against the Jew, which brought about the awful tragedies of the past. The development of race-consciousness and a peculiar obligation to Palestine, at which the merely political and racial Zionists aim, is, it may be added, a duplicate of that Teutonism from which the world has so sadly suffered in the recent past. The result of such a development must be inevitably in the end to make the Jews bad citizens of the United States or of any other country and to keep alive and increase that hostility to the Jew which results not so much from difference of religion as from the pronounced and obtrusive differences of race, nationality and political allegiance.

It is too soon to judge the future of the Zionist experiment in Palestine. If the English authorities will give fair play to all, and if the Jews will pursue the old policy of the Alliance Israelite and its schools of seeking to benefit all dwellers of the land alike, to break down, not to build up, religious, racial and social prejudices, then the Jew may perhaps overcome the present prejudice against him, and his invasion of Palestine may prove to be a blessing both to himself and to the land. The methods of those in control of the Zionist movement in Palestine while I was there were, however, aimed in the opposite direction and tended to make the Jew an object of hatred and violence wherever the opportunity for violence offered. This has been illustrated again by the recent bloody riot in Jaffa which compelled the expedition of a British warship to that port; and the order issued holding up all immigration shows that not Jaffa only but the whole country is unsafe. The Jews in Palestine are now protected only by force of British arms. Were the British troops withdrawn, the Jews would be exterminated by the angry natives, of whom the Moslems alone outnumber them in the ratio of more than ten to one; and with such action the neighboring countries would sympathize, yielding ready assistance if any were required. Mesopotamia and Egypt are seething with disaffection against British rule, and racial-religious ferment, and Palestine is to them and to the Arabs of Arabia a holy land included in the heritage of Islam. Moslem India also feels this keenly, and the British have been obliged to withdraw Moslem Indian troops from Palestine, because they will not fight against fellow-Moslems.

In this country the Jewish problem which we have hitherto had to face is not a result of religious antipathy. Religiously, politically and economically, the Jew has the same opportunity as everyone else. The Jewish problem here has been merely a matter of social prejudice, resulting from the extremely difficult task of amalgamating with great rapidity an enormous population, alien in race, culture, custom and habit. In 1880 there were, according to Jewish statistics, 250,000 Jews in this country. The Jews now claim 3,500,000, for the most part an undistributed mass huddled together in a few of the great cities—one-third of them in New York. Coming in such great numbers in so short a time and herding together thus, intentionally or unintentionally, they help one another to resist the process of Americanization. This enormously increases the incidence of social prejudice. Those who have no conscious prejudice either of religion or of race are in danger of imbibing or developing such prejudice as a method of protection of their institutions, their traditions and their habits. The Zionist movement, with its intentional development of race consciousness and race peculiarity on the part of the Jew, is an additional obstacle against the efforts of those Jews and those Christians (I use "Christian" here as a designation of the inheritors of the traditions, the culture, and the political institutions of modern civilization.) who are seeking to break down prejudice and to bring Jew and Christian together within a common recognition of the Golden Rule: that each should treat the other as he in like instance would wish to be treated by him. One of the greatest of English Jews, honored and respected by Jew and Christian alike for his learning, his philanthropy and his godly piety, says of this racial-political Zionism that it has broken his heart, and set the clock backward for his people a hundred years. The Christian lover of his country and his fellow-men may well express a similar feeling on his side.

ANTI-SEMITISM IN ENGLAND

by C. G. Montefiore

[Despite the title of this 1921 article, C. G. Montefiore, a member of England's Jewish elite and a leading advocate of Liberal Judaism, was concerned with anti-Semitism throughout Europe. His was a passionate appeal for Europeans to allow Jews entry into society, combined with a promise that Jews would become patriotic citizens of any state which would permit them the freedom to do so. He believed that the future of the Jewish people was inexorably tied to Europe. His hostility to any form of Jewish nationalism was obvious. After the war, as before it, the question of Jewish life in Europe was bound to the definition of what it meant to be a Jew.]

"Anti-Semitism in England" by C. G. Montefiore, first published in *Hibbert Journal*, 19 (July 1923), 725-38. Reproduced by permission of *Hibbert Journal*.

The growth of anti-Semitic feeling in England is one of the painful by-products of the War. Bitter things are said about the Jews now which would, I think, have been unheard of in any respectable quarter twenty years ago. One or two of the great London daily newspapers, and one of the most sober and venerable of the London weeklies, often indulge in disagreeable anti-Jewish observations and remarks. A famous monthly is even more openly and virulently "anti-Semitic." The causes of these phenomena are numerous and various; some are even inconsistent with others. But if you once heartily dislike anybody or anything, any stick will serve with which to beat the dog.

Racial, religious, and economic causes all contribute to the undesirable result. I cannot investigate these causes fully, for to do so would take far too long, and I should not be allowed the space. Moreover, I want to look at the matter in a somewhat different way.

European anti-Semitism largely depends upon the actual presence of Jews in the countries of Europe, and upon their claim to, or their possession of, complete civic, religious, and political equality. Let us assume that all the Jews of Europe chose to leave Europe, and to settle in an empty province of China, or in a large empty island in the

Pacific Ocean. Let us assume that not a single Jew, whether by race or religion, was left behind. Anti-Semitism would obviously decrease. It would hardly come within practical politics. The hatred of the Jew is due to his contiguity and ubiquity, to his claim and desire to be a European, and to his actual presence in Europe. (For the sake of simplicity, I am taking no notice of America.) Few people hate the Chinese, so long as they are in China, and stay there. But if there were seven million Chinese who wanted to live in Europe in the same way, and on the same terms of perfect equality, as the Jews now live, or claim to live, in Europe, the feelings of Englishmen as regards the Chinese would undergo a change. So, too, if the same thing were to happen in the case of Zulus or Hottentots. Then, in spite of all the grand phrases which are used about the brotherhood of man, universal philanthropy, or the love of enemies, there would probably be much hostility, bitterness, and even hatred.

Now, hatred is one thing, but hostility is another. Hatred of persons is, perhaps, never justified; but there may, perhaps, be justified hostility. Let us set out some of the reasons why, in the assumed case of Chinese, Zulus, or Hottentots, such hostility and bitterness would arise. First of all, there would be the question of colour. And with that would go the dislike of a large group of men and women of a supposed lower or inferior race living in our midst, and claiming civic and political equality. For it would be said that these men and women have other ethical ideas and ideals than ours, and that ours are higher than theirs. They have also other religious ideas and ideals than ours, and ours are higher than theirs. Again, if they marry exclusively among one another, they are an alien body in the State, whereas the citizens of a given State should, so far as possible, be homogeneous. If, on the other hand, there is any mixture of races, the result is even worse. The progeny may, likely enough, have the vices of both parents and the virtues of neither. Economically, the presence of the alien group is bad, because they tend to undersell, and to work under evil conditions. Moreover, they would probably have a lower standard of comfort, and would tend to become larger in numbers as the years went on. France for the French; England for the English. There is now, in the most literal sense, no *room* for generosity to the alien.

Such would be the arguments. And can we say, with complete candour, that there is nothing in any one of them? A book such as Stoddart's *Rising Tide of Colour* may be exaggerated, but that its fears and its opinions are wholly negligible, he would be a bold man who would assert.

The question, therefore, presents itself: Can the case of the Jews be rightly regarded as on all fours with the assumed case of the Zulus and the Hottentots, or even with the assumed case of the Chinese? Are the Jews to be rightly put on a level with those others? If so, there seems something to be said for anti-Semitism and for the anti-Semites. Hardly, indeed, is there much to be said even then for the bitter hatred, and for the often hardly veiled incitements to pogroms in Eastern countries, which distinguish the most rabid of our western anti-Semites. But there *would* be a case for the dislike of having large bodies of Jews on equal terms, and on footings of complete freedom, in European countries.

Writing as a Jew, am I, then, to suppose that Jews are as different from Europeans as the Chinese, and as inferior to Europeans as the Hottentots?

Let me briefly go through the reasons which, in the assumed incursions of Zulus, Hottentots, and Chinese, would cause a more or less justified hostility.

The colour reason falls to the ground. Jews are no less "white" than their fellow-citizens of other creeds. They are neither yellow nor black, neither brown nor red. Then comes the question of race. It is very doubtful how far the Jews of Europe can be regarded as all belonging to one and the same race. It is doubtful what percentage of them, and what percentage of the blood of any one of them, could rightly be described as purely Semitic. Whether, however, the races, whatever they be, of which they are today composed, are lower in the scale of excellence than the "Alpine" or the "Mediterranean," not to mention the great "Nordics" themselves, I cannot discuss. Nor can I touch on the possibility that, among the infiltrations into the original Semitic stock that have happened through the ages, there are not, among existing Jews, some strains of all these various European races. What I think we may safely aver is that, be the original race or races of European Jew what they may, their blood has not prevented them, or does not now prevent them, from acquiring the virtues and the faults, the ideas and the ideals, the capacities and the limitations, of the Europeans among whom, for such a very large number of generations, they have continuously dwelt. The difference of race need make no material difference in mental endowment or in ethical outlook. It would seem to be true to say that the original or basic Jewish race was not so far removed from the original race or races of Christian Europeans as to prevent Jews being, or becoming, as good and valuable citizens of the European States as those in whom no trace of Semitic blood could be discerned.

Let us, however, look at the matter in a less theoretic, and much simpler, way.

It is possible that it may be accurate to speak of the Jews as possessing certain faults and certain virtues, but it is very doubtful how far these virtues and faults are due to race, and not far more due to environment, circumstance, or education. It is certain that both special virtues and special faults tend to disappear where the Jews live in a continuing environment of liberty and emancipation. In such an environment the Jews tend somewhat rapidly to acquire both the faults and the virtues of their neighbours, so that not only do French Jews tend to become different from English Jews, English Jews from Italian Jews, and so on, but French Jews tend to become much more like Christian Frenchmen than like English Jews, English Jews tend to become much more like Christian Englishmen than like Italian Jews, and so on.

It is doubtful whether the Jew is by "nature" more of a materialist, and less of an idealist, than the European Gentile. His "materialism," when it exists, is due to other causes than to blood. The long-continued persecution, degradation, and ostracism, from which an enormous percentage of European Jews has suffered for so many generations, have produced effects in character which cannot be effaced in a year. It is, indeed, wonderful how rapidly, in the sunshine of equality, these effects—the bad ones frequently, and occasionally, alas! the good—tend to disappear. There are special virtues and special vices which persecution, degradation, cruelty, and hatred are calculated to produce. At the one end of the scale, you get heroes; at the other end, you get scum. When the immensity of Jewish sufferings is considered—for no people, no religious community, has suffered as they, and yet survived—the marvel is that the scum is as small as it is, and that the spirit, courage, capacity, and joyousness of the "race" have not been broken and dulled for ever.

It is needless to specify the vices generated by persecution: the hunted, hated, and despised animal tends sometimes not to show towards his tormentors the virtues of truthfulness and affection. Even when the persecution is relaxed, the human nature may be warped. It is the next generation only who can acquire the virtues of equality. But if active persecution is supplanted by active hatred, it is more hard for these virtues to spring up. Anti-Semitism causes the very evils of which it then proceeds to complain. The alleged materialism of the Jews, their "loudness," their vulgarity, their love of money and jewelry, their ostentation, are also largely, though not entirely, the result of secular persecution and degradation. The Jew had only one idealism, his religion. Besides this he could have no other ambition, no other joy, no other relief from misery, than money and "external goods." When emancipated, and more especially when his religious belief is weakened, his unbroken spirit tends to rush to the full enjoyment of material things. But this tendency will disappear with better education, continued equality, the full participation in all other human idealisms and creations of the spirit, and, above all, with a religious revival. It is possible, though not certain, that the European Jew needs religion even more than the European Gentile—needs it, I mean, even more in order to keep pure and "spiritual" and simple and sweet. That is why the present writer is so tremendously keen on Liberal Judaism. That, however, is another story. But even as things now are, few will venture to say that the Jews *as a whole* are "morally" inferior to their Gentile neighbours. Nor are they physically degenerate. Give them a chance, and they soon become fond of athletic exercises and games. And if there is one native and indelible tendency in the Jewish race, it is their affection for their children and the willingness of the parents to make sacrifices for their offspring.

Anti-Semitic writers and newspapers in England today make great capital of the part which, as they allege, has been played, and is being played, by Jews in the Bolshevist movement in Russia, and in anarchic and anti-social movements throughout the world. The most frantic efforts are being made to ascribe the murder of the Czar and of his family entirely to Jewish agencies and to Jewish hands. That, in the event (which most decent persons desire) of the downfall of Bolshevist rule, such efforts will assuredly lead to the massacre of thousands of wholly innocent persons, is presumably not altogether to the distaste of those who make them.

Now, assuming that there is a certain sprinkling of Jews in the Bolshevist movement and in the anarchic and anti-social movements all over the world, and assuming, which is by no means certain, that among those who compassed, and among those who connived at, the detestable murders of the Czar and of his family was a small percentage of Jews, what follows as regards the general question of Jewish morality? Very little. At present, the Jewish Russian is, for his numbers, better educated than the Gentile Russian. In every Russian party which was, or is, antagonistic to the old *regime*, Jews were, or are, therefore, to be found out of proportion to their numbers. The deeper explanation of the presence of Jews among the Bolshevist party is to be sought in the continued persecution and degradation which Russian Jews have undergone. On the whole, the Jew is not revengeful or cruel, and it is a Talmudic saying that he who is unmerciful is no descendant of Abraham. But, as I have already urged, persecution breeds scum. If there are some men of Jewish race (not of Jewish faith, and not, therefore, by Jews recognised as Jews) who have yielded to the lust of revenge, is it for the Gentile, whose systematic persecution has brought this about, to marvel? Should the Gentile, by the virulence of hatred, add fuel to the fire? He who is ostracised from human society, and forbidden to be a citizen of the country in which he lives, may sometimes sink into becoming the enemy of all society and of every organised state. Forbidden the joy of patriotism, he would destroy patriotism throughout the world. Again, the Russian Jew, like his Gentile brother, has too often abandoned religion. But the Gentile has other spiritual resources; the hunted and persecuted Jew has none. It has, moreover, to be freely admitted that the higher fruits of liberty— order, self-control, moderation—are not to be won in a day. Transplant a Russian Jew of twenty to London or New York, and the heady wine of freedom may make him mistake licence for liberty. He may use freedom for evil ends. It speaks well for the Jews as a whole that such abuses and perversions are exceptional.

In any case, such instances of "Jewish iniquity" are no evidence against "Jewish" morality. One might more legitimately argue that it is Jewish morality which has made them few.

It may, however, be said that, though Jewish morality is a high morality, is is not the *same* morality as the morality of Christian Europe. The States of Christian Europe need one and the same type of morality throughout their borders. Here the anti-Semitic argument from morality becomes inseparably mixed up with the argument from religion.

I do not think that this argument can be regarded as not worthy of full respect and serious consideration. Europe *is* Christian. England is certainly a Christian country. It would not be unreasonable that Christians should dislike the presence in this country of a compact group of persons, claiming and possessing full civic and political rights and privileges, who belong to a religion wholly different from Christianity, and with moral ideas and ideals gravely different, even if not grossly inferior. Such might be the argument not unjustly used against the Hottentots and even the Chinese.

Against Judaism and the Jews the argument has, I think, little value. For the moral ideas and ideals of Christianity and Judaism are very nearly the same. The *highest* things in the Old Testament, which, as a matter of fact, constitute the ethical elements in the religion of modern Jews, are in tune with the best ethical elements in the religious teaching of the New Testament and of Christianity. I do not deny that we find in the New Testament the command: "Love your enemies, do good to them that hate you, bless them that curse you, pray for them that despitefully use you," but it is hardly for the anti-Semites to object to a religion the sacred scripture of which does not contain these sublime injunctions. *They*, at any rate, cannot think that these commands are of any practical importance. There is, without irony or sarcasm, just *enough* difference in the ethical teachings of Judaism and Christianity to be of stimulating value; there is *not* enough to cause the presence of the dissentient minority to be of the smallest ethical danger or disadvantage to the majority. If the Jew can rightly learn to admire and to appropriate the ethical ideals and efflorescence of the New Testament, the Christian could rightly learn to appropriate more fully the highest ideals and delicacies of the Old Testament and of the Rabbis. It is sometimes said that Judaism is *this*-worldly, while Christianity is *other*-worldly. The antithesis is false; but if there were anything in it, if it were true that Judaism was specially keen on making *this* world into a true kingdom of God, then Judaism would be entirely congruous with the prevailing spirit of modern Christianity. The truth is that the teaching of modern Judaism and modern Christianity as to this world and the next world and their relations to each other have, to all intents and purposes, become the same. It would be idle to ask people with violently buzzing bees in their bonnets, such as the regular anti-Semites, to adopt any reasonable course. But if those who have milder prejudices would only consent to learn what modern Judaism actually teaches and holds, they would find that there is no ethical objection to the presence of Jews in Christian environments.

But even if the religious objection falls, the "foreign body" argument remains. The Jews refuse to marry their Gentile neighbours, and an unassimilated and unassimilable foreign body in the State is considered a disadvantage. The extremer anti-Semites find objections in both directions, for if and when the Jews do marry "Gentiles," it is alleged that the purity of the Gentile race suffers. The Jew is once more equated with the Zulu or the Chinese, and the offspring of Jew and Gentile is regarded as the offspring of white and yellow, or white and black. I will not touch upon this objection, which I believe to be unfounded and inadmissible, but as one who, for purely religious reasons, still desires the Jew to mate only with the Jew, or with the proselyte to Judaism, I will confine myself to the other.

Now, if the Jewish reluctance to marry the Gentile had any other than a religious root, Christian hostility would be perfectly justified. For then it might be argued that this very reluctance proves that a Jew cannot be a perfect French, Danish, or German patriot, as the case may be. But it has *no* other root than religion. A small minority can maintain its identity and distinctiveness in no other way. Let Jews intermarry freely with men and women of other faiths, and in a few generations Judaism must disappear. And a good thing too, would say the anti-Semites. Yes, but those who believe in Judaism and its mission cannot say so. Yet the purely religious reason for the reluctance to intermarriage takes away its political sting. It does nothing to impair the fullness and intensity of Jewish patriotism. To the Jew (except to that dangerous modern creation, the nationalist Jew), what makes a man a Jew is religion; and just as he who abandons or denies Judaism is to the Jew no Jew, be his race and ancestry what they may, so is he who has adopted Judaism a Jew in the fullest sense of the word, be his blood and lineage Aryan or Semitic. I will not waste words as to Jewish patriotism. It is difficult for an English Jew to write upon the subject with restraint. Suffice it to say that the blood which the Jews shed for England in the Great War was no less gladly offered than the blood of the purest Aryan or "Nordic" in the land. Treat the Jews as equal citizens, and you will have no cause to regret it; you will soon have reason to appreciate the fervour of their patriotism. What is rather wonderful is that in thousands of cases the patriotism has not been wanting, even when the citizenship was in default. It cannot, however, be denied that the volume and intensity of anti-Semitic hatred have in some quarters inclined some Jews to despair, and to throw up the sponge. Hence the growth of Zionism and of Jewish nationalism, which, at bottom, are a surrender to our enemies and to their contention that the Jews themselves admit that they cannot become, and that they do not want to become, citizens of the countries in which they dwell. Whatever the future of Palestine, the welfare of the immense majority of Jews depends upon those who refuse to surrender or to despair. Citizens we are, and citizens we claim to be; and not only citizens, but worthy citizens, who love, and mean to love, their European country and their European homes.

A few words must suffice as to economic objections: these, to some extent, cancel one another.

On the one hand, the Jews are disliked because they are capitalists and financiers, lovers of wealth and of money; international financiers, moreover, who promote militarism, reaction, and darkness. On the other hand, they are disliked because of their poverty, their low standard of comfort, their prolificness, their tendency to sweat and be sweated, to undercut and undersell. But they are also, as we have seen, disliked because they are the too violent enemies of the capitalist, because they are wild and anarchic socialists and communists, the plotters of red revolution and of ruin. So far as there is any truth in one, or other, or all of these allegations, they are the fruit and issue of disabilities and degradation. What occupations and professions were open for centuries to the Jew except the lower forms of acquisition? When other occupations and professions are open to them, it is not found that Jews are slow to take advantage of these newer opportunities. They soon learn the higher standards of comfort; it is even curious that among the Jewish critics of themselves there are some who think that Jews have a tendency to raise this standard unnecessarily high. Give the Jews freedom and justice, and even a short respite from hatred and prejudice, and there is no reason to suppose that these various products of disabilities and persecutions will not entirely disappear. If a group of men have *no* country, how can they learn loyalty to *any* country? Where every man's hand is against you, you may be tempted to hit back. It does no good but you may yield to the temptation. And these evil passions cannot be overcome by all in the twinkling of an eye. Is it too much to ask from Christendom, in return for centuries of persecution, a few years of patience? Certain ugly characteristics of the hunted animal—fear, cunning, untruthfulness— may have shown themselves in a few Jews who had not yet learnt to love and care for England. But the Jew learns very quickly. Indicate to him that you *want* him to learn, that you will *welcome* his learning. Even as things are, the learning is going on apace. At this very moment, in the far east of London, taught by one of the finest Jewish Englishmen alive, the sons of the alien are learning "to set the cause above renown, To love the game beyond the prize." They are learning

> to count the life of battle good,
> And dear the land that gave them birth,
> And dearer yet the brotherhood
> That binds the brave of all the earth.

Give them only a little encouragement; a little surcease from suspicion and hatred; a little breathing space; a little time.

Anti-Semitism tends to make the people it hates at last worthy of hatred. For hatred will at last breed hatred, and suspicion will breed suspicion. Equality, fairness, love: these are curative. To make the Jews as like you as possible, treat them as you treat any other English citizens. They will soon resemble you—in your very failings as well as in your virtues!

Meanwhile, the lesson for the Jews is always the same. First: Cast not off religion; for in religion—in a living harmony of religious belief and religious practice—lies your true salvation. Secondly: Never despair; keep to your old ideal—Englishmen of the Jewish faith: nothing less, nothing more.

THE JEWS UNDER THE MINORITIES TREATIES

by Israel Cohen

[This 1929 article is a brief critique of the Minorities Treaties and their impact on Jewish life in Eastern Europe. Israel Cohen, an English Zionist and prolific writer on Jewish affairs, believed that the treaties offered little protection because the procedure of the League was far too cautious. He proposed a reform of the system that would make the treaties more effective, but in so doing he assumed a greater commitment to the cause of human rights than the Great Powers were prepared to make. Here Cohen made a plea for the resuscitation of the system which in 1919 promised to provide some guarantee of rights for Eastern European Jewry. More importantly, Cohen raised the issue of the relative efficacy of quiet as opposed to vocal diplomacy in the protection of human rights.]

"The Jews under the Minorities Treaties" by Israel Cohen, first published in *Contemporary Review*, 4-11, Jan. 1929, pp. 73-80.

The political conditions of the Jews in Central and Eastern Europe have undergone a fundamental change since the Great War. They are characterised by a constitutional progress, which is due mainly to the special provisions relating to racial and religious minorities in the treaties concluded by the Allied and Associated Powers with the States in which they are domiciled. Before the war six million Jews, settled in Russia and Rumania, and forming about one half of the total number of Jews in the world, were subjected to a state of bondage and persecution which made those two countries a byword among civilised nations. As soon as the Peace Conference began to assemble, Jewish delegations both from Eastern Europe and from Western countries, particularly Great Britain and the United States, met in Paris for the purpose of formulating and submitting their demands. Their aim was twofold: to secure civil and political equality for those Jews who were not yet emancipated, and in consequence of the creation of new States and the alteration of the frontiers of old ones—to safeguard the rights of those Jews who might be transferred from the jurisdiction of one State to that of another. One half of the Jews in Russia—those living in that part which later constituted itself as the Union of Socialist Soviet Republics—had, indeed, already been emancipated by the Revolution in 1917, but the other half, domiciled in the territories that went to form the republics of Poland, Lithuania, Latvia, Estonia, and Finland, were at the mercy of elements which, so far as they were known, were scarcely encouraging. Poland, for instance, had inaugurated her new epoch of independence by an outbreak of assaults and outrages upon the Jews in a great number of towns and townlets, which showed how necessary it was from the very beginning not only to define the rights of the Polish State but also to guarantee the rights of its Jewish subjects.

The Jewish delegations in Paris were not content, however, that the Jews in Central and Eastern Europe should merely be granted civil and political equality. They wished to ensure that this equality should not be limited or nullified later by administrative caprice or ordinance, and above all that the Jews, living for the most part in compact masses, should be allowed to live their traditional life and to maintain their social, religious, and cultural institutions free from interference. As a result largely of their representations, the Peace Conference accepted a series of postulates that were designed to safeguard the rights not only of the Jews but also of the other racial and religious minorities in the States with which it had to deal. Sufficient time has now elapsed to afford a basis for inquiry into the practical working of these Minorities Treaties and for ascertaining to what extent they have achieved their purpose.

The first Minorities Treaty, affecting the lives of three million Jews, the largest Jewish community in any European country, was that concluded with Poland. It declared to be Polish nationals, *ipso facto* and without the requirements of any formality, German, Austrian, Hungarian, or Russian nationals habitually resident at the date of the coming into force of the Treaty in territory recognised as forming part of Poland. The main provisions of the Treaty were: that all Polish nationals shall be equal before the law and shall enjoy the same civil and political rights without distinction as to race, language, or religion; that those who belong to racial, religious or linguistic minorities shall be free to use their language in private or public, including the courts; that they shall have an equal right to establish and control at their own expense charitable, religious and social institutions, schools and other educational establishments; and that in towns and districts in which they form a considerable proportion instruction shall be given to their children in the primary schools through the medium of their own language, and they shall be assured an equitable share in the enjoyment of the sums which may be provided out of public funds for educational, religious, or charitable purposes. These provisions are applicable to all racial and religious minorities in Poland, who number thirteen million in a total population of twenty-seven million, and do not contain any specific reference to the Jews. But there are two Articles, 10 and 11, which were specially included in order to safeguard the interests of the Jews: the one authorising the Jewish communities to appoint local educational committees for the distribution of the public funds allocated to Jewish schools, and the other providing that "Jews shall not be compelled to perform any act which constitutes a violation of their Sabbath, nor shall they be placed under any disability by reason of their refusal to attend courts of law or to perform any legal business on their Sabbath."

As a corollary to the religious observance of the Saturday Sabbath, the Jewish delegations urged the inclusion in the Treaty of a clause permitting the Jews to engage in Sunday trading and labour, pointing out that this would only confirm a right that had been enjoyed by the Jews in Poland even under the Russian domination; but the Allied and Associated Powers were reluctant to impose upon another State an obligation that was only imperfectly realised in their own legislation. In order to ensure the strict observance of the stipulation affecting persons belonging to minorities, there was included a final Article declaring that these stipulations "constitute obligations of international concern and shall be placed under the guarantee of the League of Nations," and that "they shall not be modified without the assent of a majority of the Council of the League of Nations."

The Treaty signed by Poland on June 28th, 1919, formed, with the exception of the two clauses relating to the maintenance of Jewish schools and the observance of the Sabbath, the type of the Minority Treaties signed by several other States, viz., Austria, Hungary, Czecho-Slovakia, Jugoslavia, Bulgaria, Rumania, Dantzig, Greece, Turkey, and Mosul. The Treaty with Rumania finally swept aside the verbal quibbles by means of which the Jews had been denied their rights so long. It declared that "all persons born in Rumanian territory who are not born nationals of another State shall *ipso facto* become Rumanian nationals," a stipulation applying both to the new territories annexed to the country and to the whole of Old Rumania; and in order not to allow any doubt to be raised as to whether the Jews were also included, and perhaps to prevent the passing of a law declaring them to be excluded, there was inserted a special Article, in concise and unambiguous terms: "Rumania undertakes to recognise as Rumanian nationals *ipso facto* and without the requirement of any formality Jews inhabiting any Rumanian territory who do not possess another nationality." Moreover, there were four newly-created States, namely, Finland, Lithuania, Latvia and Estonia, which, though they did not subscribe to Minority Treaties, gave solemn declarations that they agreed to the principles of these compacts.

The signing of these various Treaties and the securing of these declarations were no easy task; but once the Treaties were concluded it was hoped that the Jews would enjoy the same rights and the same economic opportunities as their fellow-citizens. Unfortunately this hope has proved illusory, for scarcely had the ink of the signatures become dry before various provisions of the Treaties were violated in certain countries, with the result that a persistent struggle has had to be waged ever since in order to secure compliance on the part of the defaulting States with their obligations. The principal countries in which such infractions have occurred are Poland, Rumania, Hungary, Lithuania, and Greece.

The main questions in respect of which Poland has violated her pledges are those relating to the acquisition of citizenship, admission to the universities, and the financial support of Jewish schools. Although she undertook to declare as Polish citizens "*ipso facto* and without the requirement of any formality, German, Austrian, Hungarian, or Russian nationals habitually resident...in territory which is or may be recognised as forming part of Poland," she passed a law on January 20th, 1920, which made the acquisition of citizenship subject to certain formalities of an administrative nature with which in very numerous cases it was impossible to comply. The law required that those claiming Polish citizenship should show that their names were inscribed in local registers of the stable population or submit proof of their *Heimatsrecht*, a status of citizenship dependent upon several years' continuous residence in the same commune. Owing to the impossibility of conforming with these regulations, many thousands of Jews (besides large numbers belonging to other national minorities) were denied Polish citizenship and became *Staatenlos* [stateless]. This condition was a sufficient hardship if they remained in the country, but it increased in gravity if they wished to emigrate, as the Nansen passports [issued by the League of Nations] which they were given were not provided with an endorsement enabling them to return, and most States refused to *viser* such passports since they would be unable to deport their holders, if necessary to their country of origin. The Jewish members of the *Seym* [Polish Parliament] repeatedly demanded that the Polish Government should abolish the restrictions which it had imposed, but it was not until August, 1926, that it issued a circular instruction to the local administrative authorities to facilitate the acquisition of citizenship. A considerable improvement in the situation has since resulted, but there are still some fifteen thousand Jews in Poland who are *Staatenlos*—with all the galling disabilities attaching to such a condition.

The admission of Jewish students to the universities in Poland is restricted to a proportion corresponding roughly to the Jewish ratio of the population. It is true that there is no law imposing a *numerus clausus*, but the universities, in the exercise of their traditional autonomy, continue to limit the entry of Jews, and the Government cannot or will not take effective steps to suppress this injustice. The *numerus clausus*, however, is only one phase of the war that is conducted against the Jewish intellectual class, whose influence is unnecessarily feared. Although forming only twelve percent of the population of Poland, the Jews, belonging mainly to the industrial and commercial element, which is assessed abnormally heavy, are estimated to pay more than one-half of the direct taxation received by the State, yet the Government will not find them employment in its service (with some rare exceptions) nor grant to Jewish schools the subventions that it is obliged to provide. Nor is this policy of repression directed solely against the intellectual class. As was feared at the time when Poland signed her Minorities Treaty, she passed a law at the end of 1919 for compulsory Sunday closing, which was conceived as an act of economic oppression, and which has inflicted grave hardship upon Jewish employers and employed, who mostly observe their Sabbath. The Jewish deputies in the Seym have persistently demanded that the Government should relax the law in favour of those who observe the Jewish Sabbath and festivals, but although certain concessions have been made, the question has not yet been satisfactorily settled. The economic position of the Jews is further threatened by the law for the transfer of liquor licences to war veterans, which will mean their withdrawal from many thousands of Jews, who will thus be impoverished, and also by the projected Guild law, which requires artisans to undergo a course of training in vocational schools, access to which will be limited in the case of Jewish workers.

In Rumania the principal infractions are likewise in respect of the conferment of citizenship and admission to the universities, whilst even more serious has been the campaign of assault upon the Jews continued almost uninterruptedly for the last six years. A Nationality Law was passed on February 23rd, 1924, which is similar in principle to the Polish Nationality Law, as it makes the acquisition of citizenship subject to the possession of the *Heimatsrecht*. But it has imposed a twofold restriction, first, in substituting the *Heimatsrecht* or *indigenat* for habitual residence, and secondly in making that qualification date from December 1st, 1918, instead of September 4th, 1920, when the Treaty signed by Rumania came into force. The result of this Treaty violation and of the tantalising procedure for seeking redress is that in the Bukovina there are still twenty thousand Jews who are *Staatenlos*, besides many thousands in Bessarabia and Transylvania. The position of a "Stateless" person in Rumania is even more depressing than in Poland, for if he wishes to emigrate, not only is he denied the endorsement in his passport that will enable him to return, but as the holder of such a passport he forfeits all claims to Rumanian citizenship and ownership of rural property from the moment that he leaves the country.

There is no *numerus clausus* in Rumania by law, but there is one in practice. The admission of Jewish students to the universities is restricted by the university authorities to a small percentage, whilst from time to time the Rumanian students run amuck, drive out the

Jews from the college buildings, and thus create a *numerus nullus*. The agitation for the exclusion of the Jews has been fanatically fostered by Professor Cuza, of Jassy, who has poisoned the minds of the academic youth of his country, and it has been accompanied by violent demonstrations in Bucarest, Jassy, Czernowitz, Kishineff, Oradea Mare, Cluj, and other cities, resulting in the frequent closing of the universities. The anti-Semitic students have indulged in repeated assaults not only upon Jewish students but upon the Jews in general, destroying property, sacking synagogues, wounding innocent onlookers, and even throwing Jewish passengers out of trains. The agitation has already cost two lives—that of the Prefect of Jassy, Manciu, who tried to suppress a demonstration and was shot dead in court by a Rumanian student, and that of David Fallik, a Jewish student of Czernowitz, who was also shot in court by a Rumanian student. Both assassins were tried, acquitted as patriots, and then acclaimed as national heroes. The immunity of these murderers from punishment and the general insecurity of Jewish lives and property constitute an even graver breach of the provisions of the Minorities Treaty than the practical enforcement of the *numerus clausus.*

Only in Hungary was a law enacted to subject citizens belonging to national minorities to differential treatment in regard to their admission to the universities. This law, which was passed in September, 1920, was applied solely against the Jews, who were limited to six percent of the total number of students. The attention of the League of Nations was promptly called to this infraction of the Treaty of Trianon by representative Jewish bodies, who protested against Hungary being admitted to membership of the League until she rescinded the obnoxious law. The Hungarian delegate, Count Banffy, gave a solemn assurance in September, 1922, that his country would faithfully observe her obligations in respect of the treatment of racial minorities, and Hungary was accordingly welcomed into the League. But as the law continued to be enforced, the Jewish organisations renewed their protests, with the result that at a meeting of the Council of the League of Nations in 1925, Count Klebelsberg declared that the measure was only temporary, introduced owing to the abnormal post-war situation of the country, and that it would be amended directly the position improved. At length, in February last, the Hungarian Government amended the law by abolishing the Article that refers to nationality and replacing it by another Article, which provides that preference shall be given in admissions to the universities to the sons of Government officials, war veterans, peasants, and those engaged in trade. It will thus be possible to practise the same discrimination against Jewish students in the future by virtue of this economic classification. Indeed, Count Klebelsberg has made no secret of the fact that this amendment is designed mainly to satisfy or pacify the League of Nations, and that the admission of Jews to the universities is not likely to be increased by more than one-half percent.

Lithuania began her new career of independence, by giving the

Jews a model system of national autonomy, with a Ministry of Jewish Affairs supported by the State, but this ideal arrangement was soon swept away by a change of Government, bringing in its train an era of intolerance that gravely affects many phases of Jewish life in the country. An attempt to interfere with the use of Hebrew and Yiddish and with the autonomy of the Jewish schools was checked by the League of Nations, but a Sunday closing law was adopted, which has weakened the economic position of the Jews and against which they have no redress. Moreover, the Government has dissolved the organised Jewish communities and insisted that they shall be replaced by purely religious congregations on a voluntary basis, deprived of the fiscal rights which the communities possessed, so that Lithuanian Jewry is threatened with gradual disintegration. As for Greece, the most serious grievance felt by the Jews is that which affects the ancient community in Salonica. For hundreds of years they had formed the largest national group in that city, rested on Saturday, and were allowed to trade on Sunday. But with the influx of vast numbers of Greeks after the Great War, the Jews became a small minority, and a Sunday Closing Law was enacted in 1924 for all the inhabitants of the city, obviously as a measure of economic protection for the majority. This law was a violation of the pledges given by M. Venizelos in 1919, but unfortunately the terms of the Greek Treaty afford no basis of redress.

The various Treaty infractions described above have formed the subject not only of representations by the Jewish communities concerned to their respective Governments, but also of frequent communications addressed by Jewish representative organisations to the League of Nations; but the slow and excessively circumspect procedure that is observed has so far prevented any appreciable amelioration. If a petition to the League is found by the Secretariat to be "receivable," it is communicated to the Government concerned for its observations, and then the President invites two of his colleagues to examine the documents with him in committee, with a view to deciding whether the question should be brought before the Council. If the question is considered by the Council and the petitioner is not satisfied with the result, he may demand that it shall be referred to the Permanent Court of International Justice. Thereupon the Government impeached is invited to submit further observations, which are considered by the Committee of Three, who report to the Council, and then the Government, brought to bay at last, may promise to make amends. It was thanks to this cumbersome and super-cautious procedure that Hungary was able to flout the League for over seven years with its *numerus clausus* law, which, even in its amended form, is applied in a manner that constitutes an infraction of the Treaty of Trianon.

The procedure for dealing with defaulting governments must be thoroughly revised if the Minorities Treaties are not to be violated with impunity. It is not enough that the Secretariat of the League is authorised to act only when it receives a petition from an aggrieved minority: the Secretariat should be authorised to report to the Council any infractions of Treaties that it may discover through the medium of its own channels of information. Minorities should be allowed to have access to the Council, and should be immediately informed of the answers made to their complaints, in order to prevent a miscarriage of justice. It is even more important that there should be a Permanent Commission, which should watch over the national minorities in the same way as the Permanent Mandates Commission looks after the mandated territories; but at least governments that are in default in respect of their obligations under the Minorities Treaties, such as Poland and Rumania, should not sit on the Council that discusses the petitions brought against them.

The weakness of the machinery for ensuring the just treatment of the minorities has been strikingly illustrated in the case of Turkey, who, by the Treaty of Lausanne in 1923, undertook to recognise as fundamental laws a series of obligations respecting her minorities. In 1925 the Chief Rabbi of Constantinople notified the Government of "the decision of the Jews of Turkey" to renounce their minority rights, and the following year this step was confirmed by twenty "notables" of the Sephardic community. Now neither the Chief Rabbi nor the "notables" have any right to barter away the guarantees for the protection of the Jewish people in Turkey, whom they could not consult and from whom they received no mandate. The action of the Turkish Government in bringing about the renunciation of those guarantees constitutes a violation of international law. If there were a Permanent Minorities Commission, invested with the requisite authority, it would presumably be possessed of sufficient courage and energy to take effective steps to have this illegality rescinded. But without such a body, the Council of the League has not so much as taken note of this extraordinary act, which may be fraught with perilous consequences in the future. Until, therefore, the League of Nations creates an independent judicial body, which should be at once mobile and resolute, for the protection of the minorities, the Jews in Central and Eastern Europe will be largely dependent upon the goodwill and sense of honour of their own Governments in regard to their treatment under the Minorities Treaties, and as some of the more important of those Governments are largely actuated by anti-Semitic considerations, the fate of their Jewish subjects is bound to be a source of anxiety for years to come.

SOVIET RUSSIA SOLVES THE JEWISH PROBLEM

by **William Zukerman**

[The causes of anti-Semitism were still a matter of debate, and some believed that economics and not race was the basis of the hatred against the Jews. In this 1931 examination of Jewish life in the Soviet Union, William Zukerman agreed with that opinion. He further believed that the socialist state had solved the Jewish problem by incorporating Jews into the economy of the country. The Soviet Union had allowed Jews to settle on the land and to participate in industry. Thus, Zukerman wrote, anti-Semitism was a thing of the past in a land that was a leader of Jew hatred under the Czars. The U.S.S.R. had pointed the way, and it was now for others to follow this proven path. Yet, Zukerman ignored the fact that the Soviet Union prohibited this economically assimilated Jew from maintaining a Jewish identity.]

"Soviet Russia Solves the Jewish Problem" by William Zukerman, first published in *Contemporary Review*, 140 (December 1931), 741-48.

The Jewish problem in Soviet Russia is one of the most hideous inheritances taken over by the Soviet Union from the old Czaristic regime. Under that regime the entire Jewish population of the old Russian Empire was confined to a "Pale" of ten provinces, mostly in the west of Russia, which they were not permitted to leave under pain of arrest. Within that narrow "Pale," too, they were hedged in by such medieval restrictions and limitations that one can hardly credit it at the present time. Thus, for instance, they were forced to live only in the cities, and were not allowed to engage in agriculture. Since the ten provinces of the "Pale" had no big industry, they were thus also excluded from the factories. The number of their professional men was strictly regulated by the severe restrictions governing the ad-

133

mission of Jewish students to the High Schools and Universities. The only means of subsistence left to these millions of people were petty trading and small artisanship. Penned into what was practically a vast prison or concentration camp, the seven million Jews of the Czaristic Empire were condemned—as the famous Czaristic apologist, Pobiedonostzeff, put it—"one-third to starvation; one-third to emigration, and the rest to baptism."

Even before the Soviet Revolution took place, the infamous "Pale" was broken down, and the seven million cooped-up human beings were let free. Half their number were transferred from Russian rule to that of the neighbouring states of Poland, Rumania, Lithuania and Latvia. About half a million were slaughtered in the War and in those terrible massacres in the Ukraine after the War and the Revolution. The rest, amounting to something under three million, remained in Soviet Russia to work out their salvation under the new and bewildering conditions of the first proletarian Revolution. The Revolution, by its very nature, could not at first do other than add to the miseries and hardships of the great mass of this sorely tried people. While liberating them politically and socially in the fullest sense of the word, the Revolution destroyed at the same time whatever economic footing they had under the old regime. For generations the Jews had been kept by force from all productive occupations, confined almost entirely to petty trading and commerce, and both these occupations were swept away by the tremendous changes introduced by the Soviet Government. Trading was practically prohibited in Russia, and commerce, foreign and home alike, was taken over as a monopoly of the State. Economically the Jews were consequently worse hit by the Revolution than any other people. Except for an insignificant section of intellectuals, who left the former "Pale," and moved to Moscow, Leningrad and the bigger Russian cities, the great mass of the people was left literally without the slightest means of subsistence. Socially, too, the vast majority of them belonged to a class which was despised and openly discriminated against by the New Russia. Thus even in their liberation the Jews were pursued by the sinister shadow of their old restrictions, and were made to suffer because of the very discriminations and outrages to which they had been subjected for generations.

The Soviet Government, even if it realised the despairing need of these people, could not, however, call a halt to its entire programme of social reconstruction because it happened to affect adversely two million Jews. It was the misfortune of these people to be in the way of the chariot of the Russian Revolution. They had either to get out or be crushed. The drivers of the chariot would not falter in their advance, nor change their course to save these former people of the "Pale" from destruction. The only thing the Government did for them was to offer them the means of changing their economic position from one running counter to the Revolution to one moving in accord with it. And thus, as far back as 1924, the Soviet Government of the Ukrainian Republic issued its now famous decree in favour of settling Jews on the land in the Crimea and in Southern Russia. The decree was accompanied by grants of free land in those fertile Republics which at the end of 1930 amounted to 375,929 hectares, or almost a million acres. The hungry men of the former "Pale," economically ruined and without the slightest means of subsistence, and spurred on the other hand by the creative forces let loose by the Revolution and by the example of a huge country reforming itself, took up the land offer of the Soviet Government with an avidity which has no parallel in modern times. From the ruined, poverty-stricken Jewish cities and villages of White Russia and Ukraine started a trek on foot and in waggons (not even covered) which rapidly became a great stream of helpless, despairing humanity pressing toward their last hope, the Promised Land.

But modern colonisation is not a matter of land and people only. Capital and machinery were needed; houses had to be built, livestock supplied; instructors were wanted to teach these inexperienced people modern farming methods; in most places the land had to be improved, and the whole movement organised and directed. It was here that the big Jewish relief organisations of the West, especially the American Jewish Agricultural Corporation ("Agro-Joint"), stepped in and did for this movement what the League of Nations did for the colonisation of the Greeks who were expelled from Turkey after the War. With the sole exception, too, of this achievement of the League, modern history knows of no greater colonisation effort more successfully carried through than this of the Jews in Soviet Russia during the last six years. The second Conference of the Russian Jewish Colonisation Society ("Geserd"), which was held in Moscow last December, showed that at present there are in Soviet Russia 135,000 full-fledged Jewish peasants, most of whom have transmigrated from their villages in the former "Pale," and have settled on the land in Crimea, South Russia, White Russia, Caucasia, and Siberia, since 1924. Apart from these, twenty-five thousand more Jewish families in White Russia and Ukraine are engaged in farming on land near their villages. Altogether fifty thousand Jewish families, or approximately a quarter of a million souls, have found their livelihood on the soil in Russia during the last six years. Although the settlements are scattered throughout European Russia, they are mostly concentrated in four main regions in the Ukraine and Crimea: "Kalenindorf," "Oktiabr," "Naizlotopol," and "Naidorf." These regions being predominantly Jewish are, in accordance with the Soviet scheme of National autonomy, governed as autonomous Jewish districts. Schools, law courts, police force, and the entire machinery of government are conducted in the native language of the colonists—Yiddish, thus forming the nucleus of a future autonomous Jewish Republic which was promulgated in 1926 by M. Kalenin, President of the Soviet Union, as the ultimate goal of this movement.

The most important feature of the colonisation is the success which these townsmen by tradition are making of their new occupation. With the exception of the German colonists on the Volga these former Jewish traders, pedlars, and shopkeepers are rapidly proving to be the best farmers in Soviet Russia. Their indescribable need, the urge of the creative forces within them and around them, their very inexperience and consequent freedom from the traditional Russian peasant methods, stood them in good stead, and helped them to make a success, which was hardly expected of them. There is only one other country in the world where Jews can point to an achievement similar to this—Palestine. But the agricultural Jewish settlement in Palestine is the result of practically fifty years of labour and of incalculable millions of treasure, while the bigger Jewish land settlement in Soviet Russia has arisen within the last six years at a cost to the Jewish relief organisations of less than ten million dollars, the great part of which was advanced to the Soviet Government as a loan, and will be repaid after twenty years. It is not for nothing that the Soviet Travel Agency included the Jewish colonies in the Ukraine in its itinerary last summer as one of the sights of the Soviet Union and one of the accomplishments of the Revolution. The Revolution may have accomplishments vaster in scope and bigger in dimension than the Jewish colonies, but it is doubtful whether it can point to anything more vital and interesting than this return of the most urban people in the world to the soil; the transformation, within so brief a period, of a nation of traders with a commercial tradition of centuries behind them, into conquerors of the steppes.

The Jewish Colonisation Movement in Soviet Russia was started in 1924, four years before the promulgation of the Five-Years Plan. Prior to the Plan, it was fundamentally a relief measure. With the coming of the Five-Years Plan the movement, from an essentially charitable effort of foreign relief organisations, was turned into a State enterprise, backed by the resources of a great Empire, budgeted for by the State and carried upon the crest of the great wave of productivisation which is now sweeping the whole of the Soviet Union. From being a special Jewish measure, it became part of the general scheme of the reconstruction of the country; part and parcel of the Five-Years Plan. As such, its scope was immediately broadened, and its possibilities increased enormously. Before 1928 it was the American "Agro-Joint" that practically conducted the entire work, while the Government assisted; in 1930 the Soviet Government was doing the bulk of the work, while the "Agro-Joint" was playing the same part as the American engineering experts in the industrial upbuilding of the country.

But the change is not in the bigger dimensions of the work alone. More important still is the extension of the movement to include what is known as industrialisation, to supplement the previous land colonisation. The Five-Years Plan, although it includes agriculture in its programme, is primarily an industrial plan. Its chief object is to "catch up and to outstrip" the capitalist countries of the world in their industrial development, and to convert agricultural Russia into a factory State. It was therefore inevitable, as the Plan developed, that Jews, too, should be drawn into the factories more than to the land. The gigantic factories and plants which sprang up all over Russia were clamouring for workers, and they found the Jews the best material for their purpose. They were mostly city folk best fitted for urban and industrial occupations. They also possessed in abundance the quick intelligence needed for the handling of the complicated machinery of a modern industrial plant, which the average Russian peasant learns only with so much difficulty. And, above all, they were in need of work and occupation to a far greater extent than could be satisfied by the slow process of land colonisation. No capital from foreign relief organisations was required to get into the factories, nor need one wait years for the first harvest. Neither was it necessary to be torn up by the roots from home and family, to migrate to distant lands before finding work. The doors of the new factories stood wide open with the promise of immediate employment, and they flocked there in such numbers that it soon became clear that industrialisation was destined to overshadow the original land colonisation.

According to the Moscow *Izvestia, Pravda* and *Emes*, last year produced the following results: 40,000 Jews were inducted into factories and heavy industry; 30,000 Jewish youths were drawn into various training centres attached to the factories, which prepare them for skilled work; 5,000 were introduced into the coal mines of the Don Basin; 1,500 into the railway system. The plans for the next three years are even greater. They provide for: 135,000 Jewish youths to be drawn into heavy industry; 65,000 to be trained in skilled labour; 55,000 unemployed Jews, 20,000 small traders, 10,000 superfluous professional men, all to be converted into industrial labourers; 145,000 to be employed in Government offices; 200,000 more to work on the land. One could prolong these figures indefinitely. They all lead to one conclusion; that by the end of the Five-Years Plan, in 1933, the percentage of Russian Jews in heavy industry will be higher than that in any other occupation; that trading will be altogether eliminated as a source of Jewish income; that non-productive employment will be wiped out entirely. In a word, the whole of the Jewish people will have been productivised and, economically, at least, the Jewish problem in Soviet Russia will have been solved.

Even now, discarding all estimates about the future, the economic transformation of Jewish life in Soviet Russia is not far short of a marvel. At the last session of the Council of Nationalities in Soviet Russia held at Moscow in the middle of January, it was stated that at the beginning of this year 46.7 percent of the Jewish population in Soviet Russia were wage-earners, a percentage which no other nationality in Soviet Russia has yet reached. That 43 percent of this new Jewish proletariat is connected with heavy industry; that the former preponderance of Jews in the needle and the leather trades was changed to a predominance in the metallurgical industries; that the number of Jews working in the Soviet metal industries now exceeds the number of all other trades. "There is not an enterprise of State building in the Soviet Union in which Jewish labour is not now represented to a considerable extent," says the Moscow *Emes* in its review of the first two years of the "Piatiletka" (the Five-Years Plan). "In the giant mills of Kertsh, in the Dniepropetrovsk metallurgical plants, in the mines of Krivorog and the Donbas, in the factories of Moscow and Leningrad, on the Urals—everywhere, brigades of Jewish workers are holding positions by no means the rearmost in the industrial front in the great struggle for Socialism." According to the same official review, trading has already been abolished as a source of income among the Jews of Soviet Russia. Tourists in Russia confirm it. In vain will one look today for a Jewish trader on the famous Sucharefka Market in Moscow, which a few years back teemed with them. He will find men there of all other nationalities, but no Jews. The grievous problem of the declassed (of people engaged in non-productive occupations), which in 1928 and 1929 affected the Jews more than any other people in Russia, has now almost disappeared. The number of Jewish *"lishentzi"* (men without rights because they engage in trading) has been reduced to such a minimum that it no longer counts. Unemployment among the Jewish youth, the greatest curse of the Jews throughout Eastern Europe, is now non-existent in Russia. Even handicraft, which in the years immediately following the Revolution was in Russia the monopoly of the Jews, is rapidly disappearing as a source of occupation. Instead, middle-aged Jews are flocking to the land, and the Jewish youth to the factories (the old, indeed, are dying out). Between the two powerful movements of colonisation and industrialisation a nation of, literally, shopkeepers and traders is in front of our eyes being transformed into a people of land and industrial workers. The century-old legend of the Jew being the banner-bearer of commerce is fast disappearing. In Soviet Russia it has already disappeared.

The best observers of the Five-Years Plan have come to the conclusion that whatever the fate of the Plan as a whole may be, certain parts of it (as for instance oil and timber) may already be put down as successes, which they will remain even if the entire Plan fails. The productivisation of the Jews in Russia seems to be one of these assured successes. It is quite evidently going to endure, no matter how the project turns out as a whole. The reason is that this movement has causes and an existence all its own, quite separate from the Five-Years Plan. The enthusiasm for industrialisation and colonisation which has swept over the Jews of Russia, especially the Jewish youth, was by no means imposed upon them by the Government. It wells up from the very depths of the soul of a people whose creative powers, long dormant, have now been awakened, and who are pressing on toward economic salvation quite independently of the Five-Years Plan. Throughout the length and breadth of that vast country the Jewish youth has been striving and struggling with all its might, altogether independently of State exhortations, to break away from the old, despised, non-productive occupations in which their people have been hemmed by force for centuries, and to reconstruct their economic life on the new lines of productivity and social service. Even if there were no Five-Years Plan, nor yet even a Revolution, this process (which, incidentally, is not confined to the Jews in Russia only) would have gone on. The Five-Years Plan merely formed the external conditions necessary for the fulfilment of this inner urge. By a rare historic coincidence the Plan happened to coincide with the great inner urge of the Jewish people, and the same process of the Russian Revolution which, in its first stage, completely annihilated their economic life, is now building it up again. The small cart of the Jewish economic problem in Russia has been hitched up to the huge motor lorry of Russian reconstruction, with the result that it is being dragged out now from the mire of centuries towards the high road which leads to a complete solution of the Jewish difficulties.

The position of the Jews in Eastern Europe is very much the same as in Soviet Russia. In all the new, and in some of the older States, the same economic process is going on, even if not accompanied there by the fireworks of a revolution. Everywhere State co-operatives and Government monopolies are eliminating the small trader, and undermining the economic position of the Jewish middleman. This is the basis of the powerful post-War anti-Semitism which has swept across Eastern and Central Europe. It is economic anti-Semitism more than religious and racial. The entire Jewish problem and its corollary, anti-Semitism, are in the final analysis the result of a maladjustment of the medieval occupations of the Jews with modern economic conditions. Socially and politically Jews everywhere in Europe live in the twentieth century, but economically the bulk of them are still in the same conditions in which feudal discrimination and medieval fanaticism have placed them. That is the cause of all the trouble; the seat of the festering wound known as anti-Semitism. And only the adjustment of Jewish economic occupations to the needs of our modern age can serve as an antidote. That is the reason why productivisation is the greatest need of Jewish life in Eastern Europe. Progressive Jewry the world over is aware of this fact, and is everywhere working, both consciously and instinctively, toward that end. Even the Zionist movement is but a disguised expression of this urge for Jewish productivisation, and so are practically most of the other Jewish social movements of today. In Soviet Russia the movement has acquired its most conscious form, and is forging ahead towards realisation at a tempo and speed unknown anywhere else in the world. It is significant that since the Five-Years Plan has gained headway, one hears very little of anti-Semitism in Soviet Russia, and all eye-witnesses agree that this relic of medievalism, once strongest of all in Russia, is fast disappearing there now. What Soviet Russia can do, the rest of Eastern Europe can do, if it really cares to solve the Jewish problem. In this particular case, as in so many others, Soviet Russia leads the way for the rest of the world to follow.

PART
III

ANTI-SEMITISM RUN RIOT: 1933-1939

On January 30, 1933, Adolf Hitler became the Chancellor of Germany. In effect this was the end of the Weimar Republic and the beginning of the end for European Jewry. Hitler's appointment brought into power the most violent of nationalistic political parties. The Nazi dream was of a great unified German nation which by right of racial superiority would dominate Europe.

Racism was not a mere sidelight or political tool of Hitler's politics; it was a fundamental part of his, and thus his party's, ideology. Hitler saw races of men in a constant competition in which there could be no stability. A race either rose in power or it declined. For Hitler, the greatest enemy of the German race was the Jew.

Speculation about the causes of Hitler's anti-Semitism is rampant. Psychological, historical, and political explanations have been offered, and all contain elements of the answer. Hitler was, above all else, the ultimate German nationalist; he hated the country of his own birth, Austria-Hungary, because he believed it to be an empire rotted by the mixture of nationalities within its frontiers. Germans and the newly unified German state were his ideal of the perfect people and the perfect state. While Hitler evaded service in the army of Austria-Hungary, he joyously joined the forces of Germany in 1914. For him, the glory of the German nation-state was a cause worthy of his life.

The Jewish people manifested the one characteristic that this super-nationalist most loathed: they were international. To Adolf Hitler, with his view of constant racial struggle, the Jews were a parasitic race who were loyal only to themselves. They were the liberals, socialists, and international capitalists who stood opposed to everything in which he believed. Hitler, and other Germans, saw the

Jews as a major threat to the German people. Hitler carried this belief to his grave; in his last will and testament, while the Third Reich lay in rubble, he enjoined the German people to continue the struggle against "the universal poisoners of all peoples, international Jewry." Prepared by years of anti-Semitism, many angry, frustrated Germans accepted Hitler's portrayal of a "Jewish threat," and were ready to put political theory into practice.

German Jewry did not have long to wait before Nazi anti-Semitism became a reality in Germany. April 1933 signaled the start of measures aimed directly at the Jews. A boycott of Jewish businesses on the first of that month and a new Civil Service Law, which prohibited Jewish employment in the German civil service, a few days later, were but the first actions against Germany's Jews. The Nuremberg Laws of September 1935 followed. With this set of racial laws German Jewry lost its citizenship and was subjected to further disabilities. German Jewish life became desperate as the government and the Nazi party launched an unending series of psychological, legal, economic, and physical attacks against the Jews. The latter reached their pre-war height on November 9 and 10, 1938—the Night of Broken Glass. Jews were beaten in the streets, their homes were pillaged, and every synagogue in Germany was destroyed. These laws and attacks, like the Holocaust that followed them, were directed not against those who practiced the Jewish religion, but against the Jews as a people—a race.

The Nazi takeover in Germany also affected anti-Semitism in other parts of Europe. The very fact that a people as cultured and industrious as the Germans openly proclaimed and practiced such a rabid form of anti-Semitism lent that movement a certain legitimacy. Fascist anti-Semitic organizations had existed in Poland, for example, but grew larger and more vocal with Hitler's success as a guide. Two Polish-Fascist groups, the *Endeks* and the *Naras*, physically attacked Jews and called for their complete exclusion from Polish economic life. Although some in Polish politics fought against anti-Semitic legislation, by early 1938 the Fascist groups had succeeded in imposing many laws and regulations directed against Polish Jewry. The story in Rumania was much the same. Fascist parties joined together in the United Front, which saw that anti-Semitic regulations became a part of Rumanian Jewish life. Hungary, Latvia, and Lithuania were mere variations on the theme, and in March of 1938 Austria became united with Germany; Austrian Jews came under the same regulations as those of Germany. On the eve of war, then, the Jews of Central and Eastern Europe were a despised and demoralized people.

This massive increase of anti-Semitism inflamed another aspect of the Jewish Question—the refugees. Jews from Germany and Eastern Europe looked for some place where they could escape the harsh reality of political Jew-hatred; but there was no place to go. No country would accept the increasing numbers of Jews who sought a haven from the rising tide of oppression. Few Jews found homes in

Western Europe or America.

What of Palestine—the Jewish national home? Jewish immigration to Palestine had always been limited to the "economic absorptive capacity" of the land as determined by the British. But as Arab hostility to Jewish settlement turned increasingly to violence, particularly after the 1936 Arab revolt, politics rather than economics came to dominate British immigration policies. The zenith of Jewish immigration to Palestine was 1935, when more than 61,000 Jews settled there. After 1936, however, reinterpretation of the immigration regulations limited Jewish settlement to 12, 269 per year. And the British White Paper of 1939 even further closed Palestine to Jewish refugees. It is ironic that as European politics increased the need for refuge, Middle Eastern politics led Britain to close the gates of Palestine.

The Jews of Central and Eastern Europe were caught in a tightening web of hatred and violence in the six years which preceded the Second World War. The articles in this final section reveal the process by which Jews lost their rights and property, and the Western reaction to it. This was a process which set the stage for the Jewish loss of life.

THE JEWS
IN FASCIST
GERMANY

by Ludwig Lore

[In this April 1933 article Ludwig Lore detailed some of the official and unofficial acts of anti-Semitism in the Nazi state, and attempted to analyze their cause. He saw several reasons for the popularity of anti-Semitism in Germany. Germans, he wrote, were looking for a simple solution to their problems, and Jews were an easily identifiable target for German anger and frustration. Yet, above all, the German hatred of Jews was the result of the rabid nationalism that was a major element of Nazi political theory and practice. Lore saw the Jews as a race whose longevity, with neither land nor "concentrated material power," was a direct challenge to Nazi nationalism. Thus the very existence of the Jewish people became the root of German anti-Semitism, rather than any specific qualities either belonging to Jews or attributed to them.]

"The Jews in Fascist Germany" by Ludwig Lore, first published in *New Republic*, 74 (12 April 1933), 236-38. Reproduced by permission of *New Republic*.

When Reich Minister Goering, Commissioner for the Prussian Ministry of the Interior, declared in a pre-election speech that "it is not the function of the Prussian police to protect Jewish storekeepers," he served notice on the Jew in Germany that the Hitler government looks on him as an outlaw in the German nation. This broad hint, emanating from the highest official circles, was enough to inflame the Storm Troops, already drunk with enthusiasm over the success of their leader, to open excesses. During the first weeks of February, after the appointment of Adolf Hitler to the chancellorship, there were sporadic anti-Jewish acts of violence. After the Goering speech they grew in number and brutality to such an extent that already three foreign governments have protested through diplomatic channels against outrages perpetrated on Jewish citizens of the respective countries who were visiting or living in Germany. The United States intervened through Ambassador Sackett for nine Americans who had been abused and attacked by Storm Troopers, and received the assurance from Baron von Neurath that the guilty parties would be adequately punished. They were promptly indicted. But before judgment could be passed they were released under a general amnesty freeing all Nationalists who in their enthusiasm had overstepped the bounds of law and order.

It was inevitable that the Jews of Germany should be the first—after the labor movement—to feel the iron heel of National Socialist power. Of the confused and illogical demands that make up the ambitious program of that party, the anti-Semitic paragraphs alone offered an easy and immediate outlet for the energies of youthful Nazi followers. Jew-baiting had long been a favorite sport of the Storm detachments. To the starving German worker and the struggling tradesman the anti-Semitic program offered a promise of quick relief much closer to his comprehension than the vague near-Socialist theory the party and its government affect to espouse. To expel thousands of Jews from the country—that is a solution to his ills the common man can understand and appreciate, a program, moreover, that offers little difficulty in execution. Nor is this less true of thousands of intellectuals, physicians, lawyers, technicians, teachers, writers, actors and musicians who resent the competition of their Semitic colleagues. German retailers have suffered heavily from the inroads made on German trade by large department stores which are owned, according to National Socialist figures, largely by Jewish merchant princes. To them the Nazi program with its promise of immediate expropriation of all the department stores and the leasing of the various departments of these institutions to small businessmen, brings dreams of the good old days when the storekeeper, with a clerk or two, catered to a prosperous local trade and its familiar needs.

In those good old days, the Jews were not free from persecution. Germany and Saxony for decades spared no effort to stem the immigration of Jews from Russian Poland by regulations directed against its most vulnerable point, the family life of the incoming Jew. Long before the War only the children of those Jewish aliens who had come to Germany before 1882, when this legislation was passed, could acquire citizenship in Prussia. All Jewish immigrants arriving after this date were forced to renew their passports biennially. No single alien was permitted to found a family. If married he was forbidden to bring his family from its homeland in Russia, Poland or Austrian Galicia. Jews residing in Prussia had to give written promise that their sons would leave the country on or before their ninth birthday, and in many cases this regulation was brutally enforced under pitiful circumstances. With the outbreak of the World War the enforcement of these restrictions became even more severe. The Saxon Ministry for Education ordered the exclusion from its public schools of the children of alien enemies, a measure directed exclusively against the Russian Jews, most of whom had come to Saxony, attracted by its thriving fur and textile industries.

The Nazis try to make the world believe that Germany is overrun with Semites from the East to an extent that threatens its racial integrity. What are the actual facts? According to the "Statistische Jahrbuch fur das Deutsche Reich," the ratio of Jewish to general population was:

1907	0.92%
1910	0.95%
1925	0.91%

In 1925, when the last census was taken, the total number of Jews in Germany was 564,379 out of a population of 62,410,619. These figures prove that the menace of the Eastern Jew and of the Jew in general in Germany is a myth bolstered up by the clever propaganda of the National Socialists. That it could become so astoundingly effective was indubitably due to the fact that the German Jew wields an economic power out of all proportion to his numbers, having been forced to develop traits that made him the forerunner and pacemaker of the modern capitalist.

The Reich government appointed by President von Hindenburg on January 30 is headed by Chancellor Hitler, but it is largely made up of members and adherents of the German Nationalist People's party under the leadership of Dr. Alfred Hugenberg. The National Socialist German Labor party at first held only three ministerial posts (out of eleven) including the Chancellor; after the March 5 election the National Socialist group took an additional post in the Ministry. It is necessary to refer briefly to the political composition of the government because the anti-Semitism of the German Nationalists differs considerably from that of the Fascists. The Hugenberg party recruits its supporters from among important industrialist groups and from the large landholding Junker nobility. Hitler's party, though it, too, enjoys the financial support of powerful industrialists and aristocrats, is essentially the party of the petty bourgeoisie and the intellectual middle class, which look to it for tangible benefits from the expulsion of the Jews.

Hugenberg's party, though inherently the party of Prussian Junkerdom at its reactionary worst, used the anti-Semitic slogans of Stocker, the famous missionary of anti-Semitism, to win petty-bourgeois and farmer support against the growing power of capitalism. Since then, under Hugenberg, it has made its peace with the capitalist class, particularly with influential sections of the heavy industries, the line of demarcation between the nobility and the wealthy bourgeoisie having disappeared to a considerable degree. Both its middle-class followers and its anti-Semitic program have been taken over by the National Socialists. Though anti-Semitism still persists in the Hugenberg party, it is neither so aggressive nor so vociferous as in the Nazi party.

The fact that the National Socialists polled six times as many votes and elected almost six times as many representatives to the legislative bodies in all parts in the Reich has superseded any significance the Hugenberg majority in the Cabinet may originally have had. The Cabinet, moreover, gave tacit recognition to the factual supremacy of Nazi dictatorship from the start by turning over the control of the police, the judiciary and the appointment of the executive bureaucracy to its associates.

German civilization is living through a crisis of terrific magnitude. Millions are without employment. Tens of thousands of white-collar workers are vainly seeking jobs. By the tens of thousands, tradesmen and artisans have been ruined and the professions are crowded with young and old who are looking for bread. Behind these uprooted millions are other millions who have never worked, young people who learned trades and professions in which there is no work to be had, who grew into manhood without having experienced the joy of creative work, the stimulus of social labor; boys who were born into the misery of a war-wracked world, brought up in fatherless and motherless homes in which hunger and neglect were their daily companions. What wonder that, in this period of destruction in which work, the foundation of all social life, has become the privilege of the few, in which workingmen and women are drifting aimlessly through a miasma of political antagonisms, disappointed and disillusioned with the Social Democratic and the Communist parties, millions are turning to this new party as an expression of their bitter resentment with things as they are, easy victims of false and hollow catchwords? Humanity today is ripe for demagogy and false prophets. In Germany it clutched at anti-Semitism, the "Socialism of the benighted."

It was a foregone conclusion that the government created under the slogan, "Down with Marxism and the Jew!" should proceed at once after imprisoning tens of thousands of Communists and Socialists, suppressing their newspapers and periodicals and gagging the labor movement, to a crusade against the Jew. The world will probably never know how many Jews were murdered and disappeared in the fateful months of February and March, 1933. Not only have the authorities refused all information: censorship of the mails and of communications to the foreign press is being enforced by such rigorous measures that it has become possible to inform the world outside of happenings in Germany only with the greatest difficulty.

In Hanover the Reich Commissioner in the Prussian Ministry for Education and Culture, Dr. Rust, declared, on February 12, that "the public schools must be purged of all non-Germans and of all that is un-German. All that is not German must disappear from our primary and higher institutions of learning. I will strike it off with ruthless thoroughness within the terms of the law." Action followed upon words. Within two weeks 150 Jewish teachers and directors in high schools and other educational institutions were dismissed "as a preliminary measure." The same Minister issued a further ukase [order] dismissing all Jewish physicians in municipal and state hospitals.

In the Staatsschauspielhaus [state theater] in Berlin sixteen Jewish actors and actresses were dismissed without notice and the new National Socialist management instructed under no circumstances to engage Jewish talent. Among the actors thus summarily dismissed are some of the most important artists of the German stage. The Academy of Arts and Sciences in Berlin was officially advised to undergo a process of "self-purification" by the removal of Jews and other undesirable members. In consequence, Heinrich Mann and Kate Kollwitz, both Christians with radical convictions, resigned from the Academy.

It is too early to judge whether Chanellor Hitler, who was equipped, by the Reichstag decision of March 23, with powers more autocratic and dictatorial than those of the Japanese emperor or even Mussolini, believes the time ripe for the execution of that point in his program which states that "citizenship rights shall be granted only to those who are of German racial origin [*Volksgenossen*]. *Volksgenossen* are those who are of German blood irrespective of religious affiliation. No Jew can be a *Volksgenosse*. The non-citizen shall live in Germany as an alien [guest] and shall be subject to the laws governing aliens. All further immigration of non-German elements shall cease. We demand, further, that all non-Germans who entered the Reich after August 1, 1914, shall be deported from German soil." It is quite possible that the government may be forced by the pressure of public opinion to a temporary moderation, determined haters of the Jews though its leaders undoubtedly are. In a collection of Hitler's speeches published in Munich by his party a short time ago and authorized by him, we find an address delivered in April, 1922, in which he says:

This race of capitalists, which first brought unscrupulous exploitation of men by men into the world, has been able to obtain control of the fourth estate by using its influence on the Left as well as on the Right, for it has its apostles in both camps. On the Right the wealthy Jew is carrying every harmful characteristic of our productive system to such extremes that the poor devil, the man of the people, must rise in righteous self-defense; greed, unscrupulousness, hardheartedness, noxious profit worship. More and more the Jews have wormed themselves into the best families; the result was that the leading elements of our nation became alienated from their own people. This was the premise of their work on the Left. For on the Left the Jew was a vulgar demagogue. He drove national intelligence from the leadership of labor in disgust, first, by his international point of view, secondly by his Marxian theories, by declaring that property as such is robbery.

Along this path the economic intelligence of nationalist convictions could no longer follow. Thus the Jews were able, by an unscrupulous use of the press, to isolate this movement from all national elements.

The Hitler regime has rightly been called a Fascist dictatorship, for it recognizes and has adopted in the program of the National Socialist German Labor party the most important doctrines of Italian Fascism. Yet, fundamentally, anti-Semitism is not an essential of Fascist philosophy, notwithstanding the prominence it has been given by the German Fascist movement. Italian Fascism is not anti-Semitic. Its basic principles, super-nationalism and insistence on a strongly centralized, anti-democratic government, are antagonistic to the Jewish point of view. By force of circumstances the Jew has become an internationalist, the champion of political liberty and democratic institutions. The name of Karl Marx is anathema to the Fascist as much because he personifies an internationalism opposed to nationalism as for his Jewish heritage. To the National Socialist, Bolshevism is a Jewish doctrine, a poison injected by an alien race into the life of his people.

In the final analysis, tragic and ghastly as is the lot of the Jew in Germany today, it represents but one aspect, though perhaps the most important one, of the problem that the German people and the world are facing. Anti-Semitism is nationalism's best ally. They are blood brothers; they belong together. A race which, without land and without concentrated material power, maintains its identity with such dogged persistence through the centuries is the living antithesis of nationalist ideology, that concept of the nation which is premised exclusively on political domination. Nationalism and anti-Semitism today outline the political picture of official Germany.

GERMANY'S ANTI-JEWISH CAMPAIGN

by Sidney B. Fay

[Not all observers saw the Nazi's coming to power as a complete disaster for German Jewry. Some believed that the early Nazi actions against the Jews were only a phase which would soon pass; they called for calm on the part of the Western world so that Nazi anti-Semitism would not be increased as a response to either vocal condemnation or economic actions against Germany.

Sidney B. Fay, a noted historian who led that school of thought which said that Germany was not responsible for the outbreak of World War I, was a spokesman for that point of view. In this May 1933 article he wrote that stories of horrible acts against Jews were certainly exaggerated, much as were tales of German atrocities in France and Belgium during World War I. He attributed German acts against Jews to unofficial and unauthorized groups carried away in the first days of Nazi power. He also believed that Western protests against Germany would cause more rather than less trouble for Germany's Jews.

Fay reflected the all-too-common disbelief that the government of a major European state could engage in violent anti-Semitism as an official policy. This inability to recognize the true nature of the Nazi regime played a major role in Western miscalculations throughout the 1930s.]

"Germany's Anti-Jewish Campaign" by Sidney B. Fay, first published in *Current History*, 38 (May 1933), 295-300.

In the rise of the Hitler party to power in Germany its spokesmen continually uttered dire threats as to what it would do to the Jews if once it controlled the government. To appeal to racial and religious animosities was an easy way of getting votes. The Nazis capitalized all sorts of hatred against the Jews. They revived the medieval religious prejudice against a downtrodden people. They urged that Jews, because they were not "Nordic" or "Aryan," were not good Germans. Jews were accused of not being patriotic because of their economic and other affiliations with people of their own race in other countries. The Nazis declared that many of the great banks, newspapers and department stores in Germany were controlled by Jews, who sucked up the money of the poor people in the interests of international Jewry, that the leading war profiteers had been Jews, and that Jews had far more than their share, on the basis of population, of the positions in the professions, especially in law and in medicine.

With this long preparation of propaganda dinned into the ears of the Nazis at their mass meetings, it is not surprising that the Hitler victory in the Reichstag elections, with its natural feeling of exultation and excitement, should have led to a widespread series of outrageous attacks upon Jews by undisciplined Nazis. It is not necessary to suppose that the attacks were deliberately ordered by Hitler or his immediate agents. It is true, however, that in the first days after the election Nazi brown shirts picketed Jewish stores and in some cases broke windows or caused the stores to close, while the government and police took no steps to prevent such injustice. It also appears to be true that innumerable little groups of unauthorized armed Nazis for two or three days carried on a regular campaign calculated to terrorize the Jewish population. Jews in cafes were beaten up. Jewish houses were broken into at night and their inmates dragged out and maltreated. Under the influence of this terror many Jews fled abroad.

Naturally enough, the stories told by those who fled were greatly exaggerated. Sensationalist newspapers abroad magnified the horrors with tales of eyes gouged out and Jews murdered at the gates of Jewish cemeteries. Fear, credulity and racial and religious hatred combined to produce stories of "atrocities" such as were once alleged to have been practiced by the Germans in Belgium and France during the World War. How much truth there was in the stories of Nazi outrages against the Jews it is impossible at this time to ascertain. Granting, however, that most of the stories were much exaggerated, there can be no doubt that where there was so much smoke there was some fire. Even Hermann Goering, who is one of the most ruthless of the Nazi leaders, in denouncing the barrage of "foreign defamation," admitted that the national revolution accomplished by Nazis had been marked by "unavoidable" blemishes in the form of irresponsible acts of lawlessness. Such an admission by him means much.

The reports of outrages against Jews in Germany quickly stirred up a feeling of indignation and a wave of protest from Jews abroad, especially in Great Britain and the United States. Jewish societies urged their governments to protest to the German Government. They urged retaliation in the form of a movement to boycott German goods. At first sight these protests seemed to have a beneficial effect in touching a sensitive spot in the Nazi government's armor. Its official spokesmen were profuse in indignantly denying most of the charges as being grossly exaggerated and as manufactured simply to discredit the new National government which had come into power. Hitler announced that strict orders had been given to the Nazi organizations that there should be no more such acts of violence; that no one should act against individual rights except upon orders issued from above.

An editorial in the *Frankfurter Zeitung* summed up the situation on March 23, saying:

> Just as the outside world has failed, with the fewest exceptions, to form a true conception of the German state of mind since the war—otherwise the policy pursued toward Germany would have been the opposite of what it was—just as it has completely misunderstood the German youth, so now it has interpreted the recent overturn under the distortion of preconceived opinions and thus misunderstood it....
>
> Excesses there have been, but to generalize such bad isolated cases into a general picture of Germany does not express the truth. This also applies to the Jewish problem. The unbridled anti-Semitism of National Socialism during the period of agitation is fraught with danger of sudden explosions and appeared indeed to create a threatening situation for German Jews after the overturn. From the demands raised in the outside world—not only in Jewish but also in Christian circles—for succor for German Jews by international action, one would infer that pogroms were the order of the day in Germany.
>
> We should fail in our journalistic duty if we did not state emphatically that such generalizations do not correspond to the situation in Germany. Since assuming power, the men in authority, at all events, have refrained from anti-Semitic utterances, and it should be remembered that Hermann Goering has assured the Central Jewish Federation that all Jewish citizens loyal to the government would have the protection of the law for person and property.
>
> Just as one must emphasize that this "revolution" has been a bloodless one, so the idea that there are any pogroms in Germany must be repudiated. Those circles outside Germany that are propagandizing for international action for the protection of German Jews should, therefore, be made to understand that their activity, however well intentioned, misses the mark.
>
> National Socialist anti-Semitism is an internal German problem. The intervention of non-German circles distorts the whole question, implies a supererogatory vote of non-confidence in German public opinion, and puts the burden just on those German Jews who, through birth, speech, education and disposition, have felt and still feel

themselves united with the German State.

Nevertheless, in spite of this hint from the *Frankfurter Zeitung* that protests from abroad would hurt the German Jews whom it was intended to help, in spite of telegrams from numerous German Jewish organizations that the stories of the anti-Semitic attacks were greatly exaggerated and that they did not welcome foreign interference in the question, in spite of a report from the United States Department of State gathered from its Consuls in Germany indicating "that whereas there was for a short time considerable physical mistreatment of Jews, this phase may be considered terminated," the foreign campaign of protest increased in vehemence, culminating in a gigantic mass meeting in Madison Square Garden in New York on March 27. And the dangers from such a foreign agitation began to be more apparent than the benefits which had appeared at first sight.

One of the most obvious lessons of history, but one which it is most difficult for people stirred with righteous indignation to learn, is the fact that foreign threats or interference at a time of revolution usually tend to excite and increase the fanaticism of the party against whom it is directed and to injure the people on whose behalf the protest or interference is made. It was notably so in the case of the French Revolution. The Austrian declarations of Padua and Pillnitz only tended to increase the fury of the Republicans against Louis XVI and Marie Antoinette. The interference of the Austrian and Prussian armies led directly to the attack on the Tuileries on August 10, 1792, to the downfall and imprisonment of the King and Queen, and to the arrest of hundreds of "suspects" who were massacred a few days later. So also after the Bolshevist Revolution in Russia. Nothing contributed more to strengthen and consolidate the power and ruthless procedure of the Bolshevists than the intervention on the part of President Wilson and the Allies with the intention of saving the remnants of the Czarist White forces and of crushing bolshevism.

Nevertheless, it may, perhaps, be objected that the analogy is not good, because there were cases of armed intervention, and no sane person is proposing armed intervention in regard to Germany—unless serious trouble should occur on the Polish or the French frontier. But the point is that any foreign interference, even in the lesser form of widespread criticism, formal protests by governments or economic boycotts, is likely to stir the anger and excite the more violent elements in the dominant party into further acts of repression and vengeance against the unfortunate minority.

So also in Germany. The effect on Nazi public opinion of the continued campaign of protest from abroad was to increase the spirit of persecution against the Jews in Germany. Jewish doctors were dismissed from the hospitals; Jewish lawyers and judges were prevented from exercising their functions; Jewish attendance at schools and universities was to be cut down radically. There developed a strong movement to restrict the number of Jews in all the professions and the educational institutions to a number proportional to the total number of Jews in Germany, which is less than 600,000. Finally, the Nazi party organization announced a general boycott of all Jewish stores and of stores financed by Jews to begin on April 1. That is, the wrath of the Nazis at the "foreign atrocity propaganda" was turned against the Jews in Germany. They were accused of injuring Germany by secretly stirring up the propaganda abroad, whereas in reality, as was pointed out above, they had sought to restrain it. Foreign interference, as in the case of the French Revolution and the Bolshevists, appeared again to have had precisely the reverse of the effect intended.

The National Socialist party's proclamation of a boycott against Jewish stores and business establishments was announced from the Nazi Brown House at Munich on March 28. It was declared to be the answer of nationally minded Germany—"tolerated but not supported by the government"—to the demonstrations of protest in Great Britain and the United States. The boycott, it was announced, would start universally throughout Germany on Saturday, April 1, at 10 A.M., and would continue until lifted by the party management. It was to be "a measure of defense against the lies and defamation of hair-raising perversity being loosed against Germany" from abroad. The details of the execution of the boycott were carefully laid down in eleven articles, the wording of which suggested that Dr. Goebbels may have had a hand in it.

According to these eleven articles, committees of action were to be formed in every local group and organization of the National Socialist party. These committees were to carry out a systematic boycott against Jewish business establishments, goods, physicians and lawyers. The committees were to be responsible for not having the boycott hit the innocent, but were to see to it that it hit the guilty all the harder. They must popularize the boycott through propaganda and public enlightenment and watch the newspapers carefully to see that they participated in the intelligence campaign of the German people against Jewish atrocity propaganda abroad. Newspapers not doing so were to be removed from every house and no German business concern was to advertise in such papers. The committees must be formed in the smallest peasant villages in order to hit Jewish tradesmen in the rural districts.

"The committees shall also take care," the boycott plan read, "that every German having connections abroad shall use these for disseminating the truth—by letter, telegraph and telephone—that quiet and order may reign in Germany; that the German people has no more ardent wish than peaceably to do its work and live in peace with the outside world, and that it conducts its fight against Jewish atrocity propaganda as a purely defensive measure. The committees are responsible for having the whole campaign run off in complete orderliness and with the strictest discipline. Do not hurt a hair on a Jew's head. We shall settle this drive by the mere weight of these measures."

Though the boycott program was the work of the Nazi party

organization and not of the Hitler government, and though it was not to begin until April 1, it was broadcast over the government-controlled radio on March 29 and at once began to go into effect in many places. Nazi pickets placed themselves in front of Jewish stores so effectively that many had to close. The municipal authorities of Berlin and many other cities announced that they would buy no supplies except from Nazi-Nationalist business institutions. Later statements by the government limited the boycott to only April 1, with the threat that it would be resumed if foreign agitation did not cease. It soon became clear that because of pressure upon the Cabinet both from without and within, the boycott would not be repeated. The fate of the Jews of Germany, however, continued to distress the world. Such was the situation when these lines were written.

THE SOCIO-ECONOMIC BACKGROUND OF NAZI ANTI-SEMITISM

by Herman Hausheer

[By 1936, the year this article was published, it was clear that the Nazi government of Germany had launched a serious campaign against the Jews, but there was little agreement concerning either the causes of the Nazi program or its ultimate impact on German Jewry. Herman Hausheer believed that the roots of German anti-Semitism were economic—that the extreme nationalists had been able to focus hostility on the Jews by portraying them as the leaders of both international finance and international socialism. The racist content of German hatred of the Jews was, for him, a logical absurdity which would disappear "under the continued contempt and ridicule of enlightened world opinion."

In the end, he believed that German anti-Semitism was rooted in German Jewry's position in the German economy and the liberal professions. The solution was to follow the course of the Soviet Union and change Jewish ways of work to productive rather than service enterprises. Yet Germany would not allow this, and German Jews, he predicted, would become a revolutionary force in Germany as they had in Czarist Russia. The downfall of the Nazi regime would allow Jews to change their economic position and anti-Semitism in Germany would end.

Hausheer looked for rational explanations for what was essentially an irrational phenomenon. His article is further evidence that Nazi motives were so far outside the norms of Western politics that, although they were explicitly expressed, they were not believed.]

"The Socio-Economic Background of Nazi Anti-Semitism" by Herman Hausheer, first published in *Social Forces*, 14 (March 1936), 341-54. Reproduced by permission of University of North Carolina Press.

Those who have written on the Jewish question, which has been for the last two milleniums a most *vexata quaestio* of mankind, have been for the most part infected with racial and confessional prejudices. If the anti-Semitic literature is enormous, the defensive literature of the Jews is quite considerable. Unfortunately, by far the greater part of the voluminous literature relating to the Jewish question is unmistakably contentious. It arouses such strong feeling that those who write about it are wont either, like Chamberlain, Ford, Fritsch, Hitler, and Rosenberg, to take violent sides against the Jews, or, like Hertz, Kahn, and Zollschan, to espouse the Jewish cause with passion. The perusal of the voluminous anti-Semitic literature is for the most part a punishment. Neither are the refutations a constant pleasure to peruse. A perpetual war with accusations and defenses, justifications and falsifications, corrections and doctored statistics has to date been fought between anti-Semites and philo-Semites. That the victims try to defend themselves is only natural, but it cannot be said that their spokesmen always do so successfully. Many of them let themselves be stirred into an aggressive combat, where coolness and silence would be more effective. To phrase statements so that both the assimilated and the Zionistic Jews, the fanatic of race and the fanatic of environment, may agree, is probably an insuperable task. Anti-Semitism and philo-Semitism represent exaggerations. The former is inconsistent in its accusations against the Jew, while the latter displays considerable inconsistency in the enumeration of the virtues of the Jew. There is little objectivity, absence of apology and diatribe in their works. In many respects they are talking past each other. It is particularly painful to plow through the writings of the anti-Semites. Even so, however, the writings in question can still be useful sources of information. There is factual truth on both sides.

According to the last German census for which figures are available, June 6, 1925, 584,379 were Jews or nine-tenth of one percent of the total population. The anti-Jewish measures of the Nazis, however, affect not only those listed as Jews, but also a newly created class of "non-Aryans." By prescribed definition a non-Aryan is a fourth part of non-Aryan blood; a person descended in particular from Jewish parents and grandparents. It suffices if one parent or grandparent is non-Aryan. It is estimated that this category comprises approximately two million Germans, making a total of about two and a half millions in the Reich who, according to Nazi standards, are classified as Jews. Although the Jews in Germany only number about one million, they exercised an influence upon the character of national culture which is much greater than was warranted by their number.

The present anti-Jewish outbreak in Germany marks the greatest ebullition of anti-Semitism in modern times. It also symbolizes the passing of a great economic epoch in Jewish history, an epoch which began with the nineteenth century and came to a close with the World War.

The nineteenth century was indubitably the century of the greatest progress and advancement for the Jews. Aside from ushering in the great Jewish emancipation, with its political, religious, and in some instances also social, equality, the nineteenth century will go down into history as the one having the greatest Jewish prosperity as far as the Western World is concerned. For centuries past the Jews had engaged in occupations which the new economic order needed and valued most. While one may not agree with W. Sombart that the Jews were the originators of capitalism, yet they had at least a good start not only in the knowledge and experience of the mechanisms of trade and commerce, but in the possession of qualities and mental equipment essential for the capitalistic world of production for sale. Thus when modern capitalism set in they were by reason of their previous economy in the vanguard.

The nineteenth century was chiefly one of individual enterprise and competition. The Jews excelled in both these aspects through centuries of persecution and consequent need of adjustment to adverse circumstances. The economic life of the age was in the direction which favored the Jews.

No student of the Jewish problem can overlook the marvellous record of Jewish achievement and prosperity during the nineteenth century. True, in Eastern Europe, the great mass of the Jews was living in the main below decent levels of subsistence. In Western Europe, however, emancipation, even if restricted and defined both by law and traditions, opened the door to achievement. Individual Jews amassed and spent fabulous fortunes. They reached unexcelled heights in learning, philosophy, science, art, literature, in journalism, on the stage, and in the professions. The Jewish boycott in Nazi Germany (1934) disclosed that many of the most illustrious names of German culture were Jewish. In no other country had the Jews ever before achieved what they were able to do in Germany.

Nazi anti-Semitism is intimately linked with the growing revolt of the German middle classes, which the events of the post-war years have left poor in pocket as well as in morale. The World War and the inflation having ruined them almost to the point of annihilation, with their old social and economic positions destroyed and threatened, and fearing being proletarianized and losing their cultural status, they rose in revolt, being willing to give their support to any one who promised a desirable change. Thus Nazism derived its real strength neither from the believers in hereditary aristocracy nor from the great capitalists, but from the large section of the national community which, in the modern world, stands between the directors of capitalist enterprise and the main body of the working class. It recruited its supporters mainly from the urban middle classes. Side by side with the older lower bourgeoisie which depended upon small-scale production and exchange for its survival, there had grown up within modern capitalism a new class, composed of technicians, salary-earners, and various kinds of consultants. The incomes and social status of these men depend upon the evolution of modern industrial technique. The industrial workers are, in Germany and other advanced countries, a shrinking factor of the population, while the clerks, the distributors, and those who render various kinds of service increased greatly in relative numbers with every technical advance.

Then too, ever since the unavoidably growing concentration and relative diffusion of capital during the period beginning with 1890 until the World War, the rise of a *rentier* class of small and middling investors had come to characterize German social life. These small investors constituted the social sphere from which were recruited the lower and middle ranks of the civil service, the more highly paid employees, the elementary and high school teachers. The German middle class, a highly differentiated world in itself, cannot be counted as a part of the employer or capitalistic class. Subject as the middle class groups were as consumers to the price policy of cartels and trusts, they nevertheless supported the capitalistic order because part of their income was linked up with it. Through the disturbance of the industrial capitalistic order by the World War the middle class groups were wrecked. In contrast to the workers, the salaried employees received minimal wage increases. The civil service was reduced in numbers, loaded with additional work and undernourished. The incomes of the small investors from mortgages, government securities and war loans suffered from depreciation in value. The middle class groups ceased to be able to live in the accustomed style. Small wonder that they came to feel themselves economically and socially degraded. Moreover, the middle class groups, being depressed in social status, ceased to be the goal of the social aspirations of the workers. Toward the end of the war the *nouveaux riches* were confronted by the *nouveaux pauvres*. This contrast became accentuated with the progress of the war, intensifying the economic resentment and envy between those who possess and those who do not.

The leadership of the Nazi movement was assumed largely by men who belonged to the technically progressive middle class group. These men were for the most part energetic individuals; they had drive and were hard-boiled. Under the banner of aggressive nationalism they were able to marshal behind them the otherwise inarticulate and unorganized forces of the small traders, the peasants, and the youthful unemployed intellectuals. Being not versed in politics, in order to help themselves they placed their faith in the exclusive leadership of an individual who dared. Reinforced by those elements from the old aristocracy and the upper bourgeoisie which had been anxious to throw their weight on the side of any force strong enough to smash the growth of social radicalism, and by the unemployed from the lower strata of the population, all these elements became under the peculiar conditions of post-war Europe, strong enough to take the whole power of the state into their hands, and use it to suppress every articulate form of opposition.

But dictatorships have only recently become Fascist in nature. The main differential factor of Nazism is its economic program, aiming at rehabilitating the middle classes. Awakened by their painful experiences since the World War to the evils of unrestrained competition and uncontrolled production of the capitalistic system, they have sought to escape their troubles through economic planning within a self-sufficing state. By reason of their economic discontent they are groping for an overturn within the framework of capitalism, intent upon retaining property rights and profits. The various phases of economic life are to be coordinated so as to raise the standard of living of all. This is still an item of the distant future. Nazism was the only vehicle for the political radicalization of the middle class, which offered the opportunity for the destruction of *laissez-faire* capitalism without the concurrent annihilation of the middle class. Hence the Third Reich rests upon economic nationalism, seeking to eliminate social and economic waste, and saving the best in capitalism and discarding the worst of it.

In aiming to smash Marxism because it alienated the workers from the ideals of a German national state and a German national economy by seeking to repress individual initiative, to abolish private property, and to foster international class interests; in aiming to crush international financial capitalism, because the large financial capitalists sought to control the economic life of the entire nation for their own ends by speculative uses of their capital, the Nazi party and later the Nazi government unavoidably became the rallying force for all latent anti-Semitic tendencies, as individual Jews had taken a prominent part in both the socialistic movements and in international finance.

Politically insignificant anti-Semitic secret organizations flourished during the duration of the belated German Republic. There were no less than sixty-two patriotic organizations, which, while violently opposed to each other, were yet unanimously anti-Semitic in their objectives. The Hitler movement and party became their political expression. The growing misery of the middle classes rendered plausible the view that they had always been the particular favorite of the state's care throughout the last century, because they had always been in danger of being ground to dust between the upper millstone of international capitalism, often Jewish capitalism, and the nether millstone of proletarianism, often Marxian socialism.

Nazism is thus both anti-capitalistic and anti-socialistic in the sense that it contends that Marxism and international financial capitalism deliberately tended to disrupt the integrity of the political state. Marxism, Nazism contends, degraded the state to playing the role of a dispenser of aid (*Fuersorgestaat*), by surrendering its integrity to internationalism, yielding to all foreign political, economic, and cultural forces, while financial capitalism through its international connections deliberately menaced the weakened economic structure of the German nation in favor of a small group of individuals. The state became the slave of international economy. To reestablish the lost supremacy of the state, the government had to become a government of deeds. It must be executive, not legislative. It must exert authority over economic life by organizing its production, distribution, and consumption so as not to endanger its supremacy.

The new state is different from the liberal state of the nineteenth century which was mainly concerned with the maintenance of order, law, and national defense. The corporative state is primarily concerned with economic and social matters. Its agencies must make decisions quickly and act even more quickly. It places national ends above individual and group interests, balanced order above liberty, invention above tradition, and practical necessities above constitutional guarantees. It tends to be administrative rather than parliamentary, and is indifferent to the traditional division of powers. It develops a whole series of governmental proprietary corporations, which tie the state into the economic structure of the country.

Nazism places no premium upon intellectuality. Rational knowledge at its best is harmful according to the Nazis. Intellectual comprehension of facts, they say, disables the individual to make fresh and quick decisions. Nazism hates intellectualism because it mimicked sympathy for Bolshevism, which effectively changed the social economy. It identifies intellectualism with parliamentarism and hollow talk. It accepts Sorel's theory of the indecision of talkers and intellectuals. But one finds nowhere as much *Schoenrednerei*, as the Germans term excessive forensics, than in the Nazi camp. It was by means of beautiful speeches that the Nazis succeeded in corrupting the various organized economic and social groups. Contrary to Nazi theory, however, the most decisive changes since the World War have been made by intellectuals. Nazism surreptitiously argues that modern society suffers from an excessive number of intellectuals. As a consequence of the overabundance of persons offering their knowledge in the market an intellectual proletariat arose. This is always a pathological condition caused by an intellectual over-estimation of formal education, and by the stoppage in the consumption of intellectual commodities due to the general impoverishment; by the industrial technological unemployment, which forces them usually into civil service or the liberal professions, both of which are overmanned. Only a very small percentage of intellectual proletarians is due to ruined careers. Having been unable to find a place at the government troughs, the intellectual proletarians become the sworn enemies of the existing political regime. It is thus not by chance that the Jews have furnished a large quota of socialistic and financial leaders in all countries. Their pariah position within the respective national states explains their comparative innocence and irresponsibility toward the national traditions of the peoples among whom they live; their resentment and aggressive drive against the existing social order, if they do not attain recognition by way of finance, and their willingness to overthrow the social order that represses them.

Not recognizing among themselves any privileged classes, the Jews naturally favor democracy and socialism. It was the proletariat which constituted in pre-war days the organized center of social dissatisfaction and of revolutionary explosives. Jewish intellectuals, restricted in pre-war days in the exercise of the professions and in the attainment of civil positions, were hindered from climbing into those positions in which they would have risen by reason of their ability if they had not been Jews. They thus became the best soil for revolutionary tendencies. As among non-Jews the number of dissatisfied intellectuals is much smaller than among the Jews, and as the proletariat has in its political rise need of intellectual leaders, it was natural that the Jews became strongly represented. But that the Jew is by reason of race inclined toward revolutions is best refuted by the fact that the rich Jewish merchants and industrialists in Central and Western Europe and in America are the pillars of the existing political and social order. It is, however, a fact that the Jews are generally less nationalistic than the Gentiles, because they live in many different countries, travel and migrate more than the non-Jews, and are probably less addicted to being distrustful and hostile towards aliens.

In their attitude toward the pre-Nazi German state and German culture the Jews could be divided roughly into four groups. The Zionists regarded themselves as a real national minority. They looked to Palestine as their real fatherland. Numerically they were insignificant. At the other extreme was a small group which continually stressed the German national spirit. This group was opposed to the immigration of Eastern European Jews into Germany; for, like the German nationalists, it saw therein a danger to German culture. The great majority of the German Jews took their stand somewhere between these two extremes. They regarded themselves as German citizens, but tried to maintain, to a certain extent, the Jewish tradition. A fourth group of uncertain size consisted of those Jews who sought complete assimilation, and who attempted to hide or deny their Jewish ancestry.

Nazism provided the impoverished middle classes, the backbone of German cultural and national life, with an outlet for their pent-up feelings, by making the Jews responsible for all their miseries. The middle class had been in pre-war Germany the main support of *laissez-faire* capitalism. The leadership of opposition against capitalism for exclusively private gain passed after the close of the World War from the workers to the middle class.

Anti-Semitism received a fresh impetus from the economic impoverishment of Germany through the World War and the inflationary period of 1922-23. The hatred of the masses against the war and inflation profiteers was much greater than their hatred against inherited wealth. Catering to the demands of the impoverished middle class groups, the socialistic proposals of the Nazi party called for the abolition of incomes unearned by work, the ruthless confiscation of war profits, the nationalization of all trusts, profit-sharing in wholesale trade, old age pensions, the municipalization of large department stores and their leasing out at low rates to small merchants, the death penalty for usurers and profiteers, prevention of speculation in land, abolition of interest on land mortgages and confiscation of land for community purposes (Points 11-18). Mass hatred against inherited wealth came to political expression in the Nazi demand for the expropriation of the large estates, which in the interests of political opportunism soon came to mean as being directed primarily against the Jewish companies which speculate in land.

The contradictions between these various socialistic proposals and the Nazi obligations to financial interests was cleverly smoothed over by a convenient distinction which the Nazi theorists made between creative and acquisitive capital. The former, which was said to keep the wheels of industry running, was accepted and supported, while the latter, representing capital invested in business and banking, was accused of reaping big profits, subtracting thereby from the national wealth. This differentiation, although a purely verbal one, applies to no real economic dissimilarity between the various forms of capital. It was simply an essential part of Nazi romantic reasoning which they presented to their proletarian followers. The injection of the pseudo-scientific racial factor into an analysis of economic processes vitiates the validity of Nazi economic theory. Cognizant of the fact that a Jewish proletariat, a Jewish wage earning class, is practically non-existent in Germany, the Nazis made use of the anti-capitalistic feeling among the majority of the workers and the middle class discontents by sidetracking it into an antagonism against foreign and Jewish capitalism.

It is not true that international capital and international industry are exclusively in Jewish hands as the fanatics among the Nazis have so glibly claimed. There is, for instance, a very small amount of Jewish capital involved in the huge corporations of the metal industry, particularly in the field of heavy industry. However, the statement by W. Sombart and Friedrich L. Nussbaum that in Germany before the war, 13.3 percent of the directors of industrial enterprises were Jewish, although the Jews formed only about 1 percent of the total population; the statements that in 1928, 15 Jews shared 718 directorships of German companies, and that in 1931 nearly 89 percent of Berlin's stockholders were Jewish, offer a partial explanation of the rage of the Nazis.

The envy of the many poor and impoverished against the few old rich and the new rich created towards the close of the World War a general anti-capitalistic resentment. In order to stem this wave, which tended to point to dreaded Bolshevism, the leaders of the right soon recognized the necessity of transferring the general hatred against and jealousy of the rich into an anti-Semitic movement against the rich Jews.

The relatively large number of Jewish new rich, of Jewish war and inflation profiteers, rendered the desired transference on the part of reactionary, nationalistic groups, easy. A comparatively larger number of European giant fortunes are in the hands of Jews. As in past wars the majority of the army purveyors were Jews during the World War. All army purveyors of past and present wars had been without exception rich. Constituting a very small fraction of the total population, the Jews owned ten or more percent of the entire national wealth. Moreover, as a minority group they were successful in maintaining their economic leadership.

The deflection of the general hatred against capitalists and big industrialists upon the Jews was successful in spite of the fact that a series of facts argued against the anti-Semitic thesis. A considerable part of the blame for Germany's failure to stop the inflation before it got beyond all bounds must be placed on the industrial and commercial capitalists of the day, rather than on the government alone. The large-scale industrialists were the major beneficiaries from the progressive inflation. Havenstein, Hellferich, and Stinnes were the three men most responsible for the inflation, apart from the terrific pressure exerted by the Allies to force impossibly large payments of reparations. Hugo Stinnes, a Gentile, was the most prominent World War and inflation profiteer. Moreover, German industry was only to a small percentage in the hands of the Jews. The large estates were almost exclusively in the hands of the Gentiles. Then too, on the whole, the Jews had lost more as a result of the World War than they had gained.

But all these facts were deliberately ignored. The public is primarily guided by phrases and slogans, not by full-orbed information and logic. Hence the Jews as a group were simply identified with the war and inflation profiteers, the capitalists and smugglers. There is some truth in the Nazi charge that the Jews actually benefited from the inflation as it offered extraordinary opportunities for persons skillful in financial affairs. A well known Jewish financial writer admitted that the inflation had been very good business for all the Jewish owned banks. There was just enough truth in the Nazi accusations to prove that Hitler, in making them, was a master in the art of propaganda. He knew what the public needed before the public knew it. The speculators became rich; but, alas! many of them lost everything a little later. But no notice of this fact was taken. The discontented and impoverished masses were told that the Jew Hilferding was responsible for the inflation. A. Hugenberg, the arch nationalist, also one of the principal profiteers from the inflation, had the audacity to assert in 1931 that the inflation had been the result of Marxian and Jewish politics. The lightning rod had thus been found. The nationalistic press, which in part was in the possession of non-Jewish industry, deflected the popular hatred against the capitalists upon the banks, as the citadels of Jewish wealth. But it did not inform its readers that the banks are a necessary element in the capitalistic economy.

The economic difficulties of post-war Europe, which destroyed and drastically reduced the financial resources of millions of the middle classes, however, hit the Jews, with a relatively large number of individual exceptions, equally hard or harder than the non-Jews, because their capital was mainly invested in money values. It was particularly the small Jewish merchants who suffered a lot identical with the rest of the middle classes. It is a little known fact that the Jews are much more directly affected by the economic oscillations of international economy than the Gentiles, because they have a larger interest in those branches of business which are particularly exposed to large price oscillations and frequent market crises in the grain, fur, metal, jewelry, pearl, stock and bond trades, and because the mail order houses, chain and department stores have come to a large extent into their control, since the Jews were the first to introduce them in many countries, improving their organization, and thus revolutionizing retail trade.

In the field of public ethics the belated German Republic, like all other countries after the close of the World War, registered a terrific slump, which it however did not create. Public life in pre-war Germany had been indeed remarkably free from crass corruption. The seeds of speculation were planted during the war. The public morals collapsed entirely when, under the blockade of food, rations ran thin and hunger became general. There occurred an excessive number of scandals, involving high officials and millions of dollars. Most of the criminals were Gentiles. The gigantic swindles of a dozen or so Jews, largely of Eastern European origin, furnished the Nazis with fresh anti-Semitic material that brought them thousands of young and receptive recruits. The older generation of the lower middle class could not understand. The Germany of their youth had been so excessively strict and *fromm* that the pendulum inevitably swung too far the other way. They looked to Hitler, a vegetarian, a tee-totaler, a non-smoker, and as far as one could see, a man who has no fun of any kind, to save Germany's morals. Hitler, the legend grew, was going to lead the nation back to a simpler and saner life, and to put an end to *Kultur Bolschewismus*, which filled the bookshops with erotic literature. And since the great majority of doctors were Jews, the middle class readily believed that the Jews were trying to contaminate the moral health of their children.

It is quite true that under the new regime of post-war Germany Jews had come into prominence. They had been the acknowledged leaders of the socialistic parties before the outbreak of the war, and thus inevitably quite a number of them rose to political leadership, both in the federal and provincial governmental departments of the Republic. Until about 1930 their numbers in the leading positions of the civil service seemed on the increase. The civil officials, it must be remembered, comprise a far greater proportion of the population in Germany than in any other country of the world, with the exception of Soviet Russia. It includes all state and local officials as well as those directly under the central government. Nearly all hospitals, all schools and universities are public; the banks and railroads are state-controlled. The Jewish professionals, however, won their places fairly in competition with the non-Jews. It was an understandable clannishness which brought it about that large and important services came almost entirely into Jewish hands, because the chiefs chose their assistants from among young Jews. This control of positions by the Jews was in part due to the fact that the Jew had at last a chance to favor his own people, and used it imprudently. But the leading men in the government were not Jews. Some of the most outstanding among them were murdered within the first two years of the Republic.

The reason so many Jews rose to commanding position[s] during the fourteen years of the Weimar Republic is that the Jews were among her staunchest supporters. Moreover, the long tradition of anti-Semitism, which was semi-official before 1918, had developed among the Jews a solidarity which led to some job favoritism. In business, too, the democratic liberation stressed an international outlook so essential to the recovery of post-war Germany. The Jews, cosmopolitan by contact and tradition, thus often took precedence over the nationalistic financier and industrialist. However, the largest proportion of the Jews still found its way into commerce and industry, although many more than formerly entered the public administration.

Then, too, the Jews had invaded the professions in ever increasing numbers in post-war Germany, thus intensifying their struggle for existence and that of their Gentile fellow professionals. The Nazi charge that in medicine, law, the press, music, art, the theater, education, banking, in retail and wholesale trade, the Jews occupied a position completely out of proportion to the ratio of the Jewish population was statistically true. The fact that the majority of the Jews were massed in the professional fields in the large urban centers is ample proof that they were financially better off than the non-Jews, enabling them to send their children to pursue studies at the universities and technical schools.

During the period of economic depression, as unemployment rose on a fantastic scale, professional competition assumed unheard of proportions. The Gentile middle class, having been hit severely by the economic catastrophes of the post-war period, felt that the disproportionate number of Jewish professionals must be drastically reduced if they, as well as their cherished traditional status, were to survive. Hence, to satisfy the large number of unemployed academically trained professionals and the lower middle class, the Hitler regime, as promised, eliminated "Jewish influence" from all phases of German life. The most important measure concerning the Jews which has been enacted by the Hitler regime has been the law for the "restoration of the professional civil service," going into effect April 7, 1933. The decree applies to the regular civil servants, to the employees in semi-public enterprises, to employees in the social services, to judges, all court officials, notaries, teachers and professors, members of the old and the new army, the police forces of the state, including officers, army doctors and veterinarians, to elected municipal officials, office employees and workers in public enterprises.

As there were too many Jewish professors, a *numerus clausus* became the obvious means of purging the universities. Besides, the overfilling of the universities and of the academic labor market had reached an extent out of all proportion to the economic strength of the vocational world. Where the Aryan paragraph did not apply directly to the university professors and to the teachers in other schools, the provisions in regard to political unreliability were often invoked. In the middle of April, 1933, the university professors known to have been dismissed by the Nazis numbered about 125, and a month later the number was estimated to be twice as large.

The thoroughness with which the Nazis have acted in economic life is not quite so marked as in the professions. While the measures taken in regard to business have been far-reaching, there are some indications that concern over the grave economic situation has tempered Nazi ardor to cleanse business, a tacit acknowledgment of the Jewish business acumen. If a Jew is a powerful banker or broker his race is forgiven him. On September 27, 1933, Dr. Kurt Schmitt, Minister of Economics, and some months ago Dr. H. Schacht, his successor, declared emphatically that discrimination between Aryan and non-Aryan business establishments hampered economic recovery and should therefore be discountenanced.

Since Easter, 1933, the number of Jews admitted to the higher institutions of learning has been drastically restricted. In order to equalize the percentage of Jews in the professions with their percentage in the total population, the law stipulates that the maximum percentage of Jews allowed to enter college and university is to be 1.5 percent of all resident Jews in the Reich.

The strength of anti-Semitism depends to no small degree upon whether economic conditions in the various countries advance or retrogress. The more a country advances economically, the more anti-Semitism decreases in intensity. The more a country declines economically, the more anti-Semitism grows. It is always in times of political and economic upheaval that it reaches its height. Anti-Semitism is weakest where the number of Jews is small, where their economic competition is less felt, where equality of Jews has been in operation for generations, and where Jews no longer appear as parvenus, as has been the case in England, Italy, and the Scandinavian countries.

Probably the most positive achievement emerging out of the suffering of the Jews during the last two years of Nazi rule, is that they and their fellow-Jews the world over have become painfully aware of the weakness of their economic position. Jewish economy has always been the most vulnerable point in Jewish life and the one most exposed to the furies of anti-Semitism. Always after a violent outburst of anti-Semitism, the most advanced Jewish thinkers have looked to their economy as the point that needed most defense.

The fatal weakness of Jewish economy is tied up with a non-productive social class. Western European Jews have made trading, shop-keeping, finance, and the professions their chief occupations, and the middle class their mainstay. In other words, they had chosen the weakest positions in the capitalistic system, the identical positions which persecution and discrimination had forced upon them before the emancipation. As seen in perspective, the Jews failed singularly in the field of economic assimilation, while they mixed very eagerly and very successfully in the cultural, social, and religious spheres. They assimilated at the top, but not at the bottom. They embraced the culture of their neighbors most thoroughly, but retained their own economy. They intermarried largely with the higher social classes, but failed to mingle with the people. It is not at all improbable that if the Jewish economic assimilation were as thorough as the cultural; if half the Jews in Germany were engaged in factories and on the land instead of in business; if instead of practically every aristocratic family having Jewish blood in it, this blood had mingled with the laboring people, there would have been no anti-Jewish campaign in Germany, and there would have been no Jewish problem at all as recent experience in Soviet Russia leads us to believe. At any rate, the anti-Jewish feeling would not have been so intense and bitter as it now is.

It is now evident that the Jewish trouble in Germany is primarily economic in origin. The Nazi clamor of Nordic superiority is merely a pseudo-scientific subterfuge and camouflage of the economic causes. The ludicrous "grandmother" theory of racial superiority will disappear under the continued contempt and ridicule of enlightened world opinion. It would not have had a chance if it had not been backed by the valid facts of the abnormal economic position of German Jewry, as revealed by their preponderance in business and trading, and in the medical and legal professions. In spite of the valid apologies that are made for such a situation and in spite of the correct explanation of its origin, the fact remains that until 1925 as many as 49.3 percent of all Jews in Germany were engaged in trading, finance, in exchange of things instead of the production of them.

Both philo-Semites and anti-Semites agree on this, while they interpret it from their respective biases. From the point of view of the relative values of exchange and production in modern society, the trader lives on the producer, the shop-keeper and financier are at the present stage of industry the least productive, and they are in all possibility the most parasitic elements of society. Now if a people engages in these occupations to the practical exclusion of all other forms of work, if a people who do so manage on the whole to live better than the average working population around them—exemplifying Veblen's theory of "conspicuous consumption,"—if they dress better, occupy better homes, ride in motor cars and take up the best seats in the theaters, cafes and cabarets, and have the greater comforts of life, the outburst of antipathy is, to say the least, understandable. It is an easy and comparatively small matter for the whole civilized world to denounce and disprove the psychopathic Nazi theories of mythological Aryanism and the vile persecution of the Jews based upon racialism, but it has been very difficult to condemn completely the Nazi acts directed against the eccentricities of the Jewish economic positions in

Germany.

Progressive Jewish leadership has sought to remedy this root evil for the last half century. The Jewish colonization schemes in Russia, Argentina, Palestine, and the United States were so many efforts to alter the entire Jewish economy in the direction the dynamic element of the anti-Semitic groups and movements pointed to. The weakness of these experiments was that they were exclusively confined to the Jewish proletarian masses of Eastern Europe. The Western Jews supported them financially. It never dawned in their minds that they, too, were in need of a similar economic revolution, that it would be well for them to change their trading and professions to agriculture and industry. They felt they were secure in the economic positions they now occupied. But the ferocious anti-Jewish outbreak in Nazi Germany has made them very conscious of the radical need of an economic revolution. The sadistic brutality of the anti-Jewish antipathy of the Nazi regime, the uncanny depth of anti-Jewish feeling which they revealed, and the speed with which the achievements of a century and a half of Jewish emancipation have been swept aside, have wrought a revolution in their thought and social life, the same type of revolution which the Czarist pogroms ushered in among Russian Jews.

A new movement has sprung up among German Jews today. It is prosaically termed *Berufs Umschichtung* (occupational change). It is by far the most constructive Jewish answer to Nazi violence. It ought to prove to be the greatest compensation to the Jews for the griefs and disappointments of the last two years. The new movement consists of a deliberate group effort on the part of Jews to abandon their former occupations and professions, and adopt more productive, even if simpler means of earning a living. Hundreds of former Jewish lawyers, physicians, dentists, and notaries are training to become mechanics, builders, plumbers, and electricians; former shop-keepers, traders, and peddlers are learning to be bricklayers, carpenters, chauffeurs, and similar workers.

Because of its group character, because it is the outcome of national suffering, this movement is accompanied by profound emotional changes and a new vision of the Jewish position in the world that is tantamount to a profound mental revolution. The vision has come with the suddenness of a revelation. It is not a species of Zionism as the movement proceeds on the assumption that the home of the Jews is not Palestine, but in those countries where they live. Zionism was a solution of the Jewish problem on the part of the Eastern European Jews. The Jews in Germany are evolving another solution of the Jewish problem.

The new movement in solving the economic basis of the Jewish problem is already crossing the frontiers of Nazi Germany, and is penetrating the Jewish communities of Europe and America. The Anglo-Jewish *Chronicle* of Great Britain has launched a crusade against "the disorderly mob-attack of Jewish youth upon the professions."

The importance of this new manifestation or reaction to the Nazi revolt against the Jews can easily be exaggerated. This new movement does not by itself solve the Jewish problem. There are evidences that as the movement stands at present in Nazi Germany and other countries it is doomed to fail as it failed in the Argentine and Palestine.

The Nazi government being primarily a retrogressive, counter-revolutionary social force, medievalistic in mentality, its presumptive solution of the Jewish problem is sterile. Instead of driving the Jew forward, to new and progressive economic forms, they are driving him back to his old occupations of the Middle Ages. This means the perpetuation of the Jews in business, finance, and in a few professions. The basis for this deliberate Nazi policy is a misconception of Jewish mentality. If the Nazi[s] were a progressive, revolutionary force, they could have transformed Jewish life in Germany as thoroughly and constructively as it has been done in Soviet Russia.

The Nazi treatment of the Jews discloses a strangely perverse policy. It has been a policy of stern suppression of everything socially useful and productive in Jewish life. But what is worse, it has apparently been a policy of tolerance toward everything which is economically productive and socially parasitic in Jewry. While Jewish professional workers and employees have been ruthlessly dismissed from their positions and deprived of every means of livelihood, Jewish business has been less molested. And this is particularly true of Jewish bankers and financiers. The Jews have been excluded from every kind of creative work, in the arts, science, the professions and even in manual work; but they have, in many instances, been permitted to remain in business. Especially the bigger Jewish business men have suffered least from Nazi anti-Semitism.

The Nazi policy regarding the Jews is in keeping with their philosophy of a return to the medieval forms of life. In the medieval world the Jew was occupied as a trader and money lender. Hence the new movement of the Jews toward humbler, productive economic occupations runs counter to Nazi views, and is thus doomed to abject failure unless the power of the Nazis is broken by a socialistic revolt. In fact, the new occupational change among German Jews is already encountering all sorts of official suppressions and prohibitions. Jewish youth is prohibited from working on farms or as skilled workers. Hence the Jewish societies are sending their lads to training centers in Poland, Lithuania, and other foreign countries.

The Soviet Union is the only country where the experiment of changing the Jewish economy from trading to production has succeeded. In the seventeen years since the Revolution, 350,000 Jews, out of a Jewish population of a little over two and a half millions, have settled on the land; about a half million are in factories, workshops, heavy industries. Jewish trading has been completely abolished and the rush into the commercialized professions stopped. Once one of the most anti-Semitic countries, Russia is now practically free from that scourge. Jews, like their fellow-Russians, may endure many hardships, but they are, for the first time in their history, free from that particular handicap and suffering which has always been their lot because they are Jews, and which is the core of the Jewish problem. The Soviet regime must be given credit for having evolved a solution of the Jewish problem.

The occupational aspirations and ambitions of the Jews in Russia have changed as have their occupations. Gone is the famous urge for business, the restless search to excel in trading, the pathological desire of the parent to bring up his offspring as a doctor or lawyer. At the higher schools the Jews study chiefly mechanics and engineering. They are attaining the reputation of being the best factory workers.

The Jews are susceptible to the influence and example of the society in which they live. Because they lived for centuries as a threatened minority in the midst of a hostile majority, they have developed an unusual adaptability to the wishes and desires of the majority. The tendency to emulate the ruling majority is a typical Jewish trait. They thus make the best nationalists in Germany, the greatest liberals in England, the most pronounced Babbitts in the United States, and the most ardent communists in Russia.

The Jewish problem can be solved only in conjunction with the larger social and economic problem of the world. Western European Jews are realizing that their former exclusive association with the middle class is no longer possible. Political and economic pressures forced them largely to abandon their present occupations and to make new economic adjustments and affiliations. The golden age of Jewish liberalism is passed. They either will be driven back, as in Nazi Germany, to the medieval ghetto, economically, and to the greatest isolation in its history, or forward, as in Russia, to a social and economic equality, such as they have never yet known.

Nazism leaves the Jew no choice today but to seek the solution of his problem according to the model of Soviet Russia. He must work for a revolutionary economic reconstruction of his own and that of the general society around him. This is his new destiny from which there is no escape except in becoming a pariah people, a new class of European untouchables. Just as the dying Czarist regime staved off imminent collapse in 1903 by organizing ferocious Jewish pogroms, the effect of which was that the entire Jewish people threw itself wholeheartedly into the revolutionary movement, the results of which were momentous for the Russian Revolution, so the anti-Jewish hatred of Nazi Germany will have a similar effect in the history of the future. Its results will be probably still greater and more comprehensive. It will do away with the scourge of anti-Semitism that has plagued the race for milleniums.

THE JEWS
IN POLAND

by Israel Cohen

[Nazi-style anti-Semitism did not stop at the German border, and in this December 1936 article Israel Cohen described two forms of Jew hatred which were causing increasing misery for Polish Jewry. The first, supported by the government, was the attempt to destroy Jewish economic life; the second was the increasing physical attacks and calls for greater legal disabilities that came from the Polish fascists in imitation of the German methods. Cohen wrote to remind the West that anti-Semitism was not merely a problem in Germany. It was spreading to infect much of Central and Eastern Europe.

Cohen's solution to hatred of the Jews was no longer the revitalization of the Minorities Treaties, as it had been in 1929. He now believed that Polish Jewry must leave Europe, and he appealed to Britain to open the gates of Palestine wide to receive them. Cohen reflected the growing tension and fear that surrounded the Jewish Question in the late 1930s.]

"The Jews in Poland" by Israel Cohen, first published in *Contemporary Review*, 150 (December 1936), 716-23.

The calamity that has overtaken the Jews in Germany has served to divert attention from their sufferings in other countries of Central and Eastern Europe, but the campaign of terrorism in Poland to which they have been subjected during the last seven or eight months has now assumed as alarming a character as the Nazi persecution itself. Week after week, and almost day after day, since last September, brutal attacks have been made upon the Jews in some part or other of Poland, in which many have been killed and still more injured. In outward character they are reminiscent of the outrages committed by the Nazis against the Jews for some years before Hitler came into power: Jews whose only offence consists in being Jews are assailed with clubs, knives, and pistols; their houses and shops are raided and demolished, their synagogues are stoned and even bombed.

The lawlessness of which the Jews have become such helpless victims recalls the outburst of anti-Jewish hostility that marked the birth of the Polish Republic. It was because of that outbreak of anti-Semitic savagery which lasted from the end of the war until the middle of 1929 [1919 is the date intended here.—Ed.] that the Allied Powers insisted upon Poland signing a Minorities Treaty that would safeguard the lives and rights of her Jewish subjects as well as those of her other racial or national minorities. Now that seventeen years have passed, it is depressing to have to record that the Treaty has been hallowed more in the breach than in the observance, and to note that its systematic infraction has served as a prelude to the present epidemic of Jew-baiting. A survey of the wrongs that the Jews have long suffered in the political, economic, and intellectual spheres will make it possible to appreciate all the more deeply the culminating tragedy that has now befallen them.

Their fundamental grievance consists in their distressing and increasing impoverishment, for which they hold the Government largely responsible. According to the letter of the law there is no discrimination against them whatsoever. But unfortunately the facts of the situation show that the wretched position of the Jew is largely due to enactments deliberately though not avowedly aimed at them and to discrimination exercised by every branch of the administration. They form only a tenth of the total population, numbering about 3,250,000, but in consequence of Poland's fiscal system, they provide about twenty percent of the revenue; for the urban population, although only a fourth of the total population, furnish over half of the revenue, and the Jews, who form a third of the urban population, are invariably assessed at a higher rate than their Gentile neighbours.

Wherever the Government is able to interfere in economic life, it exercises its influence to the advantage of the Polish element. The Jews have been systematically driven out of the various State monopolies, such as tobacco, salt and matches, in which very large numbers of them were formerly employed. Before the war about ninety-five percent of the tobacco workers in Bialystok, Grodno, Vilna and Warsaw were Jews; but today all the factories are under Government control and Jews are excluded. They are discriminated against in regard to the grant of concessions and licences, and the few Jewish concerns that have been fortunate enough to have dealings with the Government are afraid to employ Jews lest their Jewishness become pronounced and prove a liability. Those who need credit for business purposes are unable to obtain it, or only to an insignificant extent, from the two Government banks, which follow a much more generous policy in regard to the applications of non-Jewish individuals and co-operatives. In the industrial sphere the position of the Jew has been seriously handicapped by a law that requires master artisans, who are alone able to take apprentices, to pass examinations not only in their trade but also in Polish history, literature, and geography, and to travel to a particular centre for the purpose of the ordeal—an enactment which presses heavily even upon the most expert Jewish craftsman of many years' standing and diminishes the opportunities of the younger generation to engage in manual occupations. Training for manual vocations in technical schools is also rendered difficult by official restrictions. In the Government technical schools Jews form only five percent of the pupils, and in the municipal establishments as few as two percent. The Jews have therefore been obliged to establish their own technical schools, of which they have thirty-four, but they receive only about one percent of the grants given by the Government to such institutions, although the fund from which the grants are allotted is largely derived from a supplementary tax paid by Jews in addition to their trade licences.

A similar policy of discrimination prevails in all the Universities, where a *numerus clausus* is enforced against them, although it is not officially admitted. The limitation is imposed most rigorously at the medical faculties, which Jewish students are most eager to enter in order to acquire a profession that may provide them with a livelihood; they are less keen about entering the faculties for arts and philosophy, where civil servants and teachers are trained, as they are excluded from all branches of Government employment, including the schools. In the legal profession, too, their path is obstructed, as a student before qualification must have three years' practice in a clerical capacity in a law court, positions to which few Jews are appointed. The result is that a very large number of Jewish students are compelled to wander forth into other lands in search of higher education at more hospitable universities. The number of such exiles is estimated at ten thousand, and they are dispersed in France, Belgium, Italy, Czechoslovakia and other countries. Most of them are students of medicine, but when they return home with their degrees they are obliged to sit for fresh examinations before being allowed to practise.

Whatever explanations the Government may offer in extenuation of the anti-Jewish policy pursued in the aforementioned spheres of activity, it can hardly plead freedom from responsibility for excluding Jews from its own employment. When Galicia belonged to Austria, Jews in the railway service formed eight to nine percent, in the postal service seven to eight percent, and in the State schools, as teachers, four to five percent. But now, in all these branches, they hardly make up one percent, and even this consists of survivals of former times. No Jewish teacher can obtain a post in a Polish school, and Polish teachers' seminaries have for some years refused to admit Jewish students. In the administrative departments of the Government there is hardly a single Jew, and no new Jewish officials are appointed. There are ten thousand Post Office savings banks in the country, which derive sixty percent of their deposits from Jews, but there is not a single Jewish official among them all.

According to the Minorities Treaty the Jews are to receive "an equitable share" of the State funds available for educational, religious, and charitable purposes. But, although they form a tenth of the population, the total amount which they receive for all purposes is only 200,000 *zloty* out of a budget of three milliard [billion] *zloty*. On the other hand, the position of the Jews in various municipalities has been weakened through the inclusion of suburban areas: they cannot obtain employment in the municipal service nor are they granted contracts. Their numbers in the Seym [Parliament] have been reduced to insignificance. Once they had thirty-six members in the Polish Parliament, but now, in consequence of the electoral reform, they are limited to five. Their diminished representation is a reflection of their political impotence, and this is even surpassed by their economic misery.

Their poverty is due not only to the variety of causes already described, but also to other important factors. The spread of consumers' co-operative societies, especially among the Ukrainians in Galicia, has had a ruinous effect upon thousands of Jewish tradespeople; and equally disastrous will be the consequences of the recent passing of a law that has limited the slaughtering of cattle by the Jewish ritual method to the actual requirements of the Jewish population. Previously that method was regularly practised for the slaying of all cattle in a large number of towns, and it provided a source of livelihood for some forty thousand Jews (slaughterers, butchers and assistants), but now more than half of them will be thrown out of employment. And to add to their distress and their galling provocation, Jews engaged in any form of trade are the victims of recurring boycotts.

Even ten years ago it was estimated that there were one million Jews too many in Poland, owing to the numerous economic handicaps to which they are subjected. It is commonly accepted that one-third of the Jewish population is on the verge of starvation, one-third can just eke out a bare existence, and the rest have little but the minimum comfort. About 150,000 families are dependent on loans from the Jewish communal loan funds (largely created by means of relief funds supplied by Jewish philanthropic bodies of America and Great Britain), but although the amounts granted to each individual do not average more than a few shillings they are nevertheless applied for by one-half of the Jews in Warsaw, Lodz, and Bialystok, by over two-thirds in Vilna, and by similar large proportions in hundreds of other centres. Unfortunately the Jews do not receive any benefit from the Government fund for the unemployed, as the law does not provide for the relief of small artisans and traders. But helpful as the loan funds are, their resources are utterly inadequate to the tremendous needs. The result is that beggary is rampant throughout the country, suicide has spread among all classes, and many of the younger generation are driven by despair rather than conviction to the allurements of Communism. Before the war and in the first few years after the Peace, emigration provided an outlet for the natural increase, which amounted to fifty thousand a year. But now, owing to the anti-immigration restrictions of most countries, only about one-seventh of that number are able to leave each year in quest of a new home, and the great majority seek it in Palestine.

It is against this sombre background of cumulative misery and despair that there is now raging a violent campaign of the most brutal Jew-baiting. The present outbreak has been almost continuous since last September, but there were several outrages also during the early part of last year. It is generally acknowledged that those mainly responsible are the members of the two political parties, the *Endeks* (National Democrats) and the *Naras* (National Radicals), who constantly boast of their determination to drive the Jews out of Poland. That they have been incited by the example of Nazi Germany is unashamedly admitted. "Germany's success," wrote the *Gazeta Warszawska* (April 19th, 1935), "teaches us in Poland to adopt the same policy, which will force the Jews to organise their own mass emigration. We can do that only by making the Jews realise once and for all that there will be no stopping until not a single Jew is left in Poland." And in pursuance of this barbarous policy the same crude and savage methods have been adopted that were applied by Hitler and his henchmen for some years and enabled them to rise to power. The *Endeks* and the *Naras* are likewise striking at the Jews in order to discredit the Government and to replace it, and the unequal fight is such as to make one despair of civilisation. The campaign is fomented not only by the anti-Semitic newspapers previously in existence, but also by a large number of new journals that have been started in many towns, obviously with the help of foreign money, and all devoted to the propagation of the boycott and the pogrom.

As long as Marshal Pilsudski was alive any violent manifestation of anti-Semitism was promptly and vigorously suppressed, for he understood full well that such exhibitions of barbarism, besides being reprehensible in themselves, did serious damage to Poland's prestige abroad. But since the death of the dictator, the enemies of the Government have displayed increasing audacity and a ruthless determination to make life for the Jews in Poland impossible. To enumerate all the acts of violence that they have committed in recent months would entail a long and appalling record of savagery, which has broken out in nearly all parts of the Republic and is directed indiscriminately against all Jews, irrespective of age or sex. Knives and pistols, stones and clubs, iron bars and bombs, are the weapons that are commonly used in these attacks, which are aimed not only against Jewish lives and property, but also against synagogues and even cemeteries—exactly after the Nazi model. A selection of some typical incidents during the past twelve months, in chronological order, should suffice to illustrate the general character of this campaign of terrorism.

In Vilna a bomb was exploded beneath a synagogue. At Radomsk a Jew was stabbed to death. In Grodno there were repeated assaults upon Jews in the streets, from which three died. At Sokoly, near

Bialystok, a Jewish funeral party was stoned. At Chorzow (Polish Upper Silesia), eleven Jews were seriously injured by hydrochloric acid thrown upon them in a theatre. At Czenstochowa Jews were brutally beaten, and the windows of Jewish houses and shops were smashed. At Widzew, near Lodz, uniformed anti-Semites attacked Jewish shops and poured carbolic acid upon foodstuffs. At Rybnik Jewish shops were defaced with abusive inscriptions. At Pogon, near Sosnowice, a bomb was exploded near a synagogue, and a Jewish boy was killed. In Posen and Torun Jews were forcibly ejected from cafes. At Wongrowiec riots culminated in the burning down of the house of the president of the Jewish community. At Dabrowa, near Sosnowice, the synagogue was broken into by miscreants who desecrated the Ark of the Law, tore up the sacred scrolls, and carried off the silver ornaments. At Opoczno, Odrzywole, and Przysucha, near Kielee, anti-Jewish riots raged for two days, entailing police intervention, and resulting in forty Jews being injured by looting peasants, nine of whom were shot dead by the police. In Posen the Association of Restaurant Proprietors were compelled to sign an agreement with the *Endek* students to buy only from "Aryans" in order to ensure that the students would not smash their windows. Bombs were thrown into Jewish cafes in Kielee, into the courtyard and synagogue in Kattowitz and into a synagogue at Sosnowice, into Jewish houses at Lipiny and Hrubaczow, and into Jewish shops at Yusefow and Vilna. In Bialystok a young Jew was beaten by *Endeks* and had both his hands broken; in Lodz a Jew was burnt with acid, and in Kozienice two Jewish pedlars were murdered.

This is but a very brief and typical selection of the outrages of recent months, the victims of which so far number eighty Jews killed and about five hundred injured. Probably the worst case of vandalism was the pogrom on March 9th at Przytik (Radom district), where a carefully planned assault was made upon the small Jewish community: four Jews were killed or died of injuries and over fifty were seriously injured, and twenty-two persons were arrested, including five Jews accused of illegally organising their self-defence! At the trial, which took place in June, of forty-three Poles, eighteen, including those accused of murder, were acquitted, while the rest received sentences of imprisonment ranging from six to twelve months; on the other hand, of the Jews, who were guilty of nothing worse than self-defence, three were sentenced to terms of penal servitude ranging from five to eight years and eight to imprisonment from six to ten months. Comment upon this parody of justice is superfluous.

Throughout this period of terror the Polish students at the Universities have distinguished themselves by their savage attacks upon their Jewish fellow-students, whom they wish to drive away from the seats of learning. At Posen over twenty Jewish students have been injured. At the University in Lemberg one-tenth of the 2,200 Jewish students had been assaulted between last October and February, and of the 380 Jews at the Polytechnic over sixty had been seriously injured. Instead of punishing the culprits the Polytechnic authorities ordered the expulsion of seven Jews for signing a protest against the attacks and reproaching the authorities with failure to act, and although the expulsion was subsequently annulled the students were suspended for three terms. At the University of Cracow there have been similar rowdy scenes, and at the University and the Polytechnic in Warsaw the scandal has been so disgraceful as to necessitate the temporary closing of these institutions.

The Government have certainly been active in their attempts to suppress the reign of terror, but this is now so widespread as to baffle their efforts. The *Endek* party has been repeatedly dissolved in various districts, and raids have been made upon its offices in Warsaw, Lodz and Cracow, where inflammatory literature and even bombs have been seized. Nevertheless, these Polish Nazis, after poisoning the population of Western and Central Poland, have spread their agitation to Volhynia, Polesia, and other localities in Eastern Poland, inciting the White Russian peasants, and offering prizes of anti-Semitic calendars and books for every ten members who join their movement. Hundreds of the perpetrators of the outrages have been arrested and tried, but unfortunately they form but a fraction of the large number who are guilty, and the sentences imposed are not drastic enough to have a deterrent effect.

The members of the Government are fully conscious both of the real motives of the Jew-baiters and of the disgrace they are bringing upon their country. M. Raczkiewicz, Minister of the Interior, speaking in the Seym on March 6th, made a vigorous attack upon the *Endeks*, asserting that "anti-Semitism is only a means in the hands of the *Endeks*, through which they desire to obtain power in the country." A fortnight later, after the pogrom at Przytik, Prince Radziwill, speaking in the Senate, declared that both as a politician and a Christian he must denounce the *Endek* activity and their Jew-baiting, and Count Rostworowski appealed particularly to the Catholic clergy "to use their influence and authority and try to quell the wave of hatred and strife that is sapping the life of the nation." It would be futile for the Jews to appeal to the League of Nations, for Poland has officially repudiated its right to intervene. They can but hope that the Polish Government will summon sufficient courage to adopt still more rigorous measures to stamp out an evil that is quickly degrading their country to the cultural level of that of their Nazi neighbours. And the persistent gravity of their position serves but to emphasise the necessity of widening for them the portals of the only land where they have been officially declared to be "as of right, and not on sufferance" —the land of the Jewish National Home.

ANTI-SEMITISM IN EUROPE

by Herbert J. Seligmann

[Like Israel Cohen, Herbert Seligmann saw anti-Semitism spreading throughout Europe. He believed that this growth was a deliberate German plan to use anti-Semitism for military and political purposes. Seligmann detailed the position of Jews in most European states, and wrote that in many cases Jewish life was sustained only by aid from Jews in the United States. The motive behind the German campaign to spread anti-Semitism was based on neither economics nor race. Instead, the Germans hoped to use the hatred of Jews as a means to unify the German people for war, gain influence with potential allies of Germany, and divide states that were potential enemies of the Nazi state. Seligmann, writing in 1936, believed that the appeal of anti-Semitism was so great that the scheme showed every sign of success.]

"Anti-Semitism in Europe" by Herbert J. Seligmann, first published in *New Republic*, 89 (30 December 1936), 265-68. Reproduced by permission of *New Republic*.

Modern hatred of Jews, as erected into a program of expropriation and eventually of extermination, centers in Germany. Nazi Germany is the only nation in the world having specifically anti-Jewish laws on its statute books. As James G. McDonald wrote in his now famous letter of resignation as High Commissioner for Refugees, the program of the Nazi government is "designed to reduce 'non-Aryans' to a condition of impoverished unemployment and to take away from them the most elementary civil and political rights."

The motivation of the German anti-Semitic program is now clear. At a time when Germany was in no position to challenge the Treaty of Versailles or to antagonize any foreign power, the program of internal organization for war, with the lowering of living standards dependent on such a program, called for regimentation against the enemy. This is always the means of stilling criticism and of imposing absolute uniformity on a nation.

The Jews, upon the accession of the Hitler regime forming less than one percent of the German population, furnished such an "enemy," a defenseless group against whom traditional slanders could be employed to rouse passionate hatred. The history of what has since occurred is familiar to the world. The Jews became the helpless instrument for uniting the German nation in a compact fighting mass, organized primarily for war, and fortified by spurious doctrines of "race" and "blood" which overcompensated for the feeling of inferiority and impotence of a defeated people unable to retaliate against their victorious adversaries.

The Nazi program is a symbolic projection upon the future of nationalist programs directed at all dissenting minorities. Its ramifications include the entire range of human activity, economy, the arts and sciences and military politics. In the field of economics the New Economic Anti-Semitism offers a plausible if spurious solution for the disintegration consequent on rearranged frontiers and tariff, currency and trade barriers. The compact "racial" group is to receive the spoils derived from expropriating and driving out of remunerative occupations the designated internal "enemy." This program is to be fortified by "cultural" and social exclusions and, as a necessary adjunct, the progress of scientific thought must be submitted to the Procrustean regimentation necessary to the new "racial truth." Abstract truth ceases to be valid as a goal and its methodology is to be discarded.

The military-political scheme upon which the fortification and extension of this program depend involves the entire civilized world. For the doctrine underlying the program forms a means of penetrating those nations which may be necessary as military allies, and of dividing and undermining the mutual interdependence of those nations whose opposition is to be feared. Hence, the reputedly enormous sums being spent by Nazi Germany for anti-Jewish propaganda not only in the strategically important countries of Eastern Europe but in England, France, Belgium, South America, South Africa and the United States.

That the fears of a large part of the European world center in the power of Russia has been made a useful auxiliary to the Nazi program. If, on the one hand, Jews are accused as capitalists and "international bankers," on the other, they are linked with Moscow. Nazi propaganda moves in both directions, counting upon the credulity and ignorance of economically depressed populations and the absence of critical intelligence among all masses of people.

An examination of the economic circumstances of multitudes of Jews in lands where this propaganda is most active will quickly demonstrate the tragic absurdity of the claims of Jewish "menace" or "domination." In Poland, for example, where I was reliably informed last summer that fifty-two of the fifty-four daily newspapers were anti-Semitic, and where nationalist boycott has led to increasing sporadic outbreaks of violence, the Jews form something less than ten percent of the population. The peasants are poor. But the Jews are still worse off. The Jews are predominantly an urban population. They are the marginal traders and dealers and workers. Their position, the consequence of former legal exclusion from agriculture, is now further depressed by the state organization of industry and their exclusion from employment in all government work or state monopolies.

A commonly accepted figure designates more than one million of the three million Jews in Poland as subject to slow starvation. The professional classes are little, if any, better situated than the small traders and artisans. And all groups live on a scale which, though culturally intense, can be compared on the economic side only with that of the most miserable of sharecroppers in our Southern states.

To preach, as the nationalists do, either that Jews are a "menace" or that the agrarian problems of the country can be solved by having nine million peasants crowd into the marginal positions now occupied by three million Jews, most of them miserably poor, is only part of the *reductio ad absurdum* of the extreme nationalist-anti-Semitic position in Eastern Europe.

In fact, were it not for the aid consistently and generously extended chiefly from America, since the terrible post-war years of anarchy and demoralization, by the Joint Distribution Committee— aid similar to that extended in Belgium, in Russia during the famine years, in the Near East—most of the Jewish institutions in Poland either could not have been reconstituted from the wreckage of war or would since then have had their activities curtailed, if not stopped altogether.

A similar tragic absurdity characterizes the situation in Rumania. Rumania provides two kinds of material of which Germany, in the event of war, would be in especial need. These products are, first, grain and fodder and, second, fuel in the form of oil. The political orientation of Rumania in the direction of the Nazi international program could be accelerated in two ways. First, it would be useful for this purpose to implant a general fear of democracy as tending toward communism. Second, it would be vital thoroughly to indoctrinate the entire population with fear and hatred of Jewish influence. Both means have been persistently and aggressively employed.

In Rumanian universities, as one close observer put it, the *numerus clausus* has become the *numerus nullus*. The propaganda of Professor Alexander Cuza, whose Cuzists parallel the Nazis in Germany and the Endeks in Poland, goes so far as openly to urge the extermination of Jews. The consequences of it have been attacks upon Jewish passengers in Rumanian railway trains, some of them resulting in the throwing of these passengers bodily from the railway cars while they are in motion; brutal assaults upon Jews in broad daylight in the parks of Bucharest, Chisinau and other cities; and a state of tension, punctuated by physical attack, which makes the safety and the lives of Jews precarious in many parts of Rumania, as they are in Galicia and other parts of Poland.

That there is nothing inherently necessary or inevitable in this condition of affairs I had ample opportunity to observe in those regions where the propaganda had not yet become virulently active. In a number of rural communities I saw Jews and non-Jews riding together on the roads in horse-drawn carts, working together in the fields and living in amity as neighbors. But always the Jew knew well that these relationships might be interrupted and quickly destroyed if the aggressive, persistent and well financed anti-Jewish propaganda entered the community.

Here again it is not the economic power and strength but rather the poverty and helplessness of the Jews which subject them to this warfare. No peasantry in the world, save perhaps in the Far East, is more desperately impoverished than the Jews of Bessarabia, and in fact of all northern Rumania. The same actual physical warfare conducted against the Jews of Poland goes on too against the Jews of Rumania. It is definitely part of the Nazi sphere of influence and here too it is only to the Joint Distribution Committee in America that these victims have been able to look for help.

In Austria, one consideration is uppermost in the minds of liberal observers, and that is the question of closer relations with Germany. Everyone knows that should Anschluss [union] occur, the fate of Austrian Jews would be sealed as has been the fate of Jews in the Ruhr and in Danzig. Already the concentration of all but a fraction of Austria's Jews in Vienna, the impoverishment and degradation of the professional classes and the pressure upon the merchants have created a situation in which the maintenance of Jewish community life and institutions becomes increasingly difficult. Thus the mechanics of European anti-Semitism operate to starve and degrade those Jews who are most helpless, making their plight a claim upon the humanity of the civilized world, and particularly of their fellow Jews in lands of tolerance and freedom.

Elsewhere in Europe, however bitter may be the anti-Semitic movements, however rigorous the individual acts of discrimination, the social problems of the Jews remain their own, they sustain their community activities and their institutions without appeal to or help from the outside world.

Everywhere fascist activity shows the same characteristics. In England, Mosley, who began his career as a fascist with protestations that no hatred of the Jews was involved, has made anti-Semitism the basis of his entire program. His projected East End parade in London was direct provocation designed to bring this issue to the forefront. And it has brought charges that his program has been receiving financial aid "from abroad." In the other partially or fully democratic lands, including the United States, the flood of German-financed scurrilous defamation of Jews has always a clearly defined military-political objective. This is true of the Croix de Feu of France, the Rexist movement in Belgium, of similar movements in Switzerland

and Holland. Even in Italy, hitherto exempted from anti-Semitism by reason of its small Jewish population and the distinguished service of Jews to the State, closer ties with Germany have resulted in anti-Jewish manifestations.

The tendency is one which no free people can afford to ignore. It involves minorities and principles of which, for the present, the Jews are merely agonized protagonists. As such, their fate represents a barometer of what may be expected for everything that we have been accustomed to rate and to call civilization.

The Position of the Jews in Europe[1]

Country	General Population	Jewish Population	Economic and Social Situation of Jews Restrictions on Jews
Germany	66,044,161	400,000	Germany is the only country in which Jews are discriminated against by a body of law which specifically names them. Jews are held to be not part of the "German community" and therefore have neither civil nor political rights. Boycott and exclusion of Jews from education and professions, arts, and increasingly from every employment in commerce and industry, is part of the official government program. It is the expressed intention of the government to extirpate the 400,000 Jews remaining in Germany and the laws, their judicial interpretation and execution, as well as extra-legal activity, are directed to this end. Half of the 400,000 remaining are workless, without any possibility of obtaining jobs. One in five of the entire group is esti-

mated to be on relief. Increasing exclusion and boycott can only rapidly worsen the catastrophic condition.

Austria	6,759,062	190,000	The phrase "gum-shoe" or "rubber-soled" anti-Semitism has been coined in Vienna to describe the quiet and outwardly polite exclusion of Jews from government and from semi-official employment. This exclusion applies to the professions as well as to commerce and industry.

Approximately 175,000 of the 190,000 Jews in Austria are concentrated in Vienna, where poverty is intense among professional and former middle-class as well as among working people.

Belgium	8,092,004	63,000	Jews enjoy full equality.

Rexist movement, like all fascism, has strong anti-Semitic tendencies.

Bulgaria	6,090,215	47,000	No official persecution against Jews in Bulgaria, although the government intervenes in Jewish community affairs, controlling Jewish schools and community budgets.

Strong anti-Semitic movement. Educational opportunities limited.

Czechoslovakia	14,729,536	380,000	Jews enjoy full freedom. No racial prejudices in government circles. Anti-

Semitic propaganda
checked by the law.

Anti-Semitic movements
affect earning power of
Jews, especially desper-
ately impoverished groups
in Sub-Carpathia.

Denmark	3,550,656	7,100	Jews enjoy full equality.
Estonia	1,126,383	4,500	No official discrimination. Jews still retain officially their cultural autonomy.
Finland	3,667,067	1,750	Jews enjoy full equality. Anti-Semitic propaganda punishable by law.
France	41,834,923	230,000	Jews enjoy full freedom and equality.

The fascist movement un-
der Colonel de la Rocque
has for the moment been
decisively checked by the
coalition supporting Pre-
mier Blum. Thousands of
German refugees in
France constitute a serious
problem.

Great Britain	46,178,884	340,000	Jews enjoy full freedom and equality.

A fascist movement under
Oswald Mosley directed
against Jews is meeting
strong opposition from
labor and from all liberal
forces in the nation.

Greece	6,204,684	98,000	Jews not officially dis-criminated against.

In recent years Jews have
been made a political foot-
ball, and have been beaten

physically. Anti-Semitism is an issue, though the Jews are strongly defended by public men and sections of the press.

Holland	8,392,102	115,000	Jews enjoy full freedom and equality. Propaganda of race hatred prohibited and punishable by the law.
			Because of the proximity of Germany, the refugee problem is urgent. There is a well defined anti-Semitic movement in Holland.
Hungary	8,688,349	440,000	The government does not interfere with anti-Semitic activities. Officially Jews are not persecuted.
			Anti-Semitism is strong. There is a definite *numerus clausus* in the universities.
Italy	41,176,671	52,000	No discrimination against Jews.
			Anti-Semitic utterances have become more frequent since the ties with Germany have been closer.
Jugoslavia	13,934,038	70,000	Nazi centers of anti-Jewish propaganda closed by the police.
			Strong anti-Semitism exists.
Latvia	1,900,045	97,000	Jews are excluded from the legal professions, although not by law.
			Anti-Semitism is strong in both Latvia and Lithua-

			nia. In both countries there is extreme poverty among the Jews.
Lithuania	2,340,038	177,500	All Jewish teachers' seminaries are to be closed. Jews are excluded from the professions. No official restrictions.
Norway	2,814,194	1,400	Jews enjoy full freedom and equality.
Poland	31,927,773	3,150,000	Increasing establishment of government sales monopolies—*e.g.*, matches, salt, chemicals, buses—in which Jews receive no employment; restriction of *schechita*, or kosher slaughtering, thereby depriving many Jews of this employment; sanitary regulations governing operation of bakeries, groceries and food stores enforced stringently against Jews; exclusion from schools and a rigid *numerus clausus* at universities.

Masses of Jews impoverished. Over a million are literally starving, two million others desperately struggling against overwhelming odds to sustain life. Boycott in some communities amounts almost to "hunger blockade," preventing even purchase of necessary food. The widespread economic war against Jews breaks out in sporadic acts of violence, even murder, in many localities.

Portugal	6,825,883	2,600	No discrimination.
Rumania	18,025,037	1,050,000	The *numerus clausus* approximating the *numerus nullus* in Rumanian universities. Government-controlled radio station, Radion, permits anti-Jewish broadcasts.
			Extreme poverty throughout northern Rumania, especially Bessarabia. Universal boycott accompanied by sporadic acts of violence is intensifying desperate condition of Jews throughout the land.
Sweden	6,141,571	7,200	Jews enjoy freedom and equality.
Switzerland	4,066,400	17,600	Jews enjoy freedom and equality.
			A well marked anti-Semitic movement has not gained power.

[1]These population figures are approximate only—in some instances estimates. In some countries there has been no recent census.

THE JEWISH PLIGHT IN EUROPE

by Israel Cohen

[In this 1938 article Israel Cohen made a rather desperate plea on behalf of Rumanian Jewry. His appeal to the Minorities Treaties of the League of Nations, which he had declared useless in 1936, reflected the degree of that desperation. Cohen traced the history of Rumanian hostility towards Jews, and saw in that history the seeds of the even more virulent anti-Semitism which had been bolstered by the success of Germany. Cohen wrote of a Jewish population under attack. He believed that Rumania's goal was to expel its Jewish community. His article was a further reminder that anti-Semitism in 1938 was a powerful political force which could not be equated with earlier outbreaks of hatred against Jews. As each year of the 1930s passed, the hatred became more intense and the solutions more radical.]

"The Jewish Plight in Europe," by Israel Cohen, first published in *Twentieth Century*, 123 (March 1938), 267-84.

The proclamation of their anti-Semitic policy with which the Government of Rumania under M. Goga inaugurated their regime did not denote any change in the attitude of that country towards its Jewish inhabitants. It represented but a further and reactionary development in its system of discrimination. In few countries of modern Europe have the Jews suffered oppression over as long a period or so continuously as in Rumania, and in few countries have official promises for the betterment of their conditions been so frequently and cynically broken. The solemn assurances extorted from time to time that justice will be done to the Jews have served to appease that section of the civilised world that still insists upon the practice of humanity by Governments, but within the confines of Rumania the old traditions of intolerance have steadily gathered increasing strength. The new decrees now threatened will, unless averted betimes, not only bring disaster upon the Jewish community in that country but also cause serious repercussions in other lands.

Rumania acquired her independence by the Berlin Treaty of 1878, which stipulated, among other matters, that differences of religious belief should not preclude anybody from the enjoyment of civil and political rights. The article embodying this condition was inserted in the Treaty because the Jews, although they had been settled in the country for over 1,500 years and had shed their blood in its defence, were treated as outlaws and subjected to continual persecution. The Berlin Congress had intended by means of this article to effect the complete emancipation of the Jews, but Rumania, while professing to accept this among the conditions of her independence, immediately declared all the Jews to be foreigners, whose status could be improved only by the laws pertaining to the naturalisation of foreigners. Thus were such astute statesmen as Disraeli and Bismarck, the directing spirits of the Congress, duped and defied, and the Jews were condemned to remain in their state of bondage. Down to the outbreak of the Great War scarcely three hundred native Jews altogether were admitted to the rights of citizenship, in each case by a vote of both Chambers of Parliament, while all other Jews continued to be treated as outlaws, harassed by a multiplicity of oppressive decrees.

During the Great War the position of the Jews became much worse, even though they fought for their step-mother country with singular bravery. Those who were at the front were treated like spies and enemies, while the Jewish population in general was subjected to deportations, false imprisonment, plundering, requisitions, extortionate fines, forced labour, and flogging. Hence when the war was over the opportunity was again seized to endeavour to deliver the Jews from their prolonged servitude, more especially as Rumania's Jewish population was now to be increased, through the annexation of territory from Austria, Hungary and Russia, from 241,000 to 851,000. Consequently the Rumanian Government was made to sign a Minorities Treaty similar to those signed by several other States in Central and Eastern Europe, which were designed to secure and safeguard the complete civil and political equality of religious and racial minorities. This Treaty finally swept aside the verbal quibbles by means of which the Jews had been denied their rights so long. It declared that "all persons born in Rumanian territory who are not born nationals of another State shall *ipso facto* become Rumanian nationals," a stipulation applying both to the annexed territories as well as to the whole of Old Rumania. In order not to allow any doubt to be raised as to whether the Jews were also included, there was inserted a special article, in concise and unambiguous terms: "Rumania undertakes to recognise as Rumanian nationals *ipso facto* and without the requirements of any formality Jews inhabiting any Rumanian territory who do not possess another nationality." These articles had been worded so circumspectly that it was deemed to be impossible for Rumania this time to wriggle out of her pledge. But the statesmen of the Western world had underestimated the resourcefulness of Rumanian statecraft, or rather craftiness.

By the terms of the Minorities Treaty all persons habitually domiciled in the country on the date when it was signed, September 4, 1920, were entitled to citizenship without further ado; but on February 23, 1924, a nationality law was passed which made the acquisition of citizenship subject to proof of ten years' continuous residence in the same place (known as *Heimatsrecht*) before December 1, 1918. Many Jews, owing to their compulsory migrations and the misfortunes of war, were unable to show this qualification and were thus condemned to being "Stateless," with all the handicaps and disabilities this status entails; on the other hand, those who were granted civic rights were liable to lose them upon the protest of a third party. At first a period of twenty days was allowed within which a protest could be lodged, after which the grant of citizenship held good; but on March 31, 1932, a further law was passed, extending the period for protest to thirty days.

The result of this Treaty violation is that in the Bukowina there are still about twenty thousand Jews who are "Stateless," besides many thousands in Bessarabia and Transylvania. But even this number was far too small for the anti-Semitic reactionaries, for in October 1936 they demanded that the Government should order a further revision of the grant of citizenship accorded to the minorities in the annexed provinces, on the ground that many persons had obtained it illegally. The Government refrained from seeking parliamentary authority for this inquisition, owing to representations that were made from foreign quarters against what would have been a manifest breach of the Minorities Treaty, but decided to achieve the same object by administrative decree. Accordingly, it was announced that the law of 1932 applied not merely to cases of naturalisation conferred after that date, but also to all that had been dealt with since 1924, and that consequently thirty days' grace would be allowed within which protests could be lodged against all applications that had been disposed of since the earlier date. In short, the Attorney-General had the right, without any parliamentary sanction, to rescind the citizenship of members of the minorities who had received it twelve years ago, in all cases in which he might deem the ground of protest to be valid. The inquisition was aimed at primarily, if not exclusively, against the Jews, and the result was that tens of thousands of protests have been lodged against the Jews in the Bukowina, and similar proceedings will follow in Transylvania and Bessarabia. Over four thousand persons, the great majority Jews, in Czernowitz had thus already been deprived of their citizenship before M. Goga came into power.

Even the majority of the Jews, whose citizenship cannot be impeached, have been made to realise daily that theirs is but a second-class citizenship. They are not allowed to hold positions in the Government or municipal services, though they are obliged to pay more than their due share of the income-tax revenue by which those services are mainly supported—a burden that presses with even greater injustice upon those who are "Stateless." There is no law sanctioning this discrimination, for that would be a flagrant violation of the Constitution and the Minorities Treaty, but it is the common administrative practice. Many a Jewish merchant and tradesman in Czernowitz, Cluj and Temesvar complained to me (in the course of a journey of inquiry) of the petty persecutions to which they are subjected by prying officials bent upon bribes. Bribery is the order of the day, practised from the highest circles to the lowest and prevailing throughout the country. On the other hand, the Jewish community is denied an equitable share, to which it is entitled, of the sum provided out of State funds for educational and religious purposes.

Nor is it only from the public service that Jews are excluded. They are equally barred from positions in the army, although they are obliged to discharge their military duties. They are largely represented in chambers of commerce and stock exchanges, but they are kept out of the governing councils. They may provide the bulk or even the whole of the capital of a limited company, but they are required by law to reserve a number of administrative posts for persons of Rumanian race. They cannot obtain credit from a Rumanian bank; and they have difficulty in obtaining the requisite facilities for importing goods and raw materials from abroad. Jewish landowners, like others, were expropriated through the Agrarian Reform of 1926, but the Jewish peasants, of whom there are a large number in the Bukowina, Transylvania and Bessarabia, have been denied their proportionate share of the expropriated lands.

Of all the forms of anti-Jewish persecution the most persistent and ruthless has been in connexion with the universities. Ever since the Rumanian students held their first Congress on December 10, 1922, for the purpose of demanding that the admission of Jews to the universities should be restricted to a small percentage, they have continued their violent agitation year after year. Every Government has resisted the demand for a law for a *numerus clausus*, as that would involve a gross infringement of the Minorities Treaty, but the universities have been allowed to impose such a limitation in practice. Nevertheless, the students continue their crusade, which is directed not only against students but against Jews in general. It takes the form of savage attacks with knuckle-dusters, knives, and even revolvers, upon students, both men and women, in the universities; of assaults in trains upon Jewish passengers, who are often forcibly ejected; of concerted and armed raids upon Jewish quarters. Countless persons have been injured or robbed in the disorders of the last fifteen years, and two tragic episodes stand out in the sinister record. In 1924 the police prefect of Jassy, a Christian, was shot down in the local court of law by a student, Codreanu, and in 1926 a Jewish student, David Fallik, was also shot dead in the Czernowitz law court by a Rumanian student. Both assailants were tried and acquitted, and thereupon acclaimed as national heroes.

The "spiritual" founder of this crusade is a professor who once held the Chair of Economics at the Jassy University; for the past fifty years he has conducted anti-Semitic agitation, during which time he has poisoned the minds of successive generations of students and, although he has now passed his eightieth year, he is as energetic a force for evil as ever. The Government have always made a show of condemning these disturbances, but they have so far taken no effective steps to suppress them. Indeed, they are partly responsible, for they give special grants for the congresses, which are invariably the prelude to anti-Jewish riots, and provide free railway travel to enable academic hooligans to career about the country. Some Cabinet Ministers have even defended the misconduct of the students on the ground that they have carried into civic life "the spirit of the trenches" and are animated by a strong national consciousness.

Although, since the war, the students have been the most spectacular element in the practice of Jew-baiting, it has had and has its votaries among other sections of Rumanian society, too. There have been several incidents in which Jews have been shot dead or seriously injured by Rumanian soldiers, who have been allowed to escape scot-free so that the honour of the Rumanian army might remain unblemished. All the anti-Jewish excesses that have occurred since the end of the war (assaults upon people in streets and cafes, schools and synagogues, law courts and election booths, trains and trams, the damaging and plundering of shops, the desecration of places of worship), of which there is a long and appalling catalogue, have been followed by Government statements expressing condemnation, promising investigation, and announcing that the guilty will be punished. But then the Government departments concerned indulge in dilatory tactics, the local authorities make little or no effort to arrest the culprits, and so the situation remains as before.

Alarming as the agitation was until a few years ago, it has become both more extensive and intensive since the advent of the Hitler regime in Germany, for the apostles of National-Socialism are ceaselessly busy spreading their doctrines in Rumania as in so many other countries. Professor Cuza preached anti-Semitism even before Hitler was born, but the National-Socialist movement has given a powerful stimulus to Jew-baiting in Rumania and made it more violent than it was before. The change has been largely furthered by the founding of anti-Semitic newspapers, ultimately designed to win Rumania over to the side of Germany in the international struggle. Bucharest alone now has over a dozen daily papers of this category, all distinguished by the *swastika*, while there is hardly a single town of any importance without one. None of these publications could exist without a regular subsidy, and no secret is made of the fact that the money comes mainly from Germany (through German business firms dealing with Rumania), and, in certain cases, from Italy (to foster the propagation of Fascism). The common refrain of all the anti-Semitic Press is: "Boycott the Jews and drive them out!" The leading *role* in this sinister campaign is played by the *Universul*, which constantly accuses the Jews of engaging in Communism and in the "diabolical plots of Freemasonry." The most rabid journal is the *Porunca Vremii*, which belongs to the same proprietors as the *Universul* and models itself upon the unsavoury *Sturmer*, adorning its pages with slanderous and provocative anti-Jewish caricatures and enlivening them with poems permeated with hatred.

Far more menacing, however, than students or journalists, artists or poets are politicians, who pursue the Jew with a vindictiveness that knows no scruple. Foremost among them are Cuza and his disciple Corneliu Zelea Codreanu. After collaborating for some years, Codreanu broke away from his master and founded his own party, the "Archangel Michael," from which sprang the terrorist organisation the "Iron Guard." This body attracted a vast number of followers, students anxious for jobs and peasants eager to despoil the Jews, and it perpetrated so many excesses that it was banned in 1933 by the Liberal Premier, M. Duca, who paid for his courage with his life; but it immediately reappeared under another name, *"Totul pentru Tara"* ("All for the Fatherland"), and continued to grow in numbers and influence. So formidable a position has Codreanu attained that the Government has made no attempt to curb his activities. Even when he addressed a memorandum of astounding insolence in November 1936 to King Carol, requesting that his Ministers should declare that they would answer with their heads if their foreign policy involved their country in war, and that the King should make a similar declaration, nobody dared to lift a hand against him. Close upon the party of Codreanu comes the National Christian Party of Professor Cuza and Octavian Goga, the late Prime Minister and formerly Minister of the Interior. Goga and "Gaga," as the two are called, were joined at the end of 1935 by Alexander Vaida-Voivod, a former Prime Minister and founder of the "Rumanian Front" Party, but the combination was short-lived.

The "Liberal" Party, which had been in power during the last few years, is entirely devoid of any liberal outlook, and yielded to the clamours and threats of the extremist parties both in trimming its policy and closing its eyes to public scandals. That is why it agreed to revise the naturalisation of the minorities in the annexed provinces, and proposed in the spring of 1937 to pass a Bill for the "protection of national labour." The object of this Bill was to require that at least seventy-five percent of the employees in all industrial, commercial, and allied undertakings should be citizens of Rumanian race, while twenty percent might be Rumanian citizens belonging to the minorities (including Jews) who had been naturalised in consequence of the Peace Treaty, and the remaining five percent might be foreigners. The reason advanced for this measure was that there was a large amount of unemployment among pure Rumanians, who must be helped at the expense of the rest of the population; but the total number of unemployed throughout Rumania, which has a population of over eighteen million, does not exceed fifty thousand, of whom ten thousand are intellectual workers. As such a measure would have been a gross infraction of the Minorities Treaty, the Government did not venture to submit it to Parliament, but M. Valeriu Pop, the Minister for Trade and Industry, who was responsible for the project, issued a circular to all the leading commercial and industrial enterprises urgently recommending them to increase their employees of Rumanian ethnical origin to fifty percent in the case of administrative and technical workers, and to seventy-five percent in the case of clerical workers, by the end of the year.

A similar drive was also begun, months before the Goga Government came into power, against Jews engaged in the liberal professions. This step was taken by various professional organisations without any interference on the part of the Government, which must have realised that their action was a violation of the Minorities Treaty. Thus, the Congress of Rumanian Lawyers adopted a resolution last May to exclude from membership all persons not of "pure Rumanian blood," and struck out the names of many Jewish lawyers from the register on "technical grounds." Jews and members of other minorities were refused admission to the Bar in Bucharest and other cities; while Jewish lawyers who went to the courts ran the risk of being attacked by the so-called "lawyers' police," young barristers entrusted with the task of forcibly ejecting them. The Congress of the National Federation of Liberal Professions decided last June to exclude all Jews and members of other minorities from the vocations they represented; and the Association of Secondary School Masters passed a similar resolution.

No justification of any kind has ever been advanced for this hostile crusade, which has been vigorously fostered not only by rabid politicians but also by ecclesiastical dignitaries of the highest rank. Even the new Premier, the Patriarch Miron Christea, formerly a member of the Regency Council, has given it his blessing and accused the Jews of "living on the back of other people and on our own back, on the back of Rumania, like parasites" (*Curentul*, August 19, 1937), while the Bishop of Hotin has urged his flock to boycott the Jews in order that "they shall die of hunger" (*Universul*, September 5, 1937). The only body whose leaders have uttered a word in defence of the Jews is the National Peasant Party, who were responsible for King Carol's return to his throne. Dr. Julius Maniu, their supreme head, has more than once denounced the evils of anti-Semitism, while Dr. Nicolas Lupu, vice-president of the party, declared:

We have 10,000 villages without doctors: we have districts where there are no roads. We have work for all, and we need not be chauvinistic in regard to the Jews, who are the friendliest minority in Rumania and represent no danger at all to the Rumanian State. (*Jewish Chronicle*, July 9, 1937.)

194

But the National Peasants have been denied the opportunity of administering the country, and a period of reaction has set in.

Serious as the position of the Jews was before, it became considerably aggravated through the advent to power of the National Christian Party, which, although it polled less than ten percent of the votes in the general election last December, was placed, by the singular act of King Carol, in charge of the destinies of the country. This party has always displayed the greatest enthusiasm for the doctrines and practices of Nazi Germany; indeed, it had adopted the *swastika* as its emblem, although it prefers blue shirts to brown. The programme that M. Goga announced, and the actions that he and his fellow-Ministers immediately took, under the slogan of "Rumania for the Rumanians!" left no doubt that the oppression of the Jews was to form the most distinguishing feature of their policy. A Government containing that veteran and virulent anti-Semite Professor Cuza could hardly be expected to show the Jews either justice or mercy. Hitherto the Governments of Rumania had indignantly denied that they discriminated against the Jews; now, for the first time, there was an Administration that loudly and proudly proclaimed its determination to deprive the Jews of their rights and to drive them out of the country, and it promptly carried several of its iniquitous proposals into effect. In an interview by telephone with the *Evening Standard* (December 30, 1937) the late Premier said: "There are 1,500,000 Jews in Rumania out of a population of 18,000,000. Now I intend to clear them out and to re-establish Rumanians in their jobs." A week later he considerably reduced the number whom he proposed to expel. To a correspondent of the *Daily Herald* (January 6) he said: "We have 500,000 vagabond people whom we cannot regard as Rumanian citizens. My first measure will be to declare that we cannot take responsibility for retaining this people in our State life." King Carol, in an interview with the same correspondent (*Daily Herald*, January 10), contented himself with the smaller figure of "250,000 who invaded the villages and are not a good element," but he gave the assurance: "There is no question of expulsion."

The Rumanian Government announced that there is to be an extensive revision in order to ascertain whether the Jews are entitled to their Rumanian citizenship. Jews in the annexed provinces must produce documents showing that they were permanent residents there before December 1, 1918, and those of Old Rumania must submit proofs that they are not foreign subjects, and that they complied with the military conscription regulations or were mobilised during the war. The local courts, with the help of over 150 newly appointed magistrates, are to decide in each case whether a Jew has the right to Rumanian nationality, and if it should be found that it was obtained "fraudulently" or by error he will lose it. The whole of this inquisitorial procedure (like the decree of 1936) is utterly gratuitous, in view of the application of the Naturalisation Laws of 1924 and 1932; but, considering the temper of the Government departments, it may be expected that bureaucratic zeal will not err in the direction of leniency. Those who are denaturalised may not be expelled, as King Carol has declared, although M. Goga facetiously told the *Paris Soir* that they can be transported to Madagascar, where "warships of all nations could keep watch over the island to make sure that they stay there." But the consequent loss of civil rights will deprive them of their labour permits and of the means of earning a livelihood.

Even before this vast inquisition could be carried out, or even begun, a number of harsh and oppressive measures were put into effect that render the Rumanian Jews' already modified civic rights quite illusory. As in Nazi Germany, the first to suffer were those engaged in the liberal professions. Three well-known Jewish owned democratic newspapers in Bucharest (*Dimineatza, Adeverul,* and *Lupta*) have been suppressed; several purely Jewish papers in the Bukowina have been likewise suppressed (contrary to a promise given by M. Goga to a Jewish delegation that such papers would not be interfered with); 200 journalists have been dismissed; and 120 have been deprived of their free railway passes. No Jew may henceforth be employed on a Rumanian paper. All Jewish lawyers have been suspended until the revision of Jewish citizen rights has been completed. All Jewish doctors have been removed from the State insurance panels. All who obtained their diplomas abroad are to have their licences examined; and no more licences for the practice of medicine are to be granted to doctors who are not of Rumanian ethnical origin until the revision of citizenship is over. The Engineers' Association has expelled all its Jewish members, and the Architects' Association has done likewise, with the result that Jewish architects can no longer submit plans in open competition. All Jewish actors and actresses are forbidden to appear in Rumanian theatres and opera-houses. The only three Jews engaged in the diplomatic service, as commercial attaches, have been discharged, and all Jews employed in the broadcasting services are also to be cleared out. All Jewish libraries and many Jewish-owned book-shops in Bessarabia have been closed down by the Government on the ground that they are "centres of Bolshevist propaganda"; on the other hand, anti-Semitic publications of Nazi Germany that were previously prohibited in Rumania are now allowed to circulate without restriction. No Jew may teach Rumanian history and literature even in a Jewish school, while the teaching of the Jewish religion in State schools is forbidden. No State subvention is to be granted for religious or educational purposes, and in several cities the slaughter of animals according to the Jewish ritual method is prohibited.

The system of repression was also to be applied in the sphere of industry and commerce. A special department, with a large staff of inspectors, was to be created solely to look after "the protection of national labour." M. Goga's Government decreed that ninety percent of the personnel of all industrial and commercial undertakings must consist of "ethnical Rumanians." This law was bound to prove impracticable, for, since eighty percent of the Rumanian people are villagers and peasants, there are not enough Rumanian urban workers with the requisite qualifications to provide nine-tenths of the personnel of all commercial and industrial undertakings. Indeed, under the preceding Government it was found impossible to get enough "pure Rumanians" to occupy even sixty percent of the positions in such firms. Meanwhile the Distom Company, a large Jewish concern engaged in the distribution of State monopoly products (tobacco and soap), has been dissolved and is to be replaced by a purely Rumanian enterprise. M. Goga announced that the licences for the sale of liquor would be withdrawn from all Jews and transferred to war invalids (*Curentul*, January 2), and three days later the *Neamul Romanesc* reported that 150,000 liquor licences had been withdrawn from Jewish inn and store keepers in the villages "because they poison the public health in the country districts." Not only is there no such total number of Jews in the villages, but there is no such number of liquor licences throughout the kingdom. The figures afterwards published by the Department of State Monopolies (which include alcohol) showed that the total number of licences issued was 39,000, of which Jews hold only 3,180, and they are for the most part invalids and orphans of the war themselves.

Inured as the Jews in Rumania had long been to petty persecution, they were appalled by the suddenness and severity of such a multiplicity of harsh and degrading measures. The situation was aggravated by the action of many of the newly appointed provincial prefects, who had been chosen for their anti-Semitic record, and who hastened to anticipate some of the published projects that had not yet become law. The most malevolent of these prefects was M. Robu, already known as the "Rumanian Streicher," who spread terror among the large Jewish community in Czernowitz. He immediately put into force the decree issued by M. George Cuza (son of Professor Cuza), Minister of Labour, to the effect that no Jew might employ a Christian woman servant under the age of forty. The reason given for this prohibition, obviously inspired by the National-Socialist code, was the slanderous allegation that Jews engaged such servants for immoral ends. As its enforcement would have meant that sixty thousand women and girls, mostly of the peasant class, would have been thrown out of employment, and would have aroused an outcry throughout the country, the Government found themselves obliged to postpone the execution of this offensive law until the beginning of the agricultural season. In Czernowitz numerous properties belonging to Jewish institutions and private individuals, including the imposing "Jewish House" (comprising the offices of the Jewish Community and of many organisations), were expropriated by decree "for public utility purposes" and transferred to the Greek Orthodox Metropolitan Church, and the owners were consoled with the promise of compensation. Similar cases of expropriation have occurred in other places in the Bukowina.

The alarm felt by the Jews was greatest in the rural districts, where the peasants had been promised during the general election that the Jews would no longer be allowed to live on the land and their property would be divided among them. Without awaiting any law to this effect, the peasants in many districts adopted such a menacing attitude towards their Jewish neighbours, with whom they had previously been on friendly terms, that the latter, who had been settled on the land for generations, fled to the nearest towns, where temporary shelters and soup-kitchens were provided for them by local Jewish committees. Panic prevailed in the cities too, and it was by no means confined to the Jews. Christian manufacturers complained that their sales were declining as a result of the fear of Jewish merchants to invest further capital in their businesses. There was a run on the banks of unprecedented magnitude. In the first week of January alone it was estimated that at least four billion lei (about six million pounds) had been withdrawn from 138 banks, a large proportion by non-Jews (*Jewish Telegraphic Agency*, January 8). The Governments of all the neighbouring countries, fearing that there would be an invasion of Jewish refugees, immediately gave instructions that their frontiers should be closed. Thousands of Jews in despair, knowing that Palestine was for the present closed to them, resolved to emigrate overseas: they applied to the Italian consulates for permission to settle in Abyssinia, they besieged the consulates of Mexico and of various States of South America.

Soon after M. Goga had announced his Cabinet's anti-Semitic policy, which clearly involved gross infractions of the Minorities Treaty, the Governments of Great Britain, France, and the United States, which were signatories of that Treaty (the others being Italy and Japan), instructed their diplomatic representatives in Bucharest to remind him of the interest they had always taken in its proper observance. Their action was based upon Article 12 of the Mandate, which read as follows:

> Rumania agrees that the stipulations in the foregoing Articles, as far as they affect persons belonging to racial, religious or linguistic minorities, constitute obligations of international concern and shall be placed under the guarantee of the League of Nations. They shall not be modified, without the consent of a majority of the Council of the League of Nations. . . .
>
> Rumania agrees that any Member of the Council of the League of Nations shall have the right to bring to the attention of the Council any infraction, or any danger of infraction, of any of these obligations, and that the Council may thereupon take any such action and give such direction as it may deem proper and effective in the circumstances.

The Soviet Government also made representations, with particular reference to its interest in Bessarabia, and threatened to reopen the question in the event of any ill-treatment of the population of that province.

As the diplomatic representations had no effect, the executive of the World Jewish Congress, the Anglo-Jewish Joint Foreign Committee, and other Jewish bodies, submitted petitions to the Council of the League of Nations to deal with the question at the meeting opened on January 26 in accordance with the urgency procedure. Mr. Eden and M. Delbos had long talks at Geneva with Rumania's Foreign Minister, M. Micescu, in which they emphasized that their Governments considered Rumania's anti-Jewish policy a violation of the Minorities Treaty which would have to be dealt with by the League. They sought to secure from him a promise on the part of his Government that the projected anti-Jewish measures would not be carried out before the new general elections in March, but M. Micescu would give no such promise.

Despite this failure, the Council decided that the Jewish petitions should not be dealt with under the urgency procedure, as "the position could not be usefully considered until the observations of the Rumanian Government were available." The ordinary leisurely procedure will therefore be observed. A Committee of Three, consisting of the president (M. Adle, the delegate of Iran), Mr. Eden and M. Delbos, will study the Jewish petitions and subsequently the observations that have been invited from the Rumanian Government, and they will report to the next meeting of the Council, which will be held in May. The president further announced that he and his British and French colleagues were studying "whatever unofficial action can be taken immediately to help the Jewish situation in Rumania at once," which was understood to mean renewed diplomatic representations in Bucharest. But M. Micescu no sooner returned home than he made a statement that was ominous. A. Reuter's message (February 4) reported:

> It could be stated without prejudice to any final solution, he said, that there was hope for the re-establishment of the integral sovereignty of Rumania in all questions of internal policy. The solution of the Jewish minority problem, which for the past two months had been a foreign policy issue, would, he hoped, return, as it was before 1919, to that of an internal matter.

But only a week after M. Micescu's return from Geneva, M. Goga and his Cabinet were compelled to resign owing to the ruinous effects of their policy. During their brief regime of forty-five days they had spread such a feeling of distrust and uneasiness, not only among the Jews, but throughout all commercial and industrial circles, that the economic life of the country was paralysed and the Government Treasury was depleted, while the friendship of Great Britain and

France was seriously jeopardised. King Carol therefore dismissed this incompetent and reactionary Ministry and created a new Government of "National Union," which included six former Prime Ministers, with the Patriarch Miron Christea as Premier. The selection of this ecclesiastical dignitary as head of the Administration unfortunately affords no prospect of any improvement in the treatment of the Jews, as he belongs to the same fanatical anti-Semitic school of thought as M. Goga and is an intimate friend of M. Codreanu, the leader of the Iron Guard. Only last summer he published a virulent attack upon the Jews (which purported to be his reply to an official Anglo-Jewish delegation, including the Chief Rabbi, whom he received on a visit to London), in which he said: "Don't exploit us Rumanians, and don't exploit the other nations whose wealth you seize and appropriate unto yourselves with your ethnical and Talmudical cunning" (*Curentul*, August 19, 1937). Some of the new Ministers are hardly likely to exercise a moderating influence, and any hope that the new Government will abandon anti-Semitism as a policy is dispelled by its first official statement, which contains some of the most obnoxious features of M. Goga's programme:

> The Government will re-examine all naturalisations granted after the war. This will be carried out with justice. The Government will organise the departure of all the foreign elements which fall into the illegal class. Rumania will co-operate with other countries which have large Jewish populations, in order to find new homes for them.

This transparent threat to disfranchise and expel Jews is in no way mitigated by the futile proposal to "find new homes." It clearly shows that Rumania is still bent upon violating her pledges in the Minorities Treaty, to which she owes the generous enlargement of her territory. It is, therefore, incumbent upon the League's Committee of Three to act with the utmost energy and speed in order that the catastrophe that overshadows the Jews of that country shall be averted.

A
SOLUTION TO
THE JEWISH
PROBLEM

by G. Elkelas

[The increasing intensity of European anti-Semitism greatly ex-
acerbated the problem of Jewish refugees. Hundreds of thousands of
Europe's Jews sought escape; but few countries were willing to accept
them, and Palestine could accept but a few of the many who wished to go.
G. Elkelas of Argentina proposed a solution to this problem in a December
30, 1938, letter to the editor of The Spectator. *He believed that*
worldwide Jewish immigration was causing racial problems and stimu-
lating Fascist movements. He further believed that Palestine, because of
the conflict of Arabs and Jews, was not a suitable refuge for European
Jewry. Instead, he called for the founding of an autonomous Jewish state
in some uninhabited part of the world which would be purchased from the
political owners. The key element of the plan was that there would never be
any limitations placed on Jewish immigration. Only then, he wrote, would
other states have the moral right to refuse entry to European Jewry.

His proposal raised some important issues. Among them were the
viability of Palestine as the Jewish national home, and the global
dimensions of anti-Semitism. But as important was his implicit belief that
anti-Semitism was a very effective tool for the spread of Fascism.]

"A Solution to the Jewish Problem" by G. Elkelas, first published in *The
Spectator*, 161 (30 December 1938), 1124-25.

Sir,—Since the diaspora there has always been a Jewish problem
of greater or less acuteness in all parts of the world—directly, through
the anti-Semitic propaganda of National Socialism hitherto unknown
in history; indirectly, by the forced immigration of German Jews in
masses into other countries. Left to itself it threatens the peace of the
world and it must therefore be solved as soon as possible in the
interests of all countries.

Even the free admission of the Jews to other countries does not provide a solution to the problem. Jewish immigration in masses would be liable to produce racial problems and would stimulate Fascist tendencies, thus threatening peace in the countries of refuge.

If the general opinion that the Jews represent a distinct community by their origin is justified, it is natural that they should form a political unit. Palestine has proved to be unsuited for this purpose; the Jews there are under foreign authority, immigration is restricted as in other countries, and the claims of other nations to this territory exclude the hope of permanent peace. Sentiment, religious considerations and historical tradition must not be allowed to prevent an effective solution.

Today an acute outbreak of anti-Semitism threatens directly not only all Jews but also persons of Jewish descent in every State throughout the world, although as yet it is not evident everywhere and many do not so far feel the threat. But the menace exists, and Jews everywhere have therefore a vital interest in effective measures to stem the anti-Semitic tide. They have done much already in this respect, but they do not recognise or consider the fundamental nature of the problem. They have regarded the Jewish Question only from the Jewish point of view, and so have failed to find a solution universally acceptable. *This solution lies in the formation of an autonomous Jewish State* in territory which must be bought from the political owners. This territory must be at present uninhabited so that the rise of a new racial irredenta may be prevented for all time.

It must not be thought that the plan of the creation of a State by expelled Jews is not designed to preserve and foster their religion and their customs. Nevertheless the motive force is neither love nor hate; it is a desire for reason and justice.

No details of the future racial and cultural development of the State are here considered, the one essential and unchangeable condition is that no restrictions should ever be placed on the immigration or activities of Jews or of their descendants on the ground of their origin.

When this State has become so established that it can absorb all Jews threatened by expulsion, other States will have the moral right to limit Jewish immigration to their countries, whereas today such a restriction spells ruin to hundreds of thousands of human beings.

The considerable amount of money needed to finance the plan would have to be raised by long-term loans especially from Jews of all countries. But as the realisation of the plan would be to the interest of all States public support also might be expected.

It is believed that a territory could be found which fulfills the requirements in that it is uninhabited and for sale and (after the probably necessary cultivation) promises a healthy climate.

The cultivation and development of the land would doubtless demand great physical effort on the part of immigrants. It would however be properly organised and carried through with modern machinery, and the territory could be put under the control of technical and medical experts from the beginning.

Once the scheme was recognised as a possible solution its great advantages would become evident. In the execution of the plan, which would injure no one and offer no threat to world peace, there would arise for the founders of the new State an imposing task of organisation and, for those who financed the plan, an enterprise that should provide an adequate return within a reasonable time. A new State could be built up free from the impediments of tradition, more systematically and better adapted to the needs of our time than existing States. It would thus promise rapid and brilliant development. As its population might be in the neighbourhood of one million, the territory need not be very large, even allowing for an average birthrate. Its size would be limited by cost and by political considerations, to exclude from the beginning any fear of aggression in neighbouring countries. The State that sold the territory could be interested in the sale, among others, by the application of the principle of the most favoured nation.

The carrying out of this enterprise should not be allowed to interfere with any existing plans and organisations for helping expelled Jews. Indeed these, having fewer cases to deal with, would be able to work more effectively.

The creation of such a Jewish State would not only save hundreds of thousands of Jews from an extremely critical situation but it would also cause anti-Semitism to lose ground everywhere. If there were no further reason to fear Jewish immigration, the Jewish problem would lose its acutenesss and become comparatively unimportant. Moreover, the proposed solution would benefit those Jews who are citizens of other States or who have obtained permission to work there, their position becoming identical with that of other alien nationals. And last, but not least, the moral benefit would be incalculable because from an unhappy and despised section of society would arise a community united by one will and one idea which would have saved its human dignity and could claim general esteem.—I am, Sir, &c.,

G. ELKELAS.
Argentina.

IN DEFENSE
OF GERMANY

by A German Landowner and Israel Cohen

[*The German invasion of Poland was but months away when this exchange of letters to the editor of* The Spectator *was written. The first, a letter from "A German Landowner," was, in part, a reply to a previous letter which had criticized the lack of freedom of expression in Germany. "A German Landowner" believed that this charge was exaggerated and that, in any case, limits on freedom were justified by the great success of the German government. Turning his attention to British protests of Germany's Jewish policies, the author wrote that these policies were necessary measures to insure that Jews, an alien people who had injured Aryan interests whenever possible, would be stripped of their influence. The policies, he believed, were an internal German matter which would only become more harsh with foreign criticisms. Israel Cohen replied that German Jews were not aliens in the German state, but instead had been some of its most productive citizens. The last letter is a rebuttal to Cohen from "A German Landowner."*

The central issue of the debate was the place of Jews in Europe. Were or were not Jews alien to European life and culture? This was the same issue raised by Goldwin Smith and Hermann Adler in 1881, but here, less than sixty years later, the issue must be seen in a much more radical context. No longer is this a question of increasing or decreasing disabilities against the Jews. The intervening years had seen the Jewish Question dramatically escalate in intensity. It was a problem of global impact which was viewed by many as a threat to international peace. Discussion and debate were futile as Europe stood on the threshold of war, and most of European Jewry would face a death which was the fruit born of the political-racial doctrine of anti-Semitism.]

"In Defense of Germany" by A German Landowner and Israel Cohen, first published in *The Spectator*, 162 (24 February 1939), 303; 162 (17 March 1939), 447-48; 162 (24 March 1939), 488.

FEBRUARY 24, 1939

Sir,—The amount of space that the English Press devotes to Hitler and to Germany is appreciated in this country, as it indicates the measure of interest with which events over here are followed in England. Of course, it is not surprising that English comment is very often unjust, being emotionally prejudiced. I quite understand that, for an Englishman, it is more difficult now than it ever was before to arrive at an unbiased opinion about the German Government. The recent German policy with regard to the Jews is, of course, the reason for this. The English tendency to self-righteousness brings with it an appreciable difficulty to understand foreign ways of thinking; nevertheless, it seems to me that this tendency makes for strength of character, and I do not regard it as an English failing.

I have always been glad to observe how *The Spectator* tries to present to its readers every considerable difference of opinion on questions of the day. This has also been the case with regard to Germany until quite recently, and I do not doubt that you, Sir, will soon renew your efforts to hold the balance even, after having delighted most of your readers by articles such as the "Letter from a German Clerk," published on February 10th, which is misleading, to say the least of it. Nevertheless, I regard the letter as genuine; there *are* such people in Germany, but not very many, and their opinion is entirely without weight. Now, I know very well that your readers would be inclined to say it was not possible for the opinion of even the majority of Germans to make itself heard, and it seems high time that something should be done to clear up this misunderstanding.

It is, I think, not generally known in England how our Government is informed. Nazi officials, which exist everywhere, even in the remotest village, constantly have to report on the opinions which they hear about. I know that insincere and fullsome praise of the Government would almost certainly be detected and the responsible official denounced by the Government offices, which collect and forward these reports, and are, of course, constantly comparing them. In this way the authorities do get to know what the people think, and it is my considered opinion that no German Government was ever so well informed before.

No doubt your readers will object that a Government which resorts to such measures is disgusting according to all English ideas of freedom, so it will be necessary to ask for your kind consideration of the following arguments. It is, I believe, known to some even in England that a German must be a very real danger to the Government before anything untoward happens to him. After all, it must not be forgotten that Germany is now, for better or for worse, trying out a new system of government which does not officially allow *any* freedom of speech on Government matters. But, with regard to this rule, more freedom is often allowed than many Germans think advisable, although in this respect also careful consideration is exercised. Probably no European country except Russia could be now governed, for any length of time, against the opinion of the majority of the people, and certainly not Germany. Therefore, it is in the interest of Government, even in this country, to hear the opinions of all classes. This would be impossible if opinions were suppressed to the extent mentioned by your "Letter from a German Clerk."

Of course, we Germans know that we are sacrificing much in giving up, if only for a time, almost all the liberal ideas and institutions upon which every modern State has subsisted until recently. But it was patently impossible to go on in the old way in Germany, and the new system has, up to the present, given such results in every domain that it must be continued. Also, I point out that any alternative does not exist.

With regard to the Jews, Mr. Harold Nicolson is quite right that all sympathies for Germany, which had been carefully built up in England, have received a tremendous setback by our anti-Jewish policy. But it must not be forgotten that these people really constitute the only considerable number of inhabitants which are alien in race and thought, and can only be a tremendous obstacle to all national unification as now desired in Germany. The German Jew was always first a Jew and then, as far as it suited him, a German. He never ceased to injure Aryan interests if it was at all possible to give positions and influence to men of his race. Indeed, it is only the truth to say that practical race-politics were initiated by the Jews in Germany long before Hitler took up the campaign from the other side.

Of course, I know that even those Englishmen who recognise that our opposition to the Jews was necessary do not approve of the methods employed, and, indeed, many Germans found them little to their liking. But with regard to this I would remind you that the Nazi Government has always favoured very energetic measures as soon as a certain policy had once been decided on. Also, it is to be remembered that many achievements which have strengthened Germany could not have been so completely attained by the orthodox and hesitating methods of government still favoured in England, for instance. My country has made up its mind to get rid of a considerable part of a race which it regards as harmful, and this aim could never be achieved by way of humanitarian measures alone without prejudice to private interests.

On the other hand, I am quite ready to recognise that some incidents were deplorable, as they did less harm to the Jews than to Germany itself. Of course, many German Jews are personally much to be pitied, but, in spite of this, the action against them must be regarded as a necessity for the State, which, in time of stress, is justified in demanding even much greater sacrifices from all its citizens. These ideas may seem rather crude to you, Sir, but I am afraid that an authoritarian State cannot consider any principles which stand in the way of progress as understood in this country today. If it were otherwise, we could never have reached the present position of power. It is impossible to have it both ways, and, up to the present moment, I do not think matters generally could have been managed very much better.

I recognise that I might be asked, if the Jews were really so harmful to Germany, if it was necessary to proceed against them very harshly by law. My answer would be that the German Government must be regarded as competent to decide this question, and that it has decided it, braving world opinion and all resultant injury to our foreign interests.

It must not be forgotten that our present system promises a big advance in the improvement of all conditions of life. That much has been achieved already is universally recognised, and, as to the future, one of your best-known economists and an enemy of Nazi ideas has only just published an examination of the German financial system, and gives it as his opinion that there are, at present, no signs of collapse for many years to come.

Would it not be better to recognise that Germany cannot alter, or even modify, her system to please foreign countries, and that all difficulties created by people with prejudiced opinions do harm to all, and not to my country alone? Englishmen may rest assured that their convictions are shared by many Germans, as is well known in German Government circles. These principles are even accorded a certain amount of influence, but only as long as the same objections are not also expressed by foreign critics and in a too provocative manner.—
Yours faithfully,
A GERMAN LANDOWNER.

MARCH 17, 1939

Sir,—The reason offered by "A German Landowner" for the persecution of the Jews in Germany is that they "are alien in race and thought," and that they "never ceased to injure Aryan interests." He expects your readers to be naive enough to swallow this sweeping indictment, which he does not make the least attempt to substantiate. The manifold and valuable services rendered by the Jews to the intellectual and economic development of Germany, and the sacrifices that they made for that country in the Great War, have been described so often in your columns and elsewhere during the past six years that it is surely superfluous to summarise them here afresh. But since your correspondent designates the Jews of Germany as "alien in race and thought," I should like to point out that the difference in race by no means made them "alien in thought," as two or three typical instances can show.

When Friedrich Gundolf's work, *Shakespeare und der deutsche Geist*, was published in 1911, the extreme Conservative *Deutsche Tageszeitung* wrote that it was animated by "a rare nobility of conviction, aristocracy of the soul and of the mind," and declared: "We have again received a masterpiece of German spirit." But the

"Aryan" writer did not know that the great literary critic—a teacher of Josef Goebbels—was a Jew, whose real name was Gundelfinger. Similarly, an architect, Ph. Jantscher, writing in a Nazi journal, *Der Freiheitskampf*, in 1931, against the new style of building, said: "When the veteran master, Alfred Messel, completed his Wertheim building in Berlin, a new epoch dawned for German architecture. Many architects, consciously or unconsciously, adopted this reminder of the Gothic, the German style." And Heinrich Class, in his *Deutsche Geschichte*, glorified the Wertheim building as a symbol of modern German architecture. But when it became known that Messel was a Jew, this passage was omitted from later editions of this work.

There is probably no German poet whom the Nazis have execrated so much as Heine, and no German author whom they have lauded so much as Nietzsche. Yet this is what Nietzsche wrote of Heine in his *Ecce Homo*:

> The highest conception of a lyrist, in my judgement, was manifested by Heinrich Heine. I seek in vain in all the realms of the centuries for an equally sweet and passionate music. . . .And how he wields the German tongue! It will one day be said that Heine and I were by far the first artists of the German language.

The spuriousness of the racial myth was reduced to ridicule when Germany's woman representative won the world championship in the fencing contests at the Olympic Games at Amsterdam in 1928. Her name was Helene Mayer, and her victory was acclaimed by the "Aryan" Press with the words: *"Hochachtung vor diesem blonden deutschen Madel!"* (which may be rendered: "Hats off to this blonde German lass!"). But there were some very wry faces when it was discovered that Fraulein Mayer was the daughter of a Jewish doctor.

Your correspondent writes: "My country has made up its mind to get rid of a considerable part of a race which it regards as harmful." By "my country" he means the Dictatorship in his country, and his simple identification of the one with the other unfortunately reveals to what extent he has succumbed to the Nazi ideology. He asks almost plaintively: "Would it not be better to recognise that Germany cannot alter, or even modify, her system to please foreign countries?" The answer is that nobody asks Germany to do any such thing. But those countries that still uphold the elementary principles of civilisation hope that it will not be long before Germany returns to them.—Yours faithfully,

ISRAEL COHEN.

MARCH 24, 1939

Sir,—If you would allow me a last word with regard to my letter, I should like to say only this. Your readers, not only in England but also in Germany, have resented the following sentence: "I am quite ready to recognise that some incidents were deplorable, as they did less harm to the Jews than to Germany itself." This was, as I realise, too crude and too short a statement; it has been misunderstood. I want your readers to know that German opinion bitterly resented mob violence. One of your correspondents asks me if the Jewish persecutions would have been "less deplorable if they had harmed the German State less and the Jews a little more." My answer is that I was thinking of assault and battery, and that physical violence could not have been excused in any case. Many incidents of this kind have, indeed, caused the same feeling in Germany as they did in England, and this is saying a great deal.

Mr. Israel Cohen calls my contention that the Jews "are alien in race and thought," and that they "never ceased to injure Aryan interests," a sweeping indictment; he is, of course, quite right, but it would take a whole book to substantiate this assertion; there is material enough and to spare. I do not deny that the Jews rendered valuable services to the intellectual and economic development of Germany; but after the War, as soon as they had any opportunity of injuring Aryan interests, they established a domination which speedily became intolerable.

Mr. Cohen goes on to state instances for his contention that the German Jews are not "alien in thought." Of course, the Jews have always been in Germany, and it would indeed be remarkable if some members of this clever race had not succeeded in imitating German mentality. Indeed, there *are* some exceptional cases, but only surprisingly few of them. Mr. Cohen cites only one that I can accept, *viz.*, Gundolf's work *Shakespeare und der deutsche Geist*." Messel's building in Berlin is certainly one of the best examples of modern Gothic architecture, but this style is not exclusively German; very fine old Gothic churches are to be found in England (Salisbury, York, Exeter, Lincoln), France (Rouen, Amiens) and Italy (Florence). As to Helene Mayer, I never said that the Jewish race was incapable of distinction in the athletic field, or indeed any other domain.

I do not think many Germans would be inclined to deny that Jews are alien in thought and, I would add, in feeling. In England this difference may not be so apparent with regard to English Jews, but there must be a reason for the unpopularity of this race in all countries, and I submit that it can only be the dislike of a strange and uncongenial mentality.—Yours faithfully,

A GERMAN LANDOWNER.

Index

About the Author:

Jay M. Pilzer received his Ph.D. from Duke University, and was formerly an assistant professor of history at Norfolk State University. He has done extensive research on the role of Jewry and the "Jewish Question" in European politics and society. He is presently Director of Planning and Allocations at the Jewish Federation in Nashville, Tennessee.